362.734
M495a

P9-BAW-217

Foreword

WITHDRAWN

Adoptions Without Agencies: A Study of Independent Adoptions is the first thorough, comprehensive national research study of the actual conditions under which independent, nonagency adoptions are carried out, as experienced by biological parents, adoptive parents, agencies, intermediaries and law enforcement agents.

It is neither an outcome study of the "success" of such adoptions, nor does it necessarily recommend the outlawing of all such adoptions. It does examine the elements of legal and psychological risk in independent adoptions, and their extent. Among the findings are several pertaining to social agency operation and organization that the Child Welfare League would like to underline.

Many pregnant young women turned to private physicians instead of agencies as the only means of financing medical care without resort to clinic and ward care in a public hospital.

Many young women had no idea that agencies exist that would help them; a physician or lawyer was their only recourse. Many of the young women going through the independent adoption process needed and wanted counseling, but they felt under pressure from intermediaries or parents to relinquish their child and were left with unresolved, strongly conflicted feelings. A related finding was that the biological fathers' feelings and rights were either ignored or consciously denied.

Rigidity of agency requirements and practices, despite mitigation in some agencies, remains a continuing source of criticism and anger on the

34825

part of both unmarried parents and adoptive applicants. On the one hand, agency practices discourage biological parent-applicants; on the other hand, rigid agency practices to discourage adoptive applicants are reinforced by the lack of adoptable babies.

The book includes a complete review and an analysis of the laws of all the states as they relate to independent adoptions, and closes with clear, practical recommendations for legal and agency changes that would sharply reduce and in some instances eliminate the riskiness of independent adoptions, and provide immediate and long-term benefit to all parties concerned.

The recommendations place a mandate upon all those responsible for the adoption experience — agencies, legislators, the medical and legal professions — to correct, at long last, the faults that affect the lives of those who undertake the adoption experience — biological parents, adoptive parents, and children. But without question, social agencies must take the initiative in developing more comprehensive services for unmarried parents.

Joseph H. Reid
Executive Director, CWLA

13.00
5

ADOPTIONS WITHOUT AGENCIES

A Study of Independent Adoptions

William Meezan

Sanford Katz

Eva Manoff Russo

Please remember that this is a library book,
and that it belongs only temporarily to each
person who uses it. Be considerate. Do
not write in this, or any, library book.

WITHDRAWN

CWLA

CHILD WELFARE
LEAGUE OF
AMERICA, INC.

67 IRVING PLACE
NEW YORK, N.Y. 10003

This research was supported through grant OCD-90-C-573, Children's Bureau, Office of Child Development, U.S. Department of Health, Education and Welfare.

Copyright © 1978 by the Child Welfare League of America, Inc.

ALL RIGHTS RESERVED

Neither this book nor any part may be reproduced or transmitted in any form or by any means, electronic or mechanical, including photocopying, microfilming, and recording, or by any information storage and retrieval system, without permission in writing from the publisher.

CHILD WELFARE LEAGUE OF AMERICA, INC.

67 Irving Place, New York, NY 10003

Library of Congress Catalog Card Number: 77-99283

ISBN: 0-87868-174-4

Current printing (last digit)
10 9 8 7 6 5 4 3 2 1

PRINTED IN THE UNITED STATES OF AMERICA

Preface

The risks of independent adoptions have been of major concern to the Office of Child Development and the Child Welfare League of America for some time. In 1975, the League's proposed research into this area was funded by the Children's Bureau in the Office of Child Development, enabling the Research Center staff at the League to undertake the project. The authors are grateful to OCD for its financial support and to our colleagues in the various departments of the Child Welfare League of America, who provided consultation and encouragement throughout the project.

The heads of 50 state adoption services across the country helped launch the project. They provided copies of state regulations concerning adoption, and recommended agencies in their locales whose volume of adoption service qualified them to participate as respondents in the section of the study concerned with current agency practice. Ninety-five public and voluntary agencies participated as respondents in this phase of the project. Their cooperation and the forbearance of selected personnel in filling out a lengthy, detailed questionnaire are appreciated.

Another mailed questionnaire was sent to the offices of all attorneys general and selected district attorneys in each state. We thank those public officials who took the time and effort to respond to this inquiry, along with state adoption service personnel who filled out the questionnaire at the request of their local district attorney or state attorney general office.

It would have been impossible to conduct the on-site interviewing without local cooperation and teamwork. In Iowa, Los Angeles and Miami the participation of three large public agencies in obtaining the cooperation of adoptive and biological parents (and in some cases, facilitators) was of critical importance. We are grateful to Miriam Turnbull, Catherine Williams and the staff of the Iowa State Department of Social Services; Lenore K. Campbell, Velma Jordan, Robert Jones and the staff of the Los Angeles County Department of Adoptions; and Alberta Murphy and her staff at the Florida State Department of Health and Rehabilitative Services, without whose cooperation the process of identifying a sample would have been infinitely more difficult.

Many other individuals, social agencies and local organizations were involved in recruiting interviewees and in advising the study teams on a local level. Our thanks to all of them, and in particular to Ruth Stanley and Henrietta Waters (Florida), Sarah Glickman (New York), and the staff of the Association for Jewish Children of Philadelphia.

The complicated task of coordinating the direct interviewing phase in each site (and sometimes conducting interviews as well) was handled by five extremely able and dedicated individuals. Nine highly skilled interviewers persevered over many months, traveled hundreds of miles and worked diligently around the clock. We are indebted to:

Des Moines:	Edith Zober, Coordinator
	Pamela Correll
	Pamela Luiken
Los Angeles:	Sharon Browning, Coordinator
	Marilyn Horn
	Margaret Weinberger
Miami:	Dr. Virginia Cappeller, Coordinator
	Carol Odell
	Margaret Snider
New York City:	Danica Adjemovitch, Coordinator
	Lucy Aptekar
	Tamara Engel
Philadelphia:	Shirley Sagin, Coordinator
	Roslyn Sperling

We gratefully acknowledge the research and editorial assistance of Melba McGrath, Christopher Mehne and Peter F. Zupcofska, who worked on the legal analysis, and we are indebted to Ursula Gallagher for her careful reading of and commentary on this section of the manuscript.

Dr. Deborah Shapiro, who became director of the Research Center at the League in January 1977, provided guidance and a supportive working atmosphere during the project's grueling final stages.

The seemingly endless task of coding questionnaires was facilitated by the work of Alan Reich and Karen L. Brown. To Karen L. Brown the authors extend special appreciation; in addition to typing mountains of questionnaires, correspondence and first, second and third drafts of manuscript copy, she executed innumerable research tasks beyond all job expectations. She was an essential member of the research team throughout the project.

We also extend particular thanks to the adoptive parents, biological mothers and facilitators who shared their experiences with the interviewers. Without them, this most important aspect of the study would not have been possible.

Finally, we turn to Dr. Ann Shyne, who retired on July 31, 1976, as director of research at the League. It was Dr. Shyne who conceived the research and obtained the funding for the project. Her reputation in the field of child welfare research speaks for the high level of knowledge and competence that she imparted to the project staff. Her knowledge and skill were felt during all phases of the project, even after her formal retirement. Her guidance and support made our job bearable in periods of stress, and enjoyable at other times. It is to her that this volume is dedicated.

William Meezan, *Study Director*
Sanford Katz, *Legal Consultant*
Eva Manoff Russo, *Research Assistant*

CONTENTS

ADOPTIONS WITHOUT AGENCIES

1

Introduction

An independent adoption may be defined as an adoption completed without the help or aegis of a licensed social service agency. This type of adoption is legal in most states and is generally arranged through a third party (usually a lawyer or doctor), although direct placements by the biological parents are permitted. Although some independent adoptions are adoptions of children by blood relatives or stepparents, a considerable proportion involve adoption by unrelated persons. The focus of this study is upon this latter type — adoption by unrelated persons.

Adoption is a complex process that irrevocably affects the lives of children and their biological and adoptive parents. The CWLA *Standards for Adoption Service*, developed by an interdisciplinary committee under auspices of the Child Welfare League of America,[1] recommends that, if the best interests of all parties are to be protected, the following are some of the conditions that should be met:

1. The biological mother who surrenders her baby should have an opportunity to consider alternatives and to be given help in selecting among them.
2. The biological mother's decision to surrender should not be linked to the provision of services.
3. The biological father's interests should be considered in the relinquishment of his child.
4. The child has a right to protection from unnecessary separation from his or her biological parents.

5. The child has a right to a secure, permanent home.
6. The child has a right to the best suitable home available.
7. For the child to develop a sense of identity and emotional well-being, his/her adoptive parents have the right to accurate and appropriate information about the biological parents, including full knowledge of physical and developmental factors that might affect the child's growth.
8. The adoptive parents have the right to assurance that the biological parent(s) will not intervene in the child's life after placement has occurred.
9. The adoptive parents should have available help in understanding the special needs of an adopted child and the difficulties inherent in adoptive parenthood.

No systematic data are available on the extent to which these conditions are met in either agency or independent adoptions. However, social agencies are generally believed to be aware of standards in the adoption field, to focus upon the child as a primary client and to have the professional expertise necessary to deal with human problems. Lawyers and doctors are not trained to assess the *psychological* risks to the parties in adoption, and usually do not presume to do so. This is not to say that agency adoptions are immune from such problems and risks. However, skilled agency practice seeks on a conscious level to reduce or prevent them.

In 1966, the American Academy of Pediatrics, the American College of Obstetricians and Gynecologists, the United States Children's Bureau, the Family Law Section of the American Bar Association, the American Medical Association, and the Child Welfare League of America officially endorsed a statement on interprofessional relationships in serving the unmarried mother and her child.[2] It reads, in part: "While recognizing that, in some jurisdictions, individuals, as such, may place or otherwise facilitate the adoption of minors, it should be emphasized nonetheless that physicians, social workers and lawyers, individually or jointly, when acting as individuals and not in cooperation with a qualified child placement agency, do not have the facilities and resources necessary to provide protection and services needed by all persons affected by the adoption."

The statement speaks to the respective roles of physician, lawyer and social worker, and declares that the physician and the lawyer "should avoid becoming involved with the placement of the infant or acting as an intermediary," if social services are available. The transaction in independent adoption continues to be structured around the assumption that the biological and adoptive parents are mature, competent adults, capable of making a critical decision on the basis of legal and/or medical information and a description of the physical and social characteristics of the parties involved. Extensive social work experience in the adoption field does not support such an assumption. The biological parents are often young, unprotected and under stress and may not be in a position to make sound decisions without disinterested support. The adoptive parents may have unresolved conflicts or strains that the adoption itself will not necessarily eliminate.

INDEPENDENT ADOPTIONS — THE RISKS INVOLVED

The hazards that may be involved in independent adoptions can be divided into four categories: risks to the child; risks to the biological parents; risks to the adoptive parents; and risks to society at large. These categories are not necessarily mutually exclusive. Several interests may be in jeopardy if any one given risk-producing circumstance occurs.

Risks to the Child

All available evidence indicates that a large majority of adoptions work out reasonably well for the child.[3] Most children are resilient and have the capacity for healthy growth and development, and most adoptive parents care about children and have the capacity for good parenting.

In the only major followup study concerned exclusively with independent placements, Witmer et al.,[4] found that the children in their sample who had been placed at less than 1 month of age were adjusting about as well as a control group of nonadopted children. The results for the total sample were summarized as follows: "Most of the adoptions were working out well. The proportion of poor outcomes, however, was not inconsiderable and the comparison with the control children was a bit in favor of the nonadopted children."[5]

Few comparative data on agency versus independent adoptions are available. Amatruda and Baldwin[6] found an 8% failure rate for agency adoptions and a 28% failure rate for independent adoptions. Kornitzer[7] shows only 14.4% of agency placements, but 25% of "third-party and direct placements" as problems or failures. However, Kadushin warns ". . . any conclusions must remain tentative because of the differing levels of validity of the data used in the different studies."[8]

The "success" of an adoptive placement in terms of the child's physical well-being and emotional adjustment may be in jeopardy if the home in which he or she is placed has not been adequately screened. The *CWLA Standards for Adoption Service,* while speaking strongly to the desirability of limiting adoptive placements to licensed adoption agencies, provides an alternative formula for screening homes in which children are placed independently; "It should be required by law that the state department of welfare or an agency it designates make a social study for the court of all nonagency adoptive placements, including stepparent and other relative adoptions."[9] It recognizes that a study made after the placement cannot assure the child the same protection as an adoption service that offers the biological mother counseling to determine whether adoption is the best plan, and selects the best available home for the child. A post placement study does, however, provide an opportunity to offer service to the prospective adoptive parents, and in some instances to bring to the court information that will lead to the child's removal from an undesirable home. The question remains as to whether studies of homes where children have already been placed independently meet the condition of assuring the best possible home for the child.

The child's right to a secure permanent home is at risk if no one brings an adoptive placement to the attention of the court to mandate its finalization or the removal of the child. Agencies carry the responsibility of seeing that adoptions completed under their auspices are legally finalized, but in independent placements this task is left up to the adoptive parents and their lawyers. If there is no requirement that a child's legal status be defined, some adoptive parents, fearful for one reason or another that finalization will not be granted, may never bring the adoption to court. Thus, it may be possible for the child to be left indefinitely in legal "limbo."

For the infant, the right to protection from unnecessary separation from his or her biological parents is inextricably linked to the life circumstances of those parents. The decision regarding surrender is dependent, in part, upon the extent to which alternatives and support services are available for exploration and use by parents who may have doubts about relinquishment. Whether independent adoptions provide adequate safeguards against unnecessary separation is an issue that indubitably affects the child, but it is best examined in a discussion of how this process meets the needs of biological parents.

Risks to the Biological Parents

"I don't know why everybody keeps saying they know I'll make the best decision. I sure as hell don't know that myself. It seems as if whatever I choose will be wrong."[10] This excerpt from the diary of a young, unwed mother illustrates the dilemma faced by a pregnant woman in the midst of deciding whether to relinquish her unborn child for adoption. A large proportion of surrendering mothers are adolescent and unmarried. All are involved in a complicated and stressful situation. They not only may experience difficulty in deciding which plan to choose for themselves and their children, but may be unaware of what options are open to them. As stated earlier, lawyers and medical doctors are not trained to cope effectively with many of the stresses involved in an adoption situation. In addition, they are not legally obligated to inform biological mothers of the alternatives to adoption and/or the availability of professional counseling.

It is believed that, in most instances, the primary clients for lawyers facilitating independent adoptions are the adoptive parents, and that biological parents do not have separate legal representation. Thus a pregnant woman may never receive disinterested legal counseling in planning for her unborn child. Also, biological parents are vulnerable to abuse by those persons who resort to legally questionable activity in an attempt to profit by the independent adoption. A 1975 article by Maury Levy in *Philadelphia Magazine*[11] cited cases of young women pressured to surrender, of procurers waiting outside pregnancy-testing clinics for expectant mothers, and of "baby farms" where young women were paid to become pregnant or to carry through their pregnancies. The Levy article is one of many in the popular press exposing the consequences of adoptions for profit, which are more extensively discussed in the section dealing with risks to society.

In the vast majority of independent nonrelative adoptions, the prospective parents are seeking to adopt a healthy infant. A problem arises when a child promised to a specific couple is born with a developmental or physical handicap. The adoptive parents are under no obligation to accept such a child into their home. The facilitator is under no obligation to place the child. Thus, it is possible that the responsibility for the child will be returned to the biological mother, who has already prepared herself for relinquishment and may not have immediate access to the resources necessary to plan adequately for the child. In contrast, once a mother has relinquished a child to an agency she is guaranteed that the child will be provided for, either through adoption or some alternate arrangement.

On the other hand, if a biological mother decides not to relinquish a child who has been promised to a particular family and the prospective adoptive parents have agreed to pay the medical bills, the responsibility for this expense may revert to the biological mother, since the adoptive parents' payment may be based upon relinquishment of the child. Although agencies most often do not provide the amount of money for medical care frequently available through independent sources, whatever assistance is provided is not dependent upon surrender.

The *Stanley vs. Illinois* Supreme Court decision in April 1972 has had nationwide impact with respect to the rights of unwed fathers. Although interpretations vary, it has become clear that persons or organizations responsible for arranging adoptions must no longer operate on the general premise that only the biological mother's surrender is sufficient to insure the legality of an adoption.[12] Although state legislatures and adoption agencies are required to review and perhaps change procedures and laws in light of the *Stanley* decision, individual lawyers (some with limited experience in the adoption field) may not have the awareness or resources necessary for obtaining proper termination of the father's rights, or may, for convenience, disregard even minimal safeguards in considering the claims of unwed fathers.

Risks to the Adoptive Parents

As stated earlier, for the adoptive parents to help the child develop a sense of identity and emotional well-being, they have a right to appropriate and accurate information about the child's background. This implies also the right of the child to information about his/her biological heritage. A recent study found that agencies tend to share a good deal of specific information with adoptive parents.[13] Of 150 public and voluntary agencies surveyed, the great majority reported that they usually provided information regarding age, race, ethnic group, religion, education, occupation, physical description, personality, medical and psychiatric history and intellectual capacity of the biological parents. At least three-quarters of the agencies indicated that they recommended sharing this information with the child.

Speculation concerning the amount of background information communicated to adoptive parents in an independent adoption leaves room for the possibility that critical factors in the child's background might not be revealed. The reluctance of biological mothers to divulge information that would damage the child's chances of being adopted (for instance, in the case of an interracial child), and the nonrecognition by some facilitators and adoptive parents of the importance of obtaining and communicating as full and accurate a history as possible, may all contribute to an information gap. Further, the decision regarding what information the child is entitled to know (including the fact that he or she is adopted) is one that adoptive parents are probably most often expected to reach unaided. When the adopters are in need of counseling in regard to sharing of information, as well as other feelings about the adoption such as conflicts about infertility, problems of adoptive parenthood and recognizing the special needs of adopted children, the facilitator is usually not trained to provide such a service. Agencies, on the other hand, routinely counsel adoptive parents.

Although it is rare in an agency adoption for biological and adoptive parents to be known to each other, the structure of independent adoptions permits the biological mother to place her child directly into an adoptive home. Even in cases where an intermediary is involved, an indeterminate proportion of biological and adoptive parents may be aware of each other's identities. This knowledge does not necessarily guarantee problems, but the probability of the child's whereabouts being known to the biological mother does increase the chances of harassment of the adoptive parents and/or the child. If in a particular state the termination of parental rights does not occur until an independent adoption is brought to court, an additional risk arises. The adoption remains open to challenge by the biological parent(s) at any time until finalization.

In their anxiety to receive a child into their home, adoptive parents are susceptible to the risks involved in adoptions for profit. In addition to financial strain for some, the less informed and/or the more desperate can become parties to legally questionable activities. Building a family under the threat of subsequent investigation and/or challenge to the adoption is, at the very least, an emotionally hazardous proposition.

Risks to Society

The potential risks in independent adoptions are heightened when the adoption is arranged, not by an ethical professional operating strictly within the law and motivated by a desire to facilitate the process of adoption in the best interests of all parties, but by persons whose primary goal is monetary gain.

The problem of adoptions for profit has received intermittent attention for about 25 years, but there is little indication of progress toward its resolution and, in fact, there is some evidence of its increase. It has been discussed in Congressional committees, in professional journals, and in the popular press.

A paper in the *Yale Law Review* of March 1950 states: "The market for babies is a sellers' market. As a result, a few individuals make money by selling babies as they would sell goods."[14]

One of the first pieces in the popular press of which we are aware was an article in the *Saturday Evening Post* in 1951, reviewing the risks in independent adoption and citing adoptions-for-profit operations in New York, Cleveland, Washington, Miami, and Memphis.[15]

As early as 1953, the U.S. Children's Bureau gave special attention to legally questionable adoptions, and in 1955, participants in a conference of national agencies and organizations concerned with adoption were unanimous in their opinion that placements should not be made for profit.[16] In 1955 the Senate Committee on Juvenile Delinquency looked into the "black market" in adoption, and in the 1960s federal legislation was proposed, but never enacted, that would impose criminal sanctions against persons placing any child for permanent free care or adoption across state lines for compensation.

Feature stories dealing with this problem were carried in *Look Magazine* (12/28/54), the *New York Times Magazine* (11/27/55), and *Parade* (4/5/59).

There was doubtless much more publicity that escaped our attention during the 1950s and early 1960s. What is striking was the inundation of publicity during that period, and then a phase of relative quiet on the newsfront until the 1970s, when another spate of articles appeared, including the following:

9/14/71	*Wall Street Journal* — "Black Market Babies"
2/27/72	*Miami Herald* — "Babies for Sale: The Business Is Booming"
2/20/73	*New York Times* — Adoption Costs Soar as Births Decline"
6/24/74	*Christian Science Monitor* — "Baby Sale — for Big Profits"
3/16–3/22/75	*Cleveland Plain Dealer* — "The Baby Brokers"
4/13/75	*New York Sunday News* — "How I Sold — and Almost Bought — a Baby"
12/22/76	*Chicago Daily News* — "Baby-Selling: Inside a Murky Business"
6/28/77	*New York Times* — "Baby Brokers Reaping Huge Fees"

On 9/27/74 CBS Evening News included a special feature on "black market" adoptions, and early in 1975 Channel 4 in Florida produced a series of programs on the subject. The previously cited article by Levy in *Philadelphia Magazine* reviewed many of the practices described in the newspaper and TV pieces.[17] Levy quoted the Bar Association and the county medical society as "watching the situation," but bemoaned the fact that no one was really doing anything about it.

In April 1975 the U.S. Senate Subcommittee on Children and Youth held hearings on the subject of "baby selling."[18] In written testimony prepared for this committee, Joseph H. Reid, Executive Director of the Child Welfare League of America, stated: "Of the 16,500 independent placements,[19] how many are black market? Estimates from the field indicate that the number (based on 1971 figures) may be as high as one-third — that is, 4000 or 5000 children. But these are estimates; and they are estimates based on independent adoptions that were occurring when the 'shortage' of babies was not as marked as it is today."

The newspaper items listed previously indicate in part the extent of awareness of unethical and frequently illegal practices in arranging adoptions. All indications are that this activity continues, in spite of efforts to enforce existing legislation.[20] In their desperation for a child, adoptive parents appear to be willing to use any available channel and pay whatever costs are entailed.

Public concern over the hazards of independent adoption has been focused primarily on adoptions for profit, with less attention to the larger proportion of independent adoptions that, although not involving an exchange of money beyond that which is reasonable and customary, may be open to the other risks already described. This study addresses all of these risks.

FACTORS ENCOURAGING INDEPENDENT ADOPTIONS

In spite of the possible risks, both biological and adoptive parents continue to participate in the independent adoption process. Why is this so? For adoptive parents, one primary and compelling reason appears to be the so-called "baby shortage."

Within the last several years in the United States the number of healthy infants available for adoption through agencies has decreased. The greater tolerance by society of birth out of wedlock and of single parenthood is making it possible for many young women to keep babies who might have been surrendered a decade ago. In addition, the wider availability of contraceptive methods and legal abortion may be reducing the number of unwanted pregnancies. Because of these factors, adoption agencies have experienced a much higher volume of applications than they have been able to meet from prospective adoptive parents interested in adopting only healthy, white infants.

From 1960 to 1970 the number of adoptions increased from 107,000 to 175,000 and the rate rose fairly steadily from 15.0 to 21.7 per 10,000 child population.[21] About half of these adoptions were by relatives, usually stepparents. Of the adoptions by unrelated petitioners, the proportion completed through adoption agencies rose from 57% in 1960 to 78% in 1970, while the proportion arranged independently of agencies dropped from 43% to 22%.

A decline in adoptions began in 1971, with total adoptions showing a drop of 3% from the previous year, and nonrelative adoptions declining by 7%. The decrease affected both agency and independent adoptions. In 1971, a total of 17,400 independent adoptions were completed, comprising 21% of nonrelative adoptions. Complete national statistics are not available after 1971, but figures available for those states reporting between 1972 and 1975 continue to reflect a decrease in total adoptions, with independent adoptions remaining at approximately 20% of the total.

Data collected by the Child Welfare League of America from a sample of 49 voluntary and 19 public adoption agencies indicate a sharp drop in children available for adoptive placement over the last few years.[22] The number of children accepted by the voluntary agencies decreased 52% from the first half of 1971 to the last half of 1974. Trend data from the public agency sample show a decrease of 13% in children accepted from the last half of 1972 to the last half of 1974. The continuing decline in babies available for adoption through authorized agencies is believed to have led to an increase in the number of people seeking to adopt independently.

The shortage of infants does not, however, provide an explanation for the motivations of biological mothers who relinquish their children without agency help. Nor does the current situation account for the fact that independent channels prevailed as an alternative for prospective adoptive parents during periods when agency waiting lists were a good deal shorter than they are now. One possible answer may be found in an examination of agency policies and procedures.

The number and type of services provided for biological mothers through agencies may be seen as a factor in some women's surrender through independent means. Agencies most often provide medical care through clinics and public hospitals, and other funds for maintenance may be available only through public assistance. In addition, some biological mothers and/or their parents may perceive agencies as bureaucratic and impersonal and consider the use of agency resources as a violation of their privacy and personal integrity. Independent adoptions may often be viewed as offering more confidentiality and more substantial financial assistance. Whether or not the intermediary receives payment for the "brokerage" role, adoptive parents are most often seen as providers of private medical care.

In the case of persons wishing to adopt, many agencies have dropped requirements such as proof of infertility, financial status, age, religious matching, and the like, and focus increasingly on emotional stability and capacity for parenting. However, not all have done so. (The requirement of religious matching was the deterrent to use of agencies most cited in a study reported in 1967.[23]) Furthermore, community perceptions of agency policies reflect the restrictive practices no longer common. And the formality of the application process puts off many applicants, as is well illustrated in the Festinger study of "good" applicants who withdrew.[24]

Finally, some agency practices, such as exploration of the motivation of adoptive applicants and their probable capacity for the parental role, are essential to protection of the child, but applicants may perceive such practices as intrusive.

Limitations in legal provisions and regulations, their loose interpretation and a lack of enforcement may be important factors in the continuance of legally questionable independent adoptions. Differences in the laws of the various states with respect to adoption practice may also contribute to abuses. Furthermore, the adoption field may be given low priority by law enforcement officials. Even where it is illegal to "trade, barter, buy, sell or deal in infant children,"[25] enforcement has proved exceedingly difficult and may be impossible without enlisting the support of the parties involved in the adoption. Such support is difficult to obtain when it goes against vested interests and intraprofessional loyalties.

STUDY OBJECTIVES

Preliminary consideration indicated that a good deal of speculation has occurred regarding the risks associated with independent adoptions and the factors that encouraged the continuation of these adoptions. It was felt that a comprehensive and systematic study of the many aspects involved in the process of independent adoption was needed to produce sufficiently compelling evidence to prompt corrective action.

The purpose of this project was to accumulate a volume of data on independent nonrelative adoptions. It was hoped that this substantive information would serve as a basis for modifications of law, agency practice and public attitudes. The primary goals of the study were: to determine the risks experienced by the children and their biological and adoptive parents who have been parties to independent adoptions; to identify barriers in agency policies, procedures and resources that induce biological and adoptive parents to utilize independent channels; and to identify weaknesses in state laws and regulations and in their enforcement that contribute to the risks in independent adoption and that allow adoptions for profit to continue.

REFERENCES

1. *CWLA Standards for Adoption Service.* New York: Child Welfare League of America, 1968 (revised), Chapters 1-5.
2. "A Guide for Collaboration of Physician, Social Worker, and Lawyer in Helping the Unmarried Mother and Her Child," *Child Welfare*, Vol. XLVI, No. 4, April 1967.
3. Alfred Kadushin, *Child Welfare Services*, (2nd edition). New York: Macmillan, 1974, pp. 565-571.
4. Helen L. Witmer, Elizabeth Herzog, Eugene A. Weinstein and Mary E. Sullivan, *Independent Adoptions.* New York: Russell Sage Foundation, 1963.
5. *Ibid.*, p. 256.
6. Catherine S. Amatruda and Joseph W. Baldwin, "Current Adoption Practice," *American Journal of Pediatrics*, February 1951, p. 208.
7. Margaret Kornitzer, *Adoption and Family Life.* New York: Humanities Press, 1968, p. 159.
8. Kadushin, *op. cit.*, p. 571.
9. *Standards, op. cit.*, Section 7.39.
10. Jean Thompson, *The House of Tomorrow.* New York: Harper and Row; London: Evanston, 1967, p. 39.
11. Maury Levy, "The Baby Peddlers," *Philadelphia Magazine*, February 1975.
12. For a detailed account of the implications of this decision for agency practice, see Susan K. Ginsberg, *Suggestions for Practice With Respect to the Rights of Unwed Fathers: The Aftermath of Stanley vs. Illinois.* New York: Child Welfare League of America, 1975.
13. Mary Ann Jones, *The Sealed Adoption Record Controversy: A Report of Agency Policy, Practice and Opinion.* New York: Child Welfare League of America, July 1976, p. 9.
14. "Moppets on the Market: The Problem of Unregulated Adoptions," *Yale Law Review*, Vol. 59, March 1950, p. 715.

15. "The Truth About the Black Market in Babies," *Saturday Evening Post*, December 22, 1951.

16. Michael Shapiro, *A Study of Adoption Practice*, Vol. 1. New York: Child Welfare League of America, 1956, p. 108.

17. Levy, *op. cit.*

18. Hearings before the Subcommittee on Children, and Youth of the Committee on Labor and Public Welfare, United States Senate, April 28 and 29, 1975. Washington, D.C.: U.S. Government Printing Office, 58-578-0, 1975.

19. Reid was referring to the approximate number of independent nonrelative adoptions arranged by intermediaries in 1971.

20. For example, the indictments of a number of attorneys by the Bergen County (New Jersey) Grand Jury, as reported in the *New York Times*, 7/8/76; and the investigation of several New York City law firms by the Manhattan District Attorney, as reported in the *New York Times*, *New York Post* and *New York Daily News*, May 19, 20, 1977.

21. All national data are drawn from annual reports on *Adoptions* issued by the National Center for Social Statistics, Social and Rehabilitation Service, U.S. Department of Health, Education and Welfare.

22. Michael J. Smith, *Adoption Trend Data Reports*, September 1971 through September 1972; Barbara L. Haring, *Adoption Trend Data Reports*, March 1973 through September 1974. New York: Child Welfare League of America.

23. Howard Bluth, "Factors in the Decision to Adopt Independently," *Child Welfare*, Vol. XLVI, No. 9, November 1967, pp. 504-513.

24. Trudy Bradley Festinger, *Why Some Choose Not to Adopt Through Agencies*, MARC Monograph No. 1. New York: Metropolitan Applied Research Center, April 1972.

25. As provided in Pennsylvania law.

2

Methodology

To meet the goals of the study, it was necessary to gather data from a variety of sources in a number of locations and to use several data collection techniques. The study design called for six basic components. They are listed here in terms of the chronology in which data collection was initiated.

1. Collection of copies of the most recent adoption laws and regulations from each of the states, followed by analysis of these laws and regulations.
2. A mailed questionnaire to one public and one voluntary child welfare agency in each state to obtain information concerning the agencies' knowledge of independent adoption.
3. Personal interviews with 115-125 couples (or single parents) who had adopted at least one child, aged 2 years or under, independently between 1970 and 1976. Interviewing was conducted in five sites around the country. The Los Angeles, Miami, New York City and Philadelphia areas were chosen because of the high incidence of independent adoptions in and around these sites.[1] The Des Moines area was added at the request of the Iowa Department of Social Services because of professional concern about aspects of the independent adoption process in the area.

4. Interviews in the same sites with 115-125 biological mothers who had relinquished children aged 2 years or under, between the years 1970 to 1976, independently of an adoption agency.
5. Interviews with 75 independent adoption facilitators (lawyers, doctors, clergy) in the five sites.
6. A mailed questionnaire to all state attorneys general and to the district attorneys in the 50 largest counties in the United States, to follow up the initial analysis of adoption laws and regulations by concentrating on their enforcement.

These six components of the overall project were operationally grouped into three larger units: the legal aspect, concerned with state adoption laws and regulations and their enforcement; the agency study; and the direct interviewing of adoptive parents, biological parents and facilitators.

THE LEGAL ASPECT

This phase of the study was conducted by Professor Sanford Katz of the Boston College Law School. Katz and his staff began with a detailed analysis of each state's most recent adoption laws and regulations. Although there was access to the adoption laws, it was necessary to request copies of regulations for each state directly. Therefore, a letter from the Research Center requesting copies of regulations pertaining to independent adoptions specifically or to adoptions in general was sent to the heads of adoption services in each state. The list of these officials was supplied by the League's North American Center for Adoption.[2] By November 1975 all jurisdictions (excluding Washington, D.C., which did not respond) had complied with the request. The analysis of laws and regulations and the writing up of the findings continued through March 1977.

Early in the research it was decided to postpone the inquiry into enforcement until information from both the legal analysis and the agency study could be used in formulating a questionnaire to the attorneys general and district attorneys. It was not until November 1976 that this questionnaire, designed jointly by the legal and research staffs, was mailed to every state attorney general and to the district attorneys in the 50 largest counties in the country. Difficulties were encountered in both response rate and the content of responses received. These difficulties and their implications are discussed in Chapter IX.

THE AGENCY STUDY

In addition to the request for adoption regulations, state adoption personnel were asked to designate one public and one voluntary agency in the state that would be appropriate to answer a questionnaire on independent adoptions. The criteria for selection was that the agency either had direct contact with individuals adopting or relinquishing independently, or had a large adoption program. In almost all cases, the request was met, and the agencies designated seemed appropriate to respond to the questionnaire. In states where the request was not met, or where the agency(ies) designated did not appear to qualify for the study, the research staff, in consultation with the League's field staff, chose the agency deemed most appropriate within the locale.

In early October 1975, a 25-page questionnaire was mailed to 100 public and voluntary agency executives across the country.[3] Followup letters to nonrespondents were mailed at monthly intervals. By the beginning of January 1976, 89 responses had been received. Considering the length of the questionnaire and that its completion was often delayed because of referral to another person or appropriate department, the response rate of almost 90% was gratifying. However, because some states were not represented at all, and information from other states known to have a large volume of independent adoptions was inadequate, questionnaires were mailed to eight additional agencies in January, 1976.

Of the 108 questionnaires sent out, 95 were returned. Three questionnaires were eliminated because the information requested was either not furnished at all or was so incomplete as to be useless. Thus the completion rate for usable questionnaires was 85%.

DIRECT INTERVIEWING OF ADOPTIVE PARENTS, BIOLOGICAL PARENTS AND FACILITATORS

The Staff

On-site sample identification and interviewing necessitated the hiring of qualified local staff, usually one coordinator and two interviewers in each location. Area coordinators were responsible for identifying and obtaining the three samples, assigning interviews and reviewing the completed schedules in consultation with the interviewers.

The complexities of sample identification — described later in this chapter — had been anticipated. The coordinators were chosen on the basis of extensive experience in either the adoption field or research or both, and familiarity with resource personnel in their locales who would be essential in locating the respondents. All five coordinators had casework backgrounds, and three had substantial research experience.

The interviewers were all caseworkers or former caseworkers with experience in the adoption field. In addition to knowledge, education and experience, considerations in choice of interviewers were availability (many interviews had to be conducted on evenings and weekends, often involving extensive traveling), knowledge of the surrounding area, and above all, ability to establish rapport with a wide variety of persons.

Interviewing was under way by March 1976 in all sites except New York City and continued until January 1977. Because of difficulties in locating an adequate sample, interviewing of the biological parents was the most extended operation.

The Adoptive Parent Study

In California, Florida and Iowa, the state social service departments are mandated by law to conduct an adoptive study prior to the granting of a final decree of an independent adoption. (The Florida law requiring this was new, and not fully implemented at the time of the study). Cooperation in identifying respondents and obtaining consents for interviews was obtained from the appropriate public agency in these sites. The planned procedure for obtaining the sample in these sites was as follows: 1) at the last agency contact, the agency social worker would tell the adoptive parents about the study and ask them to sign consents permitting the agency to release their names to the staff of the Child Welfare League and indicating their willingness to be interviewed; 2) the consents would be given to the coordinator, who would then assign the parent(s) to a research interviewer. Each parent who had adopted a child under 2 years of age and who had been seen within a specified time (depending upon the volume of cases) would be asked for cooperation. This method would continue until the quota of 25 was reached.

In Iowa, sample identification proceeded smoothly following a presentation by the area coordinator in March 1976 at a meeting of Department of Social Services adoption specialists from all areas of the state. Responding by mail and telephone, agency workers from the various departments had obtained enough interview consents by the beginning of May.

The Los Angeles coordinator worked directly with the independent adoption unit in the office of the Los Angeles County Department of Adoptions. Enough consents for the adoptive parents' sample were returned before March and May 1976.

Although the Miami coordinator began meeting with agency personnel as early as January 1976, sample identification proceeded more slowly, due to changes in personnel on the state and local levels and a general reorganization within the agency. In mid-April, clearance was gained for obtaining consents, but by June the consents were far short of the quota. The coordinator then requested the workers and supervisors to write to clients whose independent adoptions had been finalized in the last year. Such letters were sent out in October 1976. Simultaneously the area coordinator met with all child and family agencies in the locale that might be sources for adoptive parents who had withdrawn from their services in favor of independent adoption.

In addition, notices were put into church and synagogue bulletins and ads were run in local newspapers. Facilitators who were being interviewed at the time were also asked to help obtain potential respondents. Through all of these sources, all the consents were obtained by November 1976.

In the New York City and Philadelphia areas, where an agency home study is not mandated by law, a variety of approaches was used to obtain respondents.

In and around Philadelphia, adoptive parents were located through: contacts with adoptive parent groups; the cooperation of the Association for Jewish Children, whose postadoption workshops are open to people who have adopted independently; other social agencies; notices sent to the American Red Cross and community mental health centers; other adoptive parents who were respondents; and a facilitator participating in the study. Respondents volunteering were asked to contact the coordinator and consents were taken by the coordinator and interviewer directly. In spite of the need to "shop around" for respondents, all consents were gained by October 1976.

The attempt to locate respondents in the New York City area was similar to that in Philadelphia, although somewhat more complicated. Initial contact with a member of the Adoptive Parents Committee produced consents from persons known to her on a personal basis. In addition, the organization's newsletter "Adoptalk" carried a story about the study, urging eligible adoptive parents to volunteer.

Eight area agencies also helped identify and obtain consents from former clients who adopted independently. Finally, some respondents in the study obtained a few consents from friends who had adopted independently. Although the procedure was complicated by the number of sources, all consents were obtained by November.

After the early interviews, five families were found to be ineligible either because the child had been born in a foreign country or had come into the home after reaching the age of 2. These were replaced. Each site met its full quota of 25 interviews. In addition, three locales, in attempting to make up for ineligible interviews and meet study deadlines, went over the number required. The final sample consisted of 131 eligible adoptive parents.

Although methods of collecting the sample varied widely, the procedures in the interviewing phase were uniform. Training sessions on the 32-page questionnaire were held in each site by the project director. The training consisted of at least 2 full days of intensive work. The first day's sessions were devoted to the mechanics of the interviewing schedule, skip patterns, intent of the questions, procedures to be followed, etc. Differences between casework interviewing and research interviewing were stressed. The following day was spent in role-playing the interview, to give the personnel some idea of the actual interviewing situation, the range of responses to the questions asked in the schedule, and the use of probing questions.

A good deal of travel was involved in all sites, as the interviewers covered not only their immediate metropolitan areas, but outlying suburbs and sprawling counties. Interviewers in Iowa traveled over the entire state. Almost all of the adoptive parents (129 out of 131) were interviewed in their own homes.

As interviews were completed, each interviewer checked the schedules and clarified answers to open-ended questions. The completed schedules were given to the coordinator, who reviewed the questionnaires, consulting with the interviewer when necessary, and then forwarded the schedules to the Research Center.

All schedules were edited by the research assistant at the League. When questions arose, letters were then sent to the interviewers involved (with copies for the coordinators) requesting clarification of responses or nonresponses. In this manner, the schedules were rendered as complete and clear as possible. Periodic memos outlining common errors and ways of correction were sent to all personnel.

In New York City the method of communication differed. The interviewers, coordinator and research assistant met at intervals of no less than 2 weeks to clarify difficulties with the questionnaire.

The Biological Parent Study

The biological parents were the hardest group to locate. The method of identifying the sample in Iowa, Los Angeles and Miami was initially similar to that used in obtaining adoptive parents. It was expected that agency workers would obtain consents at their last contact with the biological mother and that 25 interviews per site would be achieved. One major difference in approach in all locales was that, unlike the other respondents in the project, biological mothers were to be paid $25 for the interview. Each of these three sites had difficulty obtaining the sample.

In Iowa, where consents trickled in slowly, meetings attended by the coordinator and the adoption specialists throughout the state revealed that both adoption specialists and workers were hesitant to have researchers contact biological mothers because of possible emotional trauma in retelling their stories. After some discussion, the adoption specialists were asked to make a greater effort. In addition, the coordinator and the two interviewers contacted hospital social workers, public health nurses, Planned Parenthood, the Women's Community Health Center and personal friends and coworkers. These contacts resulted in some referrals. In addition, advertisements were placed in the two university newspapers.[4] A few respondents were recruited in this fashion.

The quota of 25 biological mother respondents was not reached until January 1977.

The Los Angeles coordinator was able to obtain all consents through the Los Angeles County Department of Adoptions. The agency had originally stipulated that no biological mothers were to be interviewed for the research until after the adoption of their child had been legally finalized. This meant a time lag of 4 to 6 months between the consent and the interview. During this interval, some respondents changed their minds about cooperating in the research or moved and could not be located. Progress in obtaining consents was slowed by worker resistance to asking mothers to participate. Again, there was expressed fear of causing additional pain.

After the situation and time pressures of the study were explained by the coordinator, the agency gave permission for workers to contact eligible mothers who had been seen by the agency and whose court date had passed and to interview some biological mothers whose children's adoption had not yet been finalized in court. The coordinator met with the workers, went through their caseloads and drew up lists of potential respondents for them to call. This help and personal contact motivated workers to seek consents. Data collection began in March 1976, and was concluded by the end of December.

Problems in locating the Miami sample through the state agency were intensified when it came to biological parents. In addition to the difficulties mentioned earlier and worker resistance similar to that encountered in both Iowa and Los Angeles, one of the two independent adoption units in the Miami area did not routinely see biological parents.

In order to compensate for this, the Catholic Service Bureau in Miami was approached and provided a list of biological parents who had withdrawn from its service in favor of independent adoption. In addition, facilitators who had been interviewed were asked to help. Finally, advertisements were placed in the local daily newspaper and the rest of the sample was obtained.

Even greater difficulty was anticipated in Philadelphia and New York City, where, in addition to the lack of agency involvement, there was no recourse to organized groups such as those participated in by adoptive parents. In Philadelphia, the following resources were approached with no consents obtained: local court officials; county agencies supervising independent adoptions for the courts; a child welfare agency that had some mothers withdrawing in favor of private adoption; facilitators of independent adoptions; school counselors and a teacher of a class for pregnant girls; YMCA and Settlement House residences; notices in the Interfaith Religious Movement Newsletter; notices in local college newspapers; community mental health centers; pregnancy counseling centers; feminist groups; articles in local newspapers; and public service announcements on the major local radio station over a 2-week period.

Respondents for the Philadelphia sample were recruited primarily through advertising in the personal column of one large city newspaper. A few mothers were referred by hospital and social workers. The attempt to obtain biological mothers in the Philadelphia area began in April 1976 and ended January 1977, with 22 usable interviews. Considering the obstacles encountered, this number was more than had been anticipated after the early lack of success.

New York City netted 18 usable interviews following an extended effort at recruitment. Ads were placed in weekly and daily newspapers and in university, college and community college newspapers in all five boroughs of New York City. Seventeen usable responses came from three of the weekly newspapers. Only two calls were received through ads in college newspapers. Several biological mothers recruited through newspapers failed to keep appointments.

In New York City the agencies approached for recruitment of adoptive parents were unable to help in recruiting biological mothers. Additional family service and child welfare agencies in the Greater New York area and in nearby New Jersey were contacted. Some circulated notices in their newsletters. In the end, only one respondent was recruited through an agency. Approaches to YWCAs and YWHAs, the Visiting Nurse Service of New York, hospital social workers and one adoptive parents' group that had contact with biological mothers yielded no consents.

The final sample of usable biological mother interviews met the minimum quota of 115. Three additional interviews had been completed but the respondents were ineligible because the children had been over the age of 2 when placed for adoption.

Interviewer training on the 20-page questionnaire was held simultaneously with training on the adoptive parent schedules. This procedure, along with those in assignment and checking of interviews, was the same as for the adoptive parent interviews.

Arrangements for seeing biological mothers were even more flexible than in the case of adoptive parents. Many respondents did not wish to be seen in their own homes. In New York City, more than one-half of the mothers were seen in the League offices. Interviewers in other sites made whatever arrangements seemed feasible. Biological mothers were interviewed in their own homes, in other persons' homes, in offices, restaurants and even outdoors. Although obtaining the sample was extremely difficult and there were a number of "no shows," mothers who did participate were cooperative and interested in the study, although parts of the interview were painful for most.

The $25 payment was accepted by almost all — reluctantly by some. It appeared that the payment was not the primary motive in their responding. They seemed anxious to talk about their experiences, and some seemed grateful for the opportunity to express "their side" of the story. There is insufficient evidence to judge whether the sample could have been obtained without a fee.

The Facilitator Study

Originally this phase was to be the last of the on-site studies. However, because of the difficulties in obtaining the biological parents' sample and the relative ease in locating facilitators willing to participate, sample identification and interviewing were completed earlier than anticipated. The questionnaire was distributed to the four sites already operating in mid-May and early June 1976, at which time training sessions on its use were held by the project director. The New York City group received their training at the beginning of August, along with the adoptive and biological parents' questionnaires.

In Los Angeles and Miami, lists of the most active facilitators came from the files of the cooperating agencies. Iowa, Philadelphia and New York City obtained their samples primarily from the adoptive and biological parents who were interviewed. Additional names came through agencies or through other facilitators in the sample. A few heard about the study and volunteered to participate.

When recruiting of the facilitators' sample was under way, each coordinator sent out a letter prepared by the Research Center staff, explaining the study, asking for participation, and advising the prospective respondents that an interviewer would telephone to request an appointment. Interviewers were to call assigned facilitators within 2 weeks after mailing their letters.

Recruitment proceeded fairly smoothly in all sites. The full quota of 75 usable interviews (15 per site) was obtained between June and December 1976. (Only one interview had to be replaced, because of the inability of the respondent to complete the schedule.) With the exception of Iowa, where a number of doctors were interviewed, lawyers were the most easily identified and accessible respondents. Only a few clergymen were listed and even fewer were interviewed. To meet the study criteria, the facilitator had to have been involved in arranging at least one, preferably many more, independent adoptions within the last 5 years.

Interviewing of the facilitators was complicated by their work schedules. However, in spite of postponements, mix-ups in scheduling and even an occasional two-session interview, most respondents who had consented to an interview were cooperative in following through.

Assignment of interviews and checking procedures conformed to the process for the adoptive and biological parents samples.

PREPARATION FOR STATISTICAL ANALYSIS

The questionnaires for the agency study and the interviewing schedules for the adoptive parents, biological mothers and facilitators were edited and coded as received. Twenty percent of the agency questionnaires and the adoptive parent interview schedules were double-coded to insure reliability. On items showing low reliability, every questionnaire and schedule was double-coded. Because of the number of open-ended questions on the schedules for biological parents and facilitators, each of these interviews was coded twice. Discrepancies in the coding were resolved in conferences between the coders, the research assistant and the project director.

All data were transferred to IBM cards and were checked for internal consistency on the basis of initial frequencies before the statistical analysis was begun.

REFERENCE AND NOTES

1. *Adoptions in 1973*. Washington, D.C.,: U.S. Department of Health, Education, and Welfare, Social and Rehabilitation Service, (SRS) 76-03259, July 1975.
2. The North American Center for Adoption (NACA), a division of the Child Welfare League of America, concerns itself with identifying and removing obstacles to the placement of the "waiting child." The heads of state adoption services serve as resource contacts for NACA across the country.
3. It was not possible to identify appropriate public agencies for Washington, D.C., and North Dakota.
4. All sites seeking biological mothers through advertisement used the same format. The ad ran as follows: "NEEDED: Mothers who placed their child through a doctor or lawyer since 1971, to be interviewed for national survey. Reputable child welfare organization conducting survey. Confidentiality assured. $25 per interview . . ." The name and phone number of the coordinator or interviewer followed.

3

The Agencies

THE SCHEDULE

The questionnaire used in this part of the study was a 25-page document divided into five sections: 1) adoption trends within the agencies; 2) agencies' involvement in and knowledge of the independent adoption process; 3) the demographic, social and economic characteristics of the adoptive children and their biological and adoptive parents currently being served by the agency; 4) the nature of service to the adoptive parents and the requirements for eligibility; and 5) services and requirements relating to unmarried mothers.

THE DECLINE IN ADOPTION

The average number of adoptions reported by the agencies in the study for 1970 was 192. For 1974, only 4 years later, the same agencies reported an average of 114 adoptions, a decline of almost 41%. Twelve percent of the agencies reported an increase in the total number of adoptions completed, while 88% reported a decrease. Over 40% of the agencies in the study reported that total adoptions had decreased by 50% or more over this 4-year period.

These statistics become even more dramatic when one looks at the decline in adoptions of white infants, the primary type of child placed independently. The agencies reported an average of 122 white infants placed in 1970. By 1974 this figure had dropped to 47, a decrease of 61%. Only 3% of the agencies reported an increase in white infants placed, while 97% reported a decrease. Seventy percent of the agencies reported that the number of white infants placed had decreased by 50% or more since 1970.

These figures are paralleled by the other statistics on adoption trends. The agencies reported that home studies on white families decreased an average of 35%. White homes approved for adoptive placement dropped 39%. Interestingly, although there was a decrease in the number of white unmarried mothers served, this drop was only 30%, the smallest of all the decreases reported. Although only 11% of the agencies reported an increase in white homes approved for placement, almost one-quarter reported an increase in white, unmarried mothers served. This may confirm that the number of unmarried mothers choosing to rear their children as single parents is increasing.

INVOLVEMENT IN INDEPENDENT ADOPTIONS

Almost 70% of the agencies in the study reported that agency involvement in independent adoptions is mandated within their jurisdictions. Most of the remaining agencies stated that they became involved in some cases, usually at the discretion of the court.

More than half the agencies in the study had been involved in home studies in independent adoptions during the last year. Ninety-one percent of the public agencies were involved, in contrast to only 17% of the voluntary agencies. The process described by those involved clearly illustrates that home studies in independent placements are, at best, cursory. This can be seen as a risk in independent adoption, since the conditions under which the child was surrendered, the home to which the child is going, the protection of the rights of the various parties involved, including the biological father, and the timing of the study all come under much less scrutiny than they would in any agency placement. The following data are offered as evidence of these conclusions:

1. Only 12% of the agencies involved in independent adoptions reported that the biological mother is seen more than once, while 37% reported that she is not seen at all as part of the investigation.
2. Only 2% stated that the biological father is seen more than once, while 61% stated that he is never seen.

3. Twenty-one percent stated that contact with the adopting parents does not always take place during the investigation. Compare this figure with contacts reported between agency workers and adoptive parents in agency adoptions — an average of seven contacts prior to placement, five contacts between placement and finalization, and two or three contacts after finalization.
4. Fully four-fifths reported that the home study is conducted after the child is in the home, a departure from usual agency practice.
5. Eighty-six percent stated that they have less time to complete home studies in independent placements than in agency placements.
6. Fifty-five percent reported that their recommendations to the court in independent adoptions are based on different standards from those in agency adoptions. The most common difference is that in independent adoptions the agencies judge whether homes meet minimum requirements, while in agency adoptions the "best suitable home" for the child is sought.

Not only do the home studies occur after placement and appear to be less thorough in independent than in agency adoptions, but almost 90% of the agencies involved in independent placements felt that there was a reluctance by the court to remove a child from a home once he was placed. Over half the agencies stated that even when negative recommendations are made to the court, the adoption is approved in most cases. An additional 20% of the agencies said that this situation occasionally occurs. This reluctance is illustrated in the following case examples cited by agencies:

IOWA PUBLIC

An adoptive father with a history of imprisonment for incest with four daughters remarried and adopted a girl child independently. The agency recommended that the court not approve, but its recommendation was not followed.

UTAH PUBLIC

A child was placed in a home where prospective adoptive parents gave poor supervision. Complaints of child neglect were made by the neighbors. The court allowed the family to adopt. Less than 6 months after the adoption was finalized the child was badly burned in a backyard fire and had to have both legs removed.

THE RISK FACTORS

In addition to the two risks mentioned — that the adoptive placements are not scrutinized so closely in independent adoptions as they are in agency adoptions and that there is a reluctance to remove children from inadequate homes once they have been placed — the study team, through its review of the literature, identified nine possible risks that seem more likely in independent adoptions. The agencies were asked whether, through their professional relationships, they had *direct* knowledge of such risks, and if they did, to state how many such cases had come to their attention during the last year and to cite the most recent case. It should be noted that for most of these risks, agencies reported knowing of fewer than five cases over the last year, and in only one instance did more than 25% of the agencies report knowing five cases or more.

The first risk explored was the one that has received the greatest amount of publicity and has been of most concern — namely, the sale of children for high fees or "for-profit" adoption operations — commonly called the "black market." Twenty-two percent of the agencies reported direct knowledge of such activity within their area. About 20% of the agencies in each area of the country reported direct knowledge of such activity. Typical of this activity and the way it comes to agency attention are the following examples:

ILLINOIS VOLUNTARY

Couple under study with agency had a friend who suggested calling his lawyer. The lawyer had three babies available. The price was set at $8000 per infant. The couple objected to the fee. The lawyer's response was "face it — it's a seller's market today." Couple did not call back. Lawyer called again offering a price of $7000. He advised the couple that only $2000 could be listed as payment in court.

NEW JERSEY VOLUNTARY

Couple who later rejected the idea of independent placement tells us of fees quoted to them of $15,000 to $20,000. One such lawyer has couples pay an initial fee, then pay the balance after the agency investigation, so that they can quote the initial portion of the fee as the total fee (to the court).

NEW MEXICO PUBLIC

Family wrote the documentation on this case. Lawyer called, offering them a white infant. May have got name from a doctor who knew they wanted to adopt. Family had no intention of accepting but listened and were told fees would be at least $4000. Matter was reported to the disciplinary committee of the New Mexico Bar.

These cases were fairly typical of the responses received, but fees as high as $40,000 were reported.

Another common concern is the protection of confidentiality in independent adoptions; it is often noted that the biological and adoptive parents are known to each other, allowing harassment of one party by the other to occur, placing stress on the adoption. Asked about the prevalence of this problem, 42% of the responding agencies cited at least one case within the last year. Although not statistically significant, the problem seems more prevalent in the West (58%), where "open adoptions" are more common, than in the Midwest (46%), the South (38%) or the East (22%).

Typical of problems that arise because of the lack of confidentiality are the following:

NORTH CAROLINA PUBLIC

Experience with a biological mother who, during the first year after placement, placed pressure on adoptive parents by calling them for "loans" of money when she was in economic difficulties.

VERMONT PUBLIC

Mother of child "changed her mind" but of course the court termination was final — so she called and tried to visit the adopting family. They are planning to move out of state to avoid further contact.

CALIFORNIA VOLUNTARY

A biological mother calls about every 6 weeks to announce plans to visit child. She fails to follow through but keeps adoptive family insecure.

A third risk factor concerns the rights of the child to permanency. It has been reported that, since the adoptive parents are, in effect, contracting with the intermediary for a normal child, they are under no obligation to accept a child who is not normal. Because there is no agency involved, the biological mother might then become responsible for the care of the child rejected by the prospective adoptive parents. It is at this point that she may come to an agency for help, since she does not have the resources to place the child on her own.

Twenty-three percent of the agencies reported direct knowledge of the return of a child to a biological parent because of the child's physical or emotional problem. Typical of the cases reported were:

WISCONSIN PUBLIC

An unmarried mother was notified that her 2-year-old would be returned from another state because of failure to develop. Mother contacted agency and child was sent to agency. Parental rights were terminated and child was placed in an adoptive home. "Failure to develop" was due to poor quality of adoptive home.

WEST VIRGINIA VOLUNTARY

Just before independent placement, the physician who was acting as intermediary decided against proceeding because of suspected hereditary problems in the background. He told the biological parent of his decision and, in effect, returned the baby to her.

Another risk often mentioned in the literature is the possibility of a custody fight between the biological and adoptive parents prior to the final adoption procedure; because the rights of the biological mother or father may not be properly terminated in an independent adoption, the placement remains open to challenge. Asked about this, one-quarter of the agencies responded that they had knowledge of such problems during the last year. Agencies involved in home studies for independent adoptions reported knowledge of such problems significantly more often than agencies not directly involved (36% vs. 11%). Typical of the problems mentioned are the following:

KENTUCKY PUBLIC

Biological parents were divorced. Mother had custody of the child. She placed infant with couple who wished to adopt. Biological father filed custody suit, claiming that his rights were not terminated and that he had remarried and could now care for the child. Child was returned to biological father.

KANSAS PUBLIC

A mother requested adoption be set aside, asserting that her consent was invalid because she didn't have informed independent legal advice. The only advice she received was from attorney for the petitioners. District court upheld the rights of the biological mother.

FLORIDA PUBLIC

Foreign-born biological mother alleged consent was not understood when executed, and petitioned for custody of her child. Court withheld judgment on custody until final hearing on adoption. At that time adoption and custody were granted to adopting petitioner.

Another risk — of most concern to adopting parents — is that the biological mother might change her mind after the placement but before her rights have been terminated. This is a risk in states in which termination of parental rights takes place at the adoption proceeding rather than at the point of surrender, or in states in which the biological mother is given a period of time to consider her decision after the child is placed.

Twenty-four percent of the agencies in the study reported direct knowledge of incidents of this kind. Knowledge was more likely to be reported by agencies involved with home studies for independent adoptions (34% vs. 11%) and by the nonadministrative staff of the agency (39% vs. 10%). Typical of the incidents reported are the following:

LOUISIANA PUBLIC

Biological mother had understood that her rights were terminated at the time of placement. Found out prior to the interlocutory decree that this was not the case. Child was returned to her.

CALIFORNIA VOLUNTARY

Current agency applicant had child for 3 months. Child was placed through doctor. When the couple filed the adoption petition, biological mother refused consent and child was returned to her.

The sixth risk with which the study was concerned was the possibility that a couple not approved for legitimate reasons by a licensed social agency would receive a child independently, since families adopting independently come under less scrutiny and courts seem reluctant to remove children once they are placed. Thirty-one percent of the agencies reported cases in which a child was placed and the adoption approved for a family who had been rejected by a social agency. Representative of the cases are:

NEW YORK PUBLIC

Older professional couple. Man 58, Wife 45. Man had previously married, and divorced after 31 years. No previous children. He and his present wife had been trying for 6 years to have children. Their stated motivation for wanting a child was that the man wanted an "heir." Agency turned them down, but they adopted independently.

ALABAMA VOLUNTARY

Child was placed through a doctor when family agency had refused because of severe medical problems, including cancer in one of the spouses. While application was in the process of being turned down, couple adopted independently.

Another risk explored was the possibility of the adoptive family's not receiving critical information on the child's background that might affect either the child's health and development or the adoptive parents' willingness to rear the child. Thirty percent of the agencies had direct knowledge of failure to reveal to the adoptive parents a critical factor in the child's background. Case examples include:

PENNSYLVANIA PUBLIC

Child, placed by an attorney, appeared to be racially mixed. Parents were not aware of the possibility. Orphan's Court judge was told of situation in independent investigation report. He confronted the attorney, who then revealed this possibility to the adopting couple.

OREGON PUBLIC

Adoptive parents were not informed that biological mother and others in her family were severely diabetic. Adoptive parents were under the impression that biological mother was free of health problems.

The purpose of adoption is to create a new, stable permanent environment in which the child can grow and develop. Yet, one risk often mentioned regarding independent placement is that the legal processes may, for a variety of reasons, never be completed. The result is that the child may be left in a state of limbo, living with a family but not having the guarantees or privileges of an adopted child.

Asked about this type of situation, 29% of the agencies stated that they did know of such cases within the last year. Agencies with direct involvement in independent placements were more likely to report such cases (39% vs. 17%). The reasons for such cases are many, as illustrated in the following:

MASSACHUSETTS PUBLIC

Agency made a negative report to the court. Family had learned of this and their attorney delayed finalization. Has held case since 1972. We think attorney feels the longer the child is in the home, the better the chance of ultimate finalization.

WEST VIRGINIA PUBLIC

Because the rights of the putative father were not terminated, a judge in one area of our state refused to hear the adoption petition, leaving the child in "limbo."

NORTH CAROLINA PUBLIC

Adopting parents separated (and later divorced) before the adoption was finalized. Adopting mother kept the child. Adopting father was agreeable to her keeping the child and her proceeding with a single-parent adoption. Biological parents were recontacted for consents to the single adoption, but they refused to sign again. Child is now 7 years old, still living with the original adopting mother, who has now remarried. Original petition is still pending, child is in limbo and it is uncertain when and how the case will be resolved.

WISCONSIN PUBLIC

Child in adoptive home 2½ years. Placement made by physician without agency or legal consent. Prospective adoptive parents do not want to file petition. DA refuses to file a petition and court refuses to accept agency's petition to determine the status of the child.

The final risk explored is often cited in the literature — lack of counseling to the biological mother on personal matters and decisions about the placement. It has been stated that this is not provided in independent placements, that often an unmarried mother does not know the alternatives available to her, that pressure is often placed on her to surrender and that her ambivalence about this decision and other life decisions is never explored. The literature states further that, even if counseling is offered by the intermediary, the intermediary is not trained to give adequate service.

Questioned about their direct knowledge of instances in which the biological mother failed to receive needed counseling, half of the agencies in the study reported that they knew of such cases within the last year. Indicative of the situation are the following:

WYOMING PUBLIC

A disturbed, 16-year-old unmarried mother was referred for counseling after delivery and surrender. She felt she had been forced into the adoption, primarily by her mother. No one had helped her understand her situation, alternatives or consequences. Her feelings had not been dealt with.

ARIZONA VOLUNTARY

An 18-year-old, very disturbed unmarried mother went "private." The attorney and adoptive parents were paying her $100 a month and medical expense. She wanted counseling and a living situation from the agency, but her attorney and the adoptive parents dissuaded her from pursuing this.

ILLINOIS VOLUNTARY

A mother was promised fee by a lawyer but was told she was not to tell the judge. Mother cooperated, but lawyer did not pay. Mother was ambivalent about her situation and had not had the opportunity to work out her feelings. Tried to get baby back from the judge, but it was too late.

WEST VIRGINIA VOLUNTARY

Young, unmarried mother was extremely distressed when her physician who made arrangements for independent placement refused to give her any information about her child (sex, health, birth weight, etc.), and would not tell her anything about the family with whom the baby was to be placed. In exasperation she remarked, "They (the adoptive parents) know everything about me and I know nothing about them."

It can be seen that the agencies involved in this phase of the study perceive risks in independent adoptions. Over 20% of the agencies were aware of cases illustrating each of the risks explored, and from 30% to 50% were aware of instances of four of these risks. Yet despite these risks, persons still seek a child through independent channels. The researchers believed that there might be aspects of agency practice and policy that encourage both adoptive and biological parents to adopt independently. The following discussion focuses on these agency factors.

SOME ISSUES IN THE PROVISION OF SERVICE TO ADOPTING PARENTS

Four out of five agencies in the study reported that within the last year they had couples who terminated with the agency in order to adopt independently. More than 25% of the agencies stated that they knew of at least 10 such couples. Seventy-five percent of the agencies knew of cases in which the adopting couple were approached by the intermediary; most of the others did not know how the contact for the independent placement was made.

Sixty percent of the agencies in the study felt that there were problems within their agencies that might deter adopting parents from using their service. This was significantly more often thought to be the case by the public than by the voluntary agencies (73% vs. 48%). Those respondents reporting problems within their agencies cited the following:

Table 3-1

	%*
Shortage of normal, white infants and/or waiting list closed	65
Staff shortages causing delay	37
Requirements of agency eliminate certain desirable prospective adoptive parents	22
Fees prohibitive for some	17
Lack of knowledge of agency service and/or lack of outreach	9
Home study seen as an intrusion	7
Delay in freeing child due to *Stanley* decision	4
Other	11

*Percentages total more than 100% because of multiple responses by agencies.

It is apparent that the shortage of infants and delays in receiving service were seen as the primary deterrent to the use of agencies by prospective adoptive couples. Additional evidence for this included: over half of all the agencies in the study (54%) reported that they are not currently accepting applications for normal, white infants; and seven out of 10 stated that their waiting list for this type of child had been closed at some point during the last 2 years. Although not surprising in light of the adoption statistics presented earlier, these facts are distressing, especially if agencies are not exploring with prospective parents the possibility of adopting other types of child. When a couple is seeking to adopt a normal, white infant and finds the agency doors completely closed to them, the only alternative is the independent market. Although the differences are not statistically significant, there may be geographic differences in the supply of white children available for adoption. Over 80% of the agencies in the Northeast reported that their waiting lists had been closed in the last 2 years, compared with about 75% in the Midwest and the South and 56% in the West. There were no differences between public and voluntary agencies on the closing of waiting lists, nor were there differences between agencies with large and small adoption programs.

The size of the waiting list varies among agencies, with the larger volume agencies having significantly longer waiting lists, and agencies in the Midwest tending to have longer waiting lists than agencies in other parts of the country.

The shortage of white infants and the shortage in staff are manifested in yet another way within agencies — namely, the delay in the adoption application process and in the completion of home studies. Twenty-two percent of the agencies queried stated that they do not even give an initial appointment to adoptive couples inquiring about adopting normal white infants, while 36% of the agencies stated than an appointment does not take place until at least 6 months after an inquiry has been made. Reports of the time lapse between the initial inquiry and completion of the home study are even bleaker. Forty-two percent of the agencies reported that it is at least a year between inquiry and approval, while 22% of the agencies stated that it is between 6 months and a year. Only 18% of the agencies stated that the time between inquiry and completion of the home study is under 6 months. An additional 18% said they do not do such home studies.

Once the home study is completed, the wait for the placement of a child can be even more discouraging. Only 36% of the agencies reported that they can place a child within a year of approval of a home. Thirty-one percent of the agencies stated that the time elapsed is usually between 1 and 2 years, 23% said it is between 2 and 3 years, and 8% stated that it is more than 3 years between approval of a home and the placement of a child. Thus, in agencies willing to accept an application and do a home study, the time between inquiry and the placement of a child can be as long as 5 years. Few couples are willing to wait this long for a child. The conclusion indicated is that the shortage of agency-related children available for adoption leads to the use of the independent route for many families.

Although agencies may have little or no control over the number of normal, white infants available for adoption and therefore over the long waiting period between application and placement, they do have control over their own policies. The literature suggests that one reason people turn away from agencies to independent placement is the number of requirements and the amount of red tape in agencies, and the fact that to many, these requirements seem arbitrary and inappropriate.

We identified the 14 most often cited requirements and asked the agencies whether they had each requirement and, if they did, whether the requirement could be waived. The median number of requirements among the agencies in the sample was 6. The median number that could not be waived was 3.

The requirement most often cited was the furnishing of references. Almost 80% of the agencies required references and three-quarters of these stated that the requirement could not be waived. The particular requirements varied greatly. Some agencies specified from whom the references must come; others left this open. Some agencies required only three references; others required as many as eight.

More than three-quarters of the agencies had requirements about the length of the current marriage — commonly between 2 and 4 years — and more than half of these stated that this requirement could not be waived.

Sixty-six percent had maximum age requirements of adoptive applicants, and the same percentage had minimum age requirements. Agencies were more flexible on the maximum age than on the minimum; two-thirds of those reporting age requirements could waive maximum, but only one-third could waive minimum age requirements. Median minimum age reported was 21 and median maximum age was 40.

More than half (54%) of the agencies had requirements regarding the presence of biological or adoptive children in the home, and 60% of these stated that the requirements could not be waived. Few agencies would place a child in the home if there were already two children in the home, and a substantial minority would not place another child if there was already one child in the home.

Almost half of the agencies had requirements regarding the working status of adoptive mothers, and about half had requirements concerning infertility. On both these requirements, the agencies seemed flexible, with somewhat over two-thirds reporting that they could be waived. Requirements dealing with working mothers usually prohibited or limited employment during the first year the child was in the home. The infertility requirement was usually medical proof of the problem.

About one-quarter of the agencies reported minimum income

requirements, which for the most part were rather loosely defined, and about the same number had religious requirements.

About one-fifth of the agencies had requirements on housing, usually phrased as "adequate space," although one-quarter of the agencies with such requirements stated that the child had to have a separate bedroom. Half of the agencies with this type of requirement stated that it could not be waived.

Fifteen percent of the agencies had requirements concerning divorce prior to the current marriage. The requirement usually did not prevent previously divorced people from adopting but had to do with divorce finalization and reasons for the divorce.

Fewer than 5% of the agencies said they had either educational or occupational requirements.

There were no differences between large and small agencies in the number of requirements, or between agencies whose waiting lists were or were not closed at some point during the last 2 years. Voluntary agencies had somewhat more requirements for adoptive couples than did the public agencies. There were also strong regional differences, with agencies in the South reporting significantly more requirements of adoptive couples than agencies in any other part of the country.

Table 3-2
Number of Requirements, by Location of Agency

	Location of Agency			
	Northeast	**Midwest**	**South**	**West**
	(N = 21)	**(N = 20)**	**(N = 24)**	**(N = 26)**
Number of Requirements	**%**	**%**	**%**	**%**
7 or fewer	76.2	75.0	33.3	65.4
8 or more	23.8	25.0	66.7	34.6
Chi-square = 11.66, df = 3, p < .01				

Although it is difficult to judge the appropriateness of the specific requirements that given agencies have established (and many are certainly important safeguards for the child), some agencies may use their requirements to screen out couples in order to cut down on the demand for agency services. Thus, older couples, or couples with children already in the home, or where the women must continue to work, or where infertility had not been established, or couples who resent the many references the agency requires, etc., have only the independent route to enlarge their families. It seems clear that agencies should review these requirements and retain only those necessary to protect and safeguard the child.

SOME ISSUES IN THE PROVISION OF SERVICE TO BIOLOGICAL PARENTS

Unlike the problems in the delivery of service to adoptive parents in view of the large number requesting services and the shortage of adoptive children, agencies are able to be more responsive to biological parents in terms of promptness and delivery of service. Over 80% of the agencies reported that they are able to see an unmarried mother within a week of her inquiry and the rest reported that this can take place within a month. Fewer than 15% of the agencies put any residence requirement on eligibility for services to unmarried mothers, and all the agencies will see a woman who has had previous out-of-wedlock pregnancies.

Despite the promptness of service, 83% of the agencies reported that within the last year they knew of cases in which the woman terminated with the agency in order to place her child independently, and 40% of the agencies said they knew of at least five cases. It was the opinion of 70% of the agencies that the biological mothers were usually approached by an intermediary. Only 5% of the agencies reporting knew of no case in which a woman was approached.

Asked why they thought the biological parent would turn to independent adoption, the agencies most often cited financial reasons.

Table 3-3

	%*
Financial/medical or other expenses paid	68
To have knowledge of the whereabouts of the child or knowledge of the adoptive parents	22
Fear of agency and/or red tape involved	18
To be certain that child will go directly into adoption rather than into a foster home	13
Pressure from the intermediary	11
Family pressure to relinquish in this manner	10
Trust in the intermediary	10

*Percentages total more than 100% because of multiple responses by agencies.

In addition, two-thirds of the agencies felt that there were problems about the delivery of agency services that encouraged the use of the independent system. The problems most often cited by the agencies themselves were inability to provide financial assistance (62%), mandated involvement of the biological father (24%), and the stigma attached to agency service (18%). Thus, the agency-connected reasons most often cited deal with the type of support and service agencies can provide, fear of the involvement of other persons, and concern about the permanence of the placement for the child.

Agency Services: The agencies were asked about a large number of services — whether they provide these services directly, through referral or not at all. The soft services — that is, counseling and interpersonal services — are provided by most of the agencies. For example, at least 90% provide the following services directly: adoption counseling; counseling directed toward change in interpersonal relations; counseling directed toward self-understanding; continuing services for the biological parent who keeps the child; services to the biological father; and services to the biological mother's parents.

Unfortunately, because of limited resources, agencies are not able to provide the "hard" services to nearly the same degree. Less than half of these agencies, and for the most part only public agencies, can provide financial assistance during pregnancy or after delivery, medical care by a private physician, housing during pregnancy that allows the mother to remain independent, housing after delivery, or legal counseling. Just over half of the agencies can provide financial help with medical expenses. Although most of these services can be provided through referral, the referral is usually made to public assistance, which may not be acceptable to the women because of the investigation of eligibility and the stigma associated with reliance on "welfare." Thus, in order to have the services of a private physician, and sufficient money to live on during pregnancy and for a short time after delivery, unmarried mothers may feel that their only recourse is independent adoption.

Involvement of Other Persons: The requirement for the involvement of other persons in the process of rendering services to unmarried mothers has been cited in the literature and is suspected by agencies to be a deterrent to the use of agency services. Most often this is either involvement of a government agency (welfare department, court, probation, etc.), the woman's parents or the father of the child. It has been speculated that the desire to avoid such involvement, especially of the father, might encourage women to surrender their children independently. It should be noted that such involvement is often beyond the control of the agency, since the agency may be required by state law or regulation to report or involve other parties in providing the service.

Our data confirm that involvement of other parties is often required. Twenty-one percent of the agencies stated that they must report all out-of-wedlock births to a government agency, and an additional 2% said they must do this under certain circumstances.

Involvement of the biological mother's parents may be even more prevalent, depending on the service rendered and the age of the mother. Twenty-one percent of the agencies stated that they are required to report an out-of-wedlock pregnancy to the woman's parents if she is a minor. Twenty-eight percent reported that they are required to obtain consent from the woman's parents if social services are to be rendered. Half are required to obtain this consent if medical services are to be rendered to a woman who is a minor. Thirty-six percent stated that they must get parental consent if the woman planning to surrender the child is a minor. Fifteen percent said that they are required to involve the woman's parents if social services are rendered to a minor.

Since the 1972 Supreme Court *Stanley vs. Illinois* decision, agencies have been required to involve the father of the child in the surrender proceeding. Almost half of the agencies reported that they are required to involve the putative father in rendering social services to the unmarried mother. Seventy-two percent said they must get consent of the putative father for the adoption and an additional 9% stated that this is sometimes required. Thus, in over 80% of the agencies reporting, consent of the putative father is necessary in at least some cases for the adoption to take place.

Although such involvement may be desirable, over 55% of the agencies believe the involvement of others in the decision to surrender deters the unmarried mother from using their service. The involvement of the putative father was most often cited.

Fear of Lack of Permanence: Another reason cited in the literature for the avoidance of agencies by biological parents is the fear that the child will go into foster care, not directly into an adoptive home after birth and somehow get caught in the foster care system. Although this fear may not be justified, the data indicate that few children go directly into adoptive homes after birth. Only 7% of the agencies reported that all of the children go directly into adoptive placement, while 54% reported that none of their children go directly into adoptive homes.

LEGALLY QUESTIONABLE ACTIVITIES

The agencies were asked how much of the independent adoption activity in their area they thought was "for profit." More than half of the agencies responding (N = 69) stated that none or a small minority of the activity was of this type. Nineteen percent judged that most or nearly all of the activity in their area was "black market," with 26% of the agencies stating that it was half or a substantial minority. There were no regional differences in the responses.

Asked if there were specific problems in the law that allow "black market" operations to continue, 69% of the agencies said there were. The specific problems cited most often were:[3]

Table 3-4

	%*
The fact that independent adoptions are permitted allows abuses to take place	29
Law vague and open to abuses	21
Investigation not required	12
Report of fees not required	12
Problems in the law on interstate placement	12
Unclear definitions of who is allowed to place children	12
Lack of enforcement of current law	10
Other	32

*Total adds to more than 100% because of multiple responses by some agencies.

Despite the reports of risks in independent adoptions and the occurrence of "legally questionable activities," the agencies considered a remarkably high proportion of independent homes as good or better than homes where the children are placed through an agency. Almost half of the agencies reported that nearly all independent homes are as good or better in providing physical care for the child, and more than one-third consider almost all the homes as good or better in providing emotional care. Only 15% of the agencies regarded no more than half of the homes as good as agency homes in providing physical care and one-third reported that half or fewer of the homes are as good or better in providing emotional care.

SUMMARY

The data supplied by the agencies in the sample leaves one with the following impressions:

1. Adoptive home studies in independent adoptions are less thorough than those conducted in agency adoptions.
2. Once a child is placed in a home there is reluctance by courts to remove a child on agency recommendations.
3. There are risks connected with independent adoptions of which the agencies have direct knowledge, including legally questionable activities and risks that abrogate the rights of the adoptive couple, the biological parent and the child.
4. The primary reason seen for the use of the independent route by adoptive parents is the acute shortage of white, healthy infants available through agencies.
5. Agencies continue to have specific requirements for acceptance of prospective adoptive parents that may deter prospective applicants.
6. The primary reasons seen for biological mothers' choosing independent adoption are that it allows them access to medical services (in a way that agencies cannot provide) and allows the biological mother to avoid involvement of the child's father and have greater knowledge and choice of where the child is to be reared.
7. Another factor cited in agency practice that may encourage the use of independent placements is that most children do not go directly into adoptive homes, but spend some time in foster care.
8. Families who adopt independently are seen in a generally positive light by agencies.

The foregoing points are the impressions of social agencies. Whether these perceptions are accurate can be determined only through analysis of data collected directly from the parties involved in the independent adoption process — the adoptive parents, the biological parents and the facilitators. The next four chapters explore these and other points with the various parties.

4

The Adoptive Parents
Circumstances of the Adoption, Adoptive Parents' Concerns and the Risks Involved

Data from the adoptive parents were elicited through the use of a semistructured interview schedule. A total of 131 interviews were completed in the five project sites. In each site at least 25 interviews were completed.

The interview schedule was divided into four major sections: 1) the background and circumstances of the adoption; 2) risks incurred and worries about the adoption; 3) experience with social agencies with regard to the adoption; and 4) reactions to the adoption experience. This chapter deals with the first two areas; Chapter V covers the other two.

Slightly more than half the interviews were conducted with the adoptive mother alone. In the remaining half both the adoptive mother and father participated. Almost all took place in the adoptive parents' homes.

On the average, the interview took about 2¼ hours to complete. The range was from 1¼ to 4 hours. For the most part, the interviewers felt that the participants were candid and open about their experiences. Interviewer ratings showed an indication of hesitancy or evasion in fewer than 5% of the cases.

At the time of the interview, three-quarters of the adoptions had been finalized; the others were awaiting final decrees.

DEMOGRAPHIC CHARACTERISTICS OF PARENTS

If the accidental sample used in this study is in fact representative of the population of couples adopting independently, its members are significantly different from parents in the population at large and from adoption agency applicants. Although the age distribution tends to be similar to that reported in other adoption studies, distributions on ethnicity, education, socioeconomic status and religion all differ from other data reported on adoptive parents.

In 1974, the median age of a white mother at the time of the birth of her first child was 22.18. The median age at the birth of the second child was 25.14.[1] Like adoptive parents reported by the agencies in another phase of this study and in other research studies,[2] the adoptive parents in this study were older at the time of the entrance of a child into their lives. Modal age of the adoptive parents at the time of the interview was between 30 and 35 years, with a median of 34.5 years for the husbands and 32.8 years for the wives. As the age reported was the age at the time of the interview, the couples were somewhat younger at the time the child was placed. Nonetheless, it is clear that the adopting couples tend to be older than couples having children biologically.

Table 4-1
Age of Adopting Couples at Time of Interview

Age in Years	Husband (N = 124) %	Wife (N = 124) %
Under 25	—	1
25 – 29	13	23
30 – 34	40	48
35 – 44	37	27
45 – 49	6	1
50 +	3	1

In recent years there has been increased effort by adoption agencies to recruit nonwhite homes for children awaiting placement. A recent survey[3] showed that in 18.2% of the adoptive homes approved by 41 voluntary agencies and 29.9% of adoptive homes approved by 16 public agencies the prospective adoptive couples were not white. The agencies in another phase of this study reported a median of 13.25% of adoptions completed with black adoptive parents. This is in marked contrast to the couples interviewed who adopted independently. Of the 131 adoptive families interviewed, 98% were white. The two exceptions were Chicano

families living in the Los Angeles area. These statistics reflect the fact that
independent adoptions remain almost exclusively a "white" phenome-
non. Although the sample cannot be considered systematic, and the
authors are aware that some independent adoptions take place within
minority communities, it is noteworthy that not a single black family was
identified for the study.

Comparing the religious affiliations of the adoptive couples in this
study with those reported in other adoption studies,[4] we find an
overrepresentation of Jewish couples:

	Husband (N = 128) %	Wife (N = 131) %
Catholic	26	25
Protestant	35	34
Jewish	36	37
Other	—	2
None	3	2

Indicators of socioeconomic status place this group of families well
above the general population in education, occupation, income and
housing, and also well above couples adopting through agencies.

Over 60% of the men and half the women in the sample graduated
from college, while only about 5% did not finish high school.

Table 4-2
Education of Couples Adopting Independently

Education	Husband (N = 128) %	Wife (N = 131) %
Less than high school	5	5
High school graduate	13	19
Some college	16	16
Business or technical school	6	13
College graduate	21	20
Some graduate school	5	7
Graduate degree	35	20

Seventy-five percent of the men were employed in either professional or managerial positions, with an additional 9% employed in sales occupations. Fewer than half the women worked.

Table 4-3
Occupation of Couples Adopting Independently

Occupation	Husband (N = 128) %	Wife (N = 131) %
Professional	45	24
Managerial	30	1
Sales	9	—
Craftsman	5	1
Clerical	3	4
Operative/service/laborer	5	3
Part-time employment	2	11
Not employed	—	57

More than 80% of the couples had family earnings of over $15,000 and almost half the families had earnings of over $25,000. This is substantially higher than the income and occupational level of adoptive couples reported by agencies in another phase of the study, in which about one-third were of the working or lower socioeconomic classes.

Table 4-4
Family Income of Couples Adopting Independently

Income	% (N = 130)
Under $15,000	17
$15 – $20,000	14
$20 – $25,000	21
$25 – $30,000	18
$30 – $40,000	17
$40,000 +	14

With few exceptions the adoptive parents lived in private homes, and the overwhelming majority (89%) were in the process of buying or had already bought their own homes. Only 10% rented their living accommodations.

All but three of the adoptive families were two-parent households. The marriages had lasted a fairly long time, with only 13% married less than 6 years, but 64% married more than 10 years.

There had been a history of divorce in almost one-quarter of the families. In 9%, the husband had been divorced. In the same percentage the wife had been divorced, and in 6% of the cases both had been divorced. There was only one single (never married) woman.

As expected, the families tended to be small — about half had only one child in the household. Eighteen percent of the families had biological as well as adopted children. About one-third had adopted previously — nearly half of these through agencies.

Table 4-5
Children Present in the Household

Number of Children	Total Present in Household (N = 131) %	Number of Biological Children (N = 131) %	Number of Adopted Children (N = 131) %	Number Adopted Independently (N = 131) %
None	—	82	—	—
One	50	14	65	79
Two	37	2	29	19
Three	5	2	5	2
Four or more	8	—	2	1

CHARACTERISTICS OF THE CHILDREN

Of the 131 children of concern to the study, 74 (56%) were male and 57 (44%) female. In contrast to reports by agencies[5] (36% of the children accepted for adoption by 41 voluntary agencies and 78% of the children accepted for adoption by 16 public agencies were more than 3 months old), 89% of the children were placed before they were 2 weeks old and almost all (95%) were placed before the age of 3 months. At the time of the interview the children ranged in age from under 6 months to just over 5 years.

Table 4-6
Age of Child at Time of Interview

	Adoption Final (N = 98) %	Adoption Not Final (N = 33) %
Less than 6 mos.	6	55
6 mos. – 1 year	23	27
1 – 2 years	28	12
2 – 3 years	14	6
3 – 4 years	12	—
4 years or more	16	—

FINDING THE CHILDREN

There appears to be a wide range of circumstances under which the adoptive couples came to know that a child would be available for adoption. Some couples had contact only with the biological mother; others heard of a child through personal friends; still others dealt with professionals — some of whom were known on a personal or professional basis prior to the inquiry. For some couples the search for a child took relatively little time; others waited long periods for a child to be placed. Some couples had time to prepare for the placement; others were given less than a day's notice. Although some couples dealt with only one person in their search for a child, others followed a trail that involved several intermediaries. Almost one-quarter of the children were born in states other than those in which the adoptive couples lived.

The data give strong indications that interstate independent placements are more common in some areas of the country than others — over half the New York children but less than 10% of the Miami and Los Angeles children were born in other states.

Table 4-7
Interstate Placements, by Geographic Area

Interstate Placements	New York (N = 23)	Philadelphia (N = 24)	Iowa (N = 26)	Miami (N = 29)	Los Angeles (N = 26)
No	48.0	70.8	80.8	93.1	96.2
Yes	52.0	29.2	19.2	6.9	3.8
Chi-square = 23.31, df = 4, p<.001					

The following histories show the wide variety of circumstances under which children came to be placed with their prospective parents.

> This was their second adopted child. The family already knew the lawyer through the adoption of their first. Lawyer called the family to inquire whether they wished another child.

> Couple had told wife's uncle (who was a lawyer) that they wanted to adopt. He talked with them about it — then called the day the baby was born to offer them the child.

> Husband is an attorney. A professional colleague offered them the baby and the couple jumped at the opportunity.

> A friend of the adoptive mother was called by a lawyer. She had adopted two other children through the attorney. She told this couple about the baby and they called the lawyer to ask if they could have the baby instead. Lawyer said yes on the recommendation of the friend.

> Woman asked her gynecologist to keep her in mind if he learned of an adoptable baby. He told her about the child's bio-mother and referred her to bio-mother's lawyer for more information.

> Minister knew they wanted to adopt — he is a friend of theirs. A minister from another area of the state called their minister (they had gone to seminary together) asking if he knew a good Christian family for the child of one of his parishioners.

> Infertility specialist gave list of lawyers who did adoption work. Family contacted all the lawyers on the list. One of these lawyers contacted family when baby was available.

> Left names with 26 lawyers and sent resumes to all. A particular lawyer called 2 months later to tell them about a baby due in 3 months.

How the couples found out about the availability of the children is summarized in Table 4-8.

Table 4-8

Source of Information	(N = 131) %
Biological mother or her relative	5
Lawyer — no previous contact	28
— previous professional contact	10
— previous personal contact	8
Doctor — no previous contact	5
— previous professional contact	15
— previous personal contact	10
Clergy	2
Friend/relative of adoptive parents	13
Other	5

In only a small percentage of the cases did the biological mother "choose" the particular couple with whom to place her child. As can be seen in Table 4-9, in less than 10% of the cases were the arrangements for the adoption made directly between the biological mother and the adoptive couples. Most of the couples had a child placed through a professional intermediary (or several intermediaries), many of whom

Table 4-9
Exact Circumstances of Child's Placement

Circumstance	(N = 131) %
Unknown facilitator—arranged adoption	23
Professionally known facilitator—arranged adoption	15
Friend/relative facilitator—arranged adoption	5
Unknown facilitator—referred elsewhere	2
Professionally known facilitator—referred elsewhere	7
Friend/relative facilitator—referred elsewhere	4
Approached by unknown facilitator—arranged adoption	1
Approached by professionally known facilitator—arranged adoption	9
Approached by friend/relative facilitator—arranged adoption	15
Approached biological mother	4
Approached by biological mother	5
Other	2

were unknown to the couple prior to their search for a child. Some of the facilitators were able to arrange the adoption directly, but others referred the couples to other facilitators. The patterns that emerge are again divergent.

Most of the couples who adopted with the help of a facilitator dealt with more than one professional in their search for a child. Only 28% had contact with a single intermediary. As one might expect, couples whose children were born in states other than those in which they lived were more likely to have had contact with numerous intermediaries. Fifty-one percent of the couples adopting interstate were involved with three or more intermediaries, compared with 27% of the couples completing within-state adoptions.

The intermediary who brought the biological and adoptive parents together or was directly involved in arranging the placement between the biological and adoptive parents was designated the "child-placing" intermediary. Of the 121 intermediaries involved, 53% were lawyers and 37% were physicians. The others were clergy or other professionals. About half of the child-placing intermediaries were known to the adoptive couple prior to the adoption.

Of those persons who adopted through unknown intermediaries (N = 60) most were referred through friends or relatives, many of whom had adopted through this intermediary. The remaining couples were usually referred by other intermediaries, with only a small proportion of the families (7%) locating the facilitator on their own (through yellow pages, directories, etc.).

Table 4-10
Time From Contact With Any Intermediary and From Contact With the Child-Placing Intermediary to Placement of a Child

Time Between Contact and Placement	Any Intermediary (N = 118) %	Child-Placing Intermediary (N = 121) %
Under 3 months	31	40
3 - 6 months	19	22
6 - 12 months	18	16
1 - 2 years	19	12
2 years or more	14	9

In view of the various ways the couples came to have a child placed with them and the circuitous route many had to follow to locate a child, it is surprising to note that the placements took a relatively short time to complete. Almost half the couples were able to locate and have a child placed with them within 6 months of contact with any intermediary. Two-thirds of the couples had a child placed with them within 6 months of contacting the child-placing intermediary.

There was no relationship between geographic region, number of intermediaries involved, whether the child was born out of state or whether the child-placing intermediary was known prior to the contact about the adoption, and the time between contact with the first intermediary and placement. However, first-time adopters were more likely to have a child placed with them quickly than couples who had other adopted children.

Table 4-11
Time From Contact With Any Intermediary to Placement, by Whether Current Adoption Was First Adoption

	First Adoption	
	Yes	No
Length of Time From Contact With	(N = 76)	(N = 42)
Any Intermediary to Placement	%	%
Less than 6 months	55.3	38.1
6 – 12 months	21.1	11.9
1 – 2 years	14.5	26.2
2 years or more	9.2	23.8
Chi-square = 8.89, df = 3, p<.05		

The data suggest that couples seeking their first child are more anxious about obtaining a child and therefore pursue it with greater determination than couples who had adopted in the past and are familiar with the procedures.

FACILITATOR CONTACTS

Considering the brief time between the first contact with the child-placing intermediary and the placement of a child, it is not surprising that there were relatively few contacts between the child-placing intermediary and the adoptive couple prior to placement. One-third of the adoptive parents reported that they had two or fewer contacts of any type with the child-placing intermediary prior to placement. About the same number had three to five contacts, with only one-third of the adoptive parents reporting more than five contacts.

The relatively small number of contacts is significant, since a contact was considered to be any verbal exchange, including telephone conversations, the primary type of contact reported. Eighty-three percent of the adoptive couples reported phone contact with the child-placing intermediary, 59% reported contact in the intermediary's office, and only 17% indicated that the intermediary visited them in their homes. Thirty-four percent had contacts in other places, such as in court or at the hospital when they received the child.

As expected, the number of contacts with the intermediary was related to the amount of time between inquiry about the child and placement. Parents who had children placed with them shortly after inquiry tended to have fewer contacts with the intermediary than couples who had a considerable wait for a child.

Table 4-12

Number of Contacts With the Child-Placing Intermediary, by Time Between Inquiry and Placement

	Time Between Inquiry and Placement		
	Less than 3 months (N = 49)	3 months- 1 year (N = 46)	1 year or more (N = 26)
Number of Contacts	%	%	%
2 or fewer	51.0	23.9	26.9
3 – 5	26.5	37.0	26.9
6 or more	22.4	39.1	46.2
Chi-square = 10.01, df = 4, p<.05			

When the child-placing intermediary was a doctor, there tended to be fewer contacts than if the intermediary belonged to another profession.

Table 4-13
Number of Contacts With the Child-Placing Intermediary, by His/Her
Profession

Number of Contacts	Profession		
	Lawyer (N = 64) %	Doctor (N = 42) %	Other (N = 15) %
2 or fewer	29.7	50.0	20.0
3 - 5	35.9	26.2	20.0
6 or more	34.4	23.8	60.0
Chi-square = 9.80, df = 4, p<.05			

This may reflect the fact that doctors are not involved in the legal procedures. Surprisingly, couples adopting children interstate did not report a greater number of contacts with the intermediary than couples adopting children born in the same state.

The data reveal even fewer contacts with the intermediary after the child is in the home. Seventy percent of the couples reported five or fewer contacts after placement, 31% said they had only one or two contacts, and 14% reported no contact at all.

DISCUSSION WITH THE CHILD-PLACING INTERMEDIARY

The adoptive couples were asked what was discussed with the intermediary prior to the child's placement. The responses seem to fall under four major headings: information about the adoptive parents themselves; information about the biological parents; information about the child; and information about procedures. As may be seen from Table 4-14, the only subjects discussed in as many as 40% of the cases were the biological parents' background, and fees.

The analysis indicates that discussion of specific aspects of the adoption varies with circumstances. As might be expected, discussion of the biological mother's health history and medical information is more likely to occur ($p < .02$) if the intermediary is a doctor, while discussion of adoption procedures and legal fees is more likely if the intermediary is a lawyer ($p < .001$). The adoptive couples are more likely to discuss their own backgrounds ($p < .001$) and current situation ($p = .05$) as well as

Table 4-14
Topics of Discussion With the Child-Placing Intermediary Prior to Placement

Topic Discussed	%
Adoptive Parents	
Background, current life styles	28.9
Current information (feelings about rearing a child not their own, readiness to adopt, etc.)	26.5
Biological Parents	
Background	47.9
Mother's health	28.9
Current situation (reason for relinquishment, feelings about each other, etc.)	27.3
Child (health, race, etc.)	28.1
Procedures	
Legal procedures	30.6
Fees	43.8

procedures (p < .01) and fees (p < .001) if the intermediary is not known prior to the contact related to the adoption.

After placement, the focus of discussion with intermediaries seemed to be the procedural aspects of the adoption, such as legal arrangements. Only one-third of the couples reported talking about the child's progress. Some of the contacts reported were described as a continuation of social conacts with a previously known intermediary and were not concerned with the adoption.

BACKGROUND INFORMATION

To get an accurate picture of how much information the adoptive couple had about the child's background, a series of structured questions were asked regarding specific items. The couples were asked how much (considerable, some, none) information they had received with respect to each item. Table 4-15 reports the results.

Table 4-15
Information Reported by Adoptive Parents on Background Factors of Child

		Considerable %	Some %	None %
Bio-mother's:	Family background	28.2	53.4	18.3
	Health-medical history	29.8	52.7	17.6
	Education	42.8	40.5	16.8
	Occupation	45.4	34.6	20.0
Bio-father's:	Family background	6.9	38.9	54.2
	Health-medical history	11.5	33.6	55.0
	Education	23.7	35.9	40.5
	Occupation	29.5	27.1	43.4
Child's medical history		64.9	22.9	12.2
Child's experience before placement		79.8	16.3	3.9
Reason child was surrendered		53.4	32.8	13.7
Bio-parents' feelings about each other		29.2	23.9	46.9
Bio-parents' ability to care for child		38.9	32.8	28.2

In only three of the 13 areas queried did more than half of the adoptive parents feel that they had "considerable" information. Almost 20% of the families reported that they had no information in each of the areas regarding the biological mother. Between 40% and 55% reported they had no information in each of the areas concerning the biological father.

Table 4-16
Amount of Information, by Geographic Region

	Region				
Amount of Information	Philadelphia (N = 25) %	Iowa (N = 26) %	Miami (N = 29) %	New York (N = 25) %	Los Angeles (N = 26) %
High/Medium High	16.0	26.9	48.2	64.0	65.4
Medium Low/Low	84.0	73.1	51.7	36.0	34.6

Chi-square = 20.10, df = 4, $p < .001$

To obtain a picture of the factors associated with having information about the child's family background, an index of background information was constructed by obtaining a mean score for the 13 information items reported in Table 4-15. Based on this mean score, the sample was divided into four groups — high, medium high, medium low, and low information. Families in Los Angeles, New York and Miami reported a higher level of information than families in Philadelphia and Iowa.

It was suspected that couples in areas where there is mandatory involvement of social agencies might have more information because of contacts with agency personnel. If this were the case, one would expect New York couples to be as low on information as couples from Philadelphia, since no agency contact is mandated in these sites. This supposition was not supported by the data. The results may simply be a function of individual facilitators.

Couples whose intermediary was a doctor were more likely to have high or low information scores, when compared with couples involved with intermediaries of other professions.

Table 4-17
Amount of Information, by Profession of Child-Placing Intermediary

| | Profession | |
| | Doctor (N = 42) | Lawyer/Other (N = 79) |
Information	%	%
High	33.3	15.2
Medium high/medium low	31.0	55.7
Low	35.7	29.1
Chi-square = 8.14, df - 2, p<.02		

This nonlinear relationship may be due to the fact that the doctor is more likely to have medical information on the child and his biological parents. This may be the only type of information the doctor has, or he may also be in possession of social information that a lawyer gathered. Thus, the doctor may be more likely to fall into either the highest information category or the lowest.

As one might expect, the fewer the number of contacts with the intermediary, the less information an adoptive couple is likely to have, but the difference misses statistical significance ($.10 > p > .05$). Interestingly, the time between approaching the intermediary and the placement, whether or not there was office contact with the intermediary, and whether or not the intermediary was known prior to the adoptions, is unrelated to the amount of information a couple received.

Asked if they were satisfied with the information they had about the child, 37% of the couples reported satisfaction, feeling that they had all the important information on the child. Thirteen percent reported that they were generally satisfied but felt that they were missing information in specific areas. Thirty-three percent stated that they were not satisfied. In addition, almost 18% of the couples reported that they were satisfied with the information they had because they did not want to know about the child's background. As shown in Table 4-18, satisfaction was related to the amount of information the couples had.

Table 4-18
Satisfaction With the Information, by Amount of Information

| Amount of Information | Satisfied With Information | | | |
	Yes—Got All (N = 48) %	Somewhat (N = 17) %	No (N = 43) %	Yes—Do Not Want More (N = 23) %
High	43.8	17.6	11.6	0
Medium High/Medium Low	35.4	52.9	53.5	56.5
Low	20.8	29.4	34.9	43.5
Chi-square = 22.84, df = 2, p<.001				

Those who felt they got all the information did, in fact, receive significantly more information than those who were less satisfied in this area, although 21% of the satisfied couples fall into the lowest information group. Further, the couples who stated that they were satisfied because they did not want information got the least amount of information about their children, with more than 40% falling into the lowest information category and none falling into the highest. It appears that almost one-fifth of the sample considered background information unimportant.

When the couples were asked whether they wanted additional background information about the child, almost two-thirds replied in the affirmative. The two areas of desired information most frequently cited were the medical background of the child and information concerning the biological father. Couples who were not satisfied with the information they had were more likely to desire additional information than other couples.

Table 4-19
Satisfaction With the Background Information, by Desire for Additional Information

	Satisfied With Information			
Want Additional Information	Yes—Got All (N = 48) %	Somewhat (N = 17) %	No (N = 43) %	Yes—Do Not Want More (N = 23) %
No	60.4	5.9	2.3	69.6
Yes	39.6	94.1	97.7	30.4
Chi-square = 51.60, df = 3, p<.001				

Twenty-five percent of the sample reported that they worried about insufficient background information. The data suggest that the continued concern centers on medical information. Respondents adopting through doctors expressed significantly less concern than others in the sample (p < .05). In addition, concern about insufficient background information was related to whether the couples had information on the medical history of the child (p < .01), the biological mother (p < .05) and the biological father (p = .05). Only two other information items were found to have a relationship with expressed concern — biological father's education and biological mother's occupation.

RECOGNITION OF THE CHILD'S ADOPTIVE STATUS

An issue with which the study was concerned was whether the couples recognized that there are differences between rearing biological children and rearing adoptive children — that adoptive children have an additional dimension to their lives with which they must cope. To measure this awareness the adoptive couples were asked, "Do you think there are problems in rearing an adopted child that are different from those in rearing a biological child?"

About half of the adoptive couples (N = 62) felt that there were problems in rearing an adoptive child that were different from those in rearing a biological child. Those stating that there were different problems cited several factors accounting for the special problems, including: 1) there is no connection with the biological family, which can lead to identity problems (N = 31); 2) the adoptive parents have to help the child feel comfortable with his adoptive status (N = 29); 3) the extended family or the community may make the child feel different or inferior (N = 10); and 4) the child must deal with an added dimension in his or her life (N = 7). The explanations offered most often by those who felt there were no special problems included: 1) children are the same whether adopted or biological and their adopted child feels like their own (N = 31); 2) there is no difference if the child is adopted as an infant (N = 6); and 3) there is no difference if the child is given a good home and love (N = 5).

With concerns about identity and the unconnectedness to the biological family being the primary reasons cited for the special situation of the adopted children, it is not surprising that couples who were worried about not having sufficient background information were more likely to be aware of the special problems in rearing an adopted child (67% vs. 41%). Couples who adopted through a lawyer also were more likely to feel there are special problems than couples adopting through intermediaries of other professions (58% vs. 39%). In addition, couples who adopted through an unknown intermediary were more likely to be aware of the special problems than couples who adopted through a known intermediary (60% vs. 39%).

In the analysis of awareness of special problems in rearing an adopted child, there was no difference between the couples by the age of the couple, family income, whether they had adopted in the past, or the number of contacts they had with the intermediary.

CONCERN ABOUT THE BIOLOGICAL MOTHER

Over half of the adoptive parents reported that they knew the name of the biological mother. This includes the 10 couples who had a child placed directly by the mother and 57 of the couples who had a child placed through an intermediary. In cases where the placement was by an intermediary, there were geographic differences, with couples in New York and Los Angeles less likely to know the identity of the biological mother than couples in other areas.

With more than half of the adoptive parents knowing the identity of the biological mother, it was expected that many would be concerned about the biological parents interfering in the child's life. This was not found to be the case. Only 23 couples (17.7%) reported that this caused them any worry, and for the most part the concern was minor.

In contrast, there was considerable concern that the biological mother might change her mind about relinquishment. Sixty-one percent of the couples reported that they worried about this prior to the placement of the child, and 45% reported this concern after the child was placed but before finalization.

For the most part, the fears expressed were general. Many of the adoptive couples knew that until the final adoption decree, the biological mother had the option of refusing to sign a final consent. This knowledge caused general anxiety as expressed by some of the parents:

> (We were concerned) only because of the nature of the legal process, which gives the mother this option.

> We knew that the bio-mother had the right to change her mind and that it was hard for any mother to give up her baby.

> (We were worried) because we knew the mother had the right to take the baby before the adoption was finalized.

Some couples related this fear to previous experiences, and knew that they were taking a risk by adopting independently. Examples of this response were:

> (We) had prior experience where the mother had changed her mind after the birth of the baby.

> We were worried because of things we had heard. There is always the possibility of a problem in private adoptions.

> We were worried because she might change her mind. Our lawyer doesn't like private adoptions because girls change their minds often and there is too much risk.

Many of the variables associated with worry about a change of mind before placement were also associated with that worry between placement and finalization. Only the relationships at the first point in time are presented. Unless otherwise noted, each relationship holds for the second point.

Younger adoptive mothers were less concerned about this problem than older ones.

Table 4-20
Adoptive Parents' Concern About the Biological Mother's Changing Her Mind
Before Placement, by Age of Adoptive Mother

Concern Bio-Mother's Changing Mind	Adoptive Mother's Age	
	Under 30 (N = 30) %	Over 30 (N = 94) %
None	56.7	33.0
Some	36.7	35.1
Considerable	6.7	31.9
Chi-square = 8.92, df = 2, p<.025		

Older women may be under greater pressure to start or expand their families, and therefore be more anxious than younger women about issues that might impede the adoption.

Couples who had previously adopted independently were less likely than first-time independent adopters to worry about the biological mother's changing her mind. Couples who have coped with the uncertainty of independent adoptions in the past and found their fears groundless are less likely to continue to be concerned about this possibility.

Table 4-21
Adoptive Parents' Concern About the Biological Mother's Changing Her Mind
After Placement, by Previous Independent Adoption Experience

Concern Bio-Mother's Changing Mind	Other Independent Adoptions	
	No (N = 103) %	Yes (N = 28) %
None	48.5	78.6
Some	32.0	17.9
Considerable	19.4	3.6
Chi-square = 8.59, df = 2, p<.02		

It appears also that the greater the number of contacts with the intermediary, the less the worry about the biological mother's changing her mind. The opportunity to talk to the intermediary, to clarify concerns and issues, diminishes this anxiety.

Table 4-22

Adoptive Parents' Concern About the Biological Mother's Changing Her Mind After Placement, by Number of Contacts With Intermediary Before Placement

	Number Contacts Before Placement		
	0 - 2	3 - 5	6 or more
Concern Bio-Mother's	(N = 43)	(N = 37)	(N = 41)
Changing Mind	%	%	%
None	53.5	54.1	56.1
Some	18.6	29.7	39.0
Considerable	27.9	16.2	4.9
Chi-square = 9.80, df = 4, p <.05			

One relationship was related only to worry about a change of mind after placement. Couples who had children placed with them quickly were less concerned about the mother's changing her mind after the child was placed. Longer waiting may increase anxiety by giving couples the opportunity to think about what might go wrong.

Table 4-23

Adoptive Couples' Concern About the Biological Mother's Changing Her Mind After Placement, by Length of Time Between First Contact and Placement

	Length of Time	
	Under 6 Months	6 Months or More
Concern Bio-mother's	(N = 58)	(N = 60)
Changing Mind	%	%
None	63.8	43.3
Some/Considerable	36.2	56.7
Chi-square = 4.17, df = 1, p<.05		

The amount of information about the biological mother and her relationship to the child's father were not associated with the degree of worry in this area.

Despite the generally high level of concern about the biological mother's changing her mind before the adoption was final, it should be noted that such concern ceased at the time of finalization. Of the 98 couples whose adoptions were finalized at the point of the interview, only three expressed any concern that the biological mother would attempt to regain custody of the child.

CONCERN ABOUT THE BIOLOGICAL FATHER

Each of the couples was asked if they knew whether the biological father had given his consent to the adoption. Thirty-eight percent had no information about this. The same proportion knew that he had consented to the adoption, and 24% knew that his consent was not obtained. When one analyzes these data, strong geographic differences are apparent.

Table 4-24
Information About the Biological Father's
Consent, by Geographic Area

	Region				
Had Information	Philadelphia (N = 25) %	Iowa (N = 26) %	Miami (N = 29) %	Los Angeles (N = 26) %	New York (N = 25) %
No information	72.0	15.4	58.6	3.8	40.0
Knew whether bio-father consented	28.0	84.6	41.4	96.2	60.0
Chi-square = 36.00, df = 4, p<.001					

It is noteworthy that in states with strong consent statutes[6] the adoptive parents are aware of the biological father's status significantly more often than in states with weaker consent statutes. Similarly, in states with strong consent statutes adoptive couples are more likely to worry about the biological father's refusing to give his consent for the adoption. Of the 29 couples who reported this as a concern, all but four were from Iowa or California (p < .001).

Several other variables were associated with whether a couple was concerned about the biological father's consent. Couples who had three or more contacts with the intermediary were more likely to be concerned about this (27% versus 9%). Perhaps with more contacts, there is a greater likelihood of discussing the biological father, which raises the anxiety of the adoptive parents.

Couples who had longer periods of time between inquiry and placement tended to worry more about the biological father. A third of those who waited more than a year, but only 14% who waited less, expressed this worry. Again, couples with longer waits may have more time to become aware of issues dealing with the biological father, and thus be more concerned.

There was also a relationship between concern of the adoptive parents and the year in which the child was placed. Using the age of the child at the time of the study as an indicator of when the child was placed (since most of the children were placed as infants), couples adopting recently were less concerned about the biological father than couples who had children placed 6 to 24 months prior to the interview. Couples whose children had been in the home for more than 24 months were also less concerned.

Table 4-25
Worry About Biological Father's Refusing
Surrender, by Child's Age

Worry Bio-Father's Refusing Surrender	Child's Current Age		
	Under 6 Months (N = 24) %	6 – 24 Months (N = 63) %	2 Years or More (N = 44) %
No	87.5	62.5	90.9
Yes	12.5	37.5	9.1
Chi-square = 11.61, df - 2, p<.005			

This relationship may reflect the initial impact of the *Stanley vs. Illinois* and subsequent decisions. Couples adopting soon after the *Stanley* decision and its implementation may have been more aware of the rights of the biological father than couples adopting recently or before its implementation.

Having information about the biological father was not associated with this concern. Couples who knew about the biological father's background, relationship, etc., were no more likely to express concern about the biological father's refusing to surrender than those who did not have this information.

CONCERN ABOUT THE CHILD'S PHYSICAL CONDITION

Each couple was asked if, before placement, they were concerned whether the child had a physical problem of which they were unaware. Thirty-seven percent of the couples said this was of concern to them. Much of the reason for worry was stated in general terms. For example:

> We wanted a healthy child and were concerned about this.
>
> Concerned that the child would be healthy — a normal concern like anyone expecting to have or get a child.

Other couples were worried about specific health problems that might arise:

> We were concerned that the child might be born with handicaps through birth injuries.
>
> We were worried that the baby would be born with handicaps, brain damage, etc.
>
> We were concerned about retardation.
>
> The bio-parents might have been on narcotics and the baby could be born addicted.

Still others saw this as a risk in independent adoption and considered whether they would accept such a child:

> I didn't want to accept (a child) if ill or there was gross physical or mental impairment.
>
> She (the child) may be malformed or retarded — through private adoptions you take what you get and in agency adoptions you get a healthy child.

Couples wishing more information about the child were more likely to be concerned about this possibility. This was not surprising, since information about health was the most frequently cited need.

Table 4-26
Worry About Child's Physical Condition,
by Desire for Additional Information

Concern Prior to Placement About Child's Physical Condition	Want Additional Information	
	No (N = 47) %	Yes (N = 84) %
No	76.6	56.0
Yes	23.4	44.0
Chi-square = 4.77, df = 1, p<.05		

Concern about the child's physical condition was also related to the number of contacts between the intermediary and the adoptive parents, and to the time it took to have a child placed. Couples with few or a great many contacts with the intermediary, and couples who waited short or long periods were less likely to be concerned about the child's physical condition than couples who had a moderate number of contacts and those who waited a moderate time.

Table 4-27
Worry About Child's Physical Condition Before Placement, by Number of Contacts With Intermediary Prior to Placement

| Concern Prior to Placement About Child's Physical Condition | Number of Contacts | | |
	0 – 2 (N = 43) %	3 – 5 (N = 37) %	6 or more (N = 41) %
No	76.7	48.6	61.0
Yes	23.3	51.4	39.0
Chi-square = 6.81, df = 2, p<.05			

Table 4-28
Worry About Child's Physical Condition Before Placement, by Time Between Inquiry and Placement

| Concern Prior to Placement About Child's Physical Condition | Time Between Inquiry and Placement | | |
	Less than 3 months (N = 49) %	3 – 12 months (N = 46) %	12 months or more (N = 26) %
No	69.4	47.8	76.9
Yes	30.6	52.2	23.1
Chi-square = 7.55, df = 2, p<.05			

That adoptive parents with many contacts and long waits had more information than other couples may account for their lesser concern. Those with few contacts may not have had time even to consider this possibility.

The adoptive parents were also asked if they were currently

concerned about the child's physical condition. Thirteen percent said this was a source of worry and reported such problems as:

> Child had recurring ear infections.
>
> . . . has many colds, is getting over double hernia and his feet are turned in.
>
> He is showing signs of diabetes and she is worried that he may have inherited this.

The child's current age was the only factor found to relate to current concerns about the child's health. Couples with children more than a year old tended to have more concern about the child's physical condition than couples with younger children (19% vs. 5%). Since these concerns were based on the child's current health, it may be that health problems do not arise until the child has been in the home for a significant time.

CONCERN ABOUT THE CHILD'S EMOTIONAL CONDITION

The adoptive couples were asked, "Before (the child) was placed with you, were you worried if he/she may have inherited some mental or emotional problem from his/her parents?" Almost 30% of the couples expressed such concern. In reviewing the reasons for this worry, it was evident that the anxiety expressed related to mental retardation, not emotional illness. Typical responses were:

> Did have some concern that the child might be retarded or borderline. Did not know at what level the bio-mother was functioning.
>
> Fear was present — we didn't know for certain because of limited information.

Such responses suggest that this fear is connected with lack of information about the child. Four specific pieces of information (biological mother's family background, biological father's family background, biological mother's occupation and biological parent's ability to care for the child) were found to be related to whether the adoptive parents expressed concern about the child's developmental or emotional well-being. On each item, couples with only some or no information were more likely to be concerned than couples with considerable information.

In addition, respondents who had adopted other children (either independently or through agencies) were less likely to express this concern (15% vs. 35%). Evidently, a previous adoption experience in which a concern was not realized diminishes that concern in a second experience.

In response to a question on current concern about the child's emotional development, only eight respondents expressed any concern, and it tended to be minor. As with the current physical concerns, this worry was expressed more often by couples whose children were older.

COSTS OF THE ADOPTION

Questions were asked about the financial aspects of the adoption including: total costs; a breakdown of the costs; how they were paid; whether there was an attempt to increase the costs; whether the couples felt the costs were justified; whether they worried about being able to pay the fees; and whether the adoption caused financial strain.

All but 11 couples gave the interviewer an approximation of the total costs. Of the 11 who did not, seven were couples whose costs had not yet been determined, while four couples refused to answer. The total costs of the adoption reported were as follows:

Table 4-29
Total Costs of the Adoption
(N = 120)

Cost	%
Under $1000	13
$1000 – 2499	45
$2500 – 3999	24
$4000 – 5999	12
$6000 or more	6

The median cost of the adoptions reported was $2223.

Almost all respondents paid attorney's fees and medical expenses for the biological mother. In addition, 15% of the adoptive parents paid the biological mother's housing costs for a time during her pregnancy, and the same percentage of couples paid other costs of the biological mother. In addition, 35% of the adopters incurred other expenses, including transportation costs and investigators' charges for seeking the biological father. Table 4-30 presents the data.

Table 4-30
Costs of Legal Fees, Medical, Housing and Other Costs for the Biological Mother, and Other Costs Paid by the Adopting Couple

	Legal (N = 113) %	Medical (N = 118) %	Housing (N = 122) %	Other Payment (N = 121) %	Other (N = 120) %
None	4	15	85	84	65
$1 - 249	6	—	1	8	18
$250 - 499	19	8	5	5	11
$500 - 999	53	22	3	3	1
$1000 - 1999	10	42	7	—	3
$2000 +	9	13	—	—	3

For the majority of the adoptive couples (59%), all the costs were set before the placement of the child. The rest did not know the costs of the adoption until placement, including some who did not know what the adoption would cost until finalization.

The payment of fees most commonly occurred at two points — at or before placement, and at or prior to finalization. This was reported by 42% of the couples. Nineteen percent established escrow accounts from which the intermediary drew money as needed. Some couples paid in one lump sum (18%) either at placement, at finalization or at some point in between. The other couples paid in installments.

For the most part, the adoptions were paid for by check or by setting up trust funds or escrow accounts. Eighty-eight percent of the couples reported this as the only method of payment. However, 12% of the couples reported that some cash was given to the intermediary during the adoption process.

Nineteen couples (15%) reported an attempt to boost the costs of the adoption prior to finalization. In eight of these cases there was a request for more funds for medical fees for the mother. In seven cases there was a demand for larger fees for the intermediary. In two cases, the money was to be used for room and board for the mother, a cost that had not been agreed upon originally. In the other two cases, the biological mother was reported to have demanded a cash payment to relinquish her child.

Most of the couples (72%) felt that the costs of the adoption were justified and reasonable, and another 5% thought that the costs were justified but high. However, more than 20% of the respondents felt that at least some of the costs were inflated — over half of these thought that the lawyer's fee was excessive.

Almost one-quarter of the couples reported that the adoption caused them financial strain. Twenty percent were worried about being able to meet the costs of the adoption. This financial strain was dealt with in various ways, including depletion of savings, borrowing money, general reduction in the standard of living, and the wife's taking a job. Not surprisingly, high income families felt much less strain and worry than families with incomes under $30,000.

Concern about the ability to pay was also more common among couples whose adoption costs were $4000 or more than among those whose costs were less than $4000 (43% vs. 15%).

CONCERN ABOUT THE LEGALITY OF THE ADOPTION

The adoptive parents were asked, "Prior to the child being placed with you, were you ever concerned about the legality of the way his/her adoption was handled?" Fifteen percent (N = 19) of the couples reported that they had concerns in this area. Some expressed these in general terms about the adoption taking too long or the potential for abuse in independent adoptions. Other respondents gave vivid examples of why they were concerned about the legality of the adoption:

> "We knew we were paying a lot of money. The lawyer was 'procuring' a baby — he was involved with an abortion group. In a roundabout way the lawyer mentioned that sometimes a girl is in her 23rd week but is told she is in her 25th so she cannot have an abortion and they will have another child to get adopted. We lied to the social worker about the fee — the lawyer told us to. We also lied about payment in court."

> "Lawyer #1 told us that lawyer #2 wanted one-third of the amount in a personal check and two-thirds in cash. This made us suspicious."

> "The lawyer told us that the adoption would have to be completed in Mexico. When we tried to transfer to a different lawyer to see about finalizing where we lived, the lawyer threatened to take the baby back."

"We did not live in New York, but knew it would be very difficult to adopt privately in (state), so we took a New York address and said we lived there."

Concern about the legality of the adoption was strongly related to its cost.

Table 4-31
Concern About the Way the Adoption Was Handled, by Costs of the Adoption

	Total Costs of Adoption		
Concern About Legality	Less than $4000 (N = 99) %	$4000 or more (N = 21) %	All Costs Not Yet Known/ Would Not Reveal (N = 11) %
No	91.9	66.7	63.6
Yes	8.1	33.3	36.4
Chi-square = 13.54, df = 2, p<.005			

Couples whose adoption costs exceeded $4000 and those whose costs were not yet final or who would not reveal their costs to the interviewer were much more likely than others to be concerned about the legality of the way the adoption was handled.

Apparently, couples who were asked to pay high fees were aware that they might have been involved in a violation of the law. This is borne out by the data. Couples who felt that the fees were justified were less likely to be concerned about the legality of the adoption than couples who felt that the fees were not justified by the service they received.

Table 4-32
Concern About the Way the Adoption was Handled, by Justification of Costs

	Cost Justified	
Concern About Legality	Yes (N = 94) %	No (N = 33) %
No	91.5	72.7
Yes	8.5	27.3
Chi-square = 5.88, df = 1, p<.025		

There was no relationship between concerns in this area and whether the couple had adopted independently in the past, where the couple was living, whether the child was born in the same state, or whether there was more than one intermediary involved.

INDICATIONS OF LEGALLY QUESTIONABLE ACTIVITIES

For obvious reasons, couples were not asked directly about the legality of their efforts to obtain a child. However, the interview was so structured as to permit specific indications of illegal activity to emerge. These indicators included: 1) the high total costs of the adoption; 2) whether the biological mother received payments beyond medical and housing costs; 3) whether cash was given to the intermediary; 4) whether all costs of the adoption were declared in court; 5) whether there was an attempt to increase the fee; 6) whether the adoptive parents were concerned about the legality of the adoption; and 7) whether the adoptive parents felt the costs were justified.

On each schedule a judgment was made by the coder and checked by the research staff as to whether legally questionable activity was indicated in the interview. It should be noted that the mere presence of one of the elements listed did not classify a case as legally questionable. For example, high fees might be justifiable if the intermediary or someone he or she employed had to do extra work to free the child for adoption. A case was classified as legally questionable only if a number of elements were present and concrete information were available. Some of the cases classified in this way were cited in the previous section. Some additional examples help clarify this point.

"The child was born in the state of _____. That was where the biological mother lives. According to our lawyer, it is illegal in _____ to transport a child out of state for the purpose of adoption. When the lawyer found this out, he said the adoption could not go through. About a week later he telephoned and said 'You can pick up your child at the railroad station.' I assume this was illegal, although I never asked and the lawyer never said so." (The adoption cost $3000.)

The total cost of the adoption was about $5000. The lawyer received his legal fee half in cash and half in a check. There was in addition to the legal fee a payment of $1500 to the lawyer's "source" for finding the child in (another state). The payment to the source in _____ was not declared in court. They do not know what the lawyer declared as his fee.

The total cost of the adoption was $5500. The biological mother and her family were from _____ and moved to _____ for the last 4 months of the pregnancy. The costs included rent for all these people and a Nassau vacation after the placement.

The couple could not finalize in their state because the baby came from (another state) and the judge refused to finalize. Lawyer advised they would have to legalize in Mexico. Mr. O flew to Juarez to meet the lawyer's contact there. Next day they went to court, but the Mexican judge was on vacation. The "contact" said he had been a judge and was qualified to sign the adoption papers. They went to a notary and had the adoption certificate notarized. Later the adoptive parents received a revised birth certificate from (other state) on the basis of the Mexican adoption. The judge in (home state) told them that the adoption might not stand up if it was contested. The cost of the adoption was $4450. The intermediary attempted to raise the fee by telling them she had forgotten to bill them for expenses like long-distance calls, medical costs, attorney's fees in the state from which the child came, etc. They actually paid the lawyer $4200, but at one point she "became frightened by a TV expose" and told them she had "miscalculated expenses" and voluntarily returned $600.

The adoption cost $7500. Paid the lawyer $6000 in cash in five installments. The lawyer tried to raise fee when the baby was picked up at the hospital because he said he had additional expenses. "We refused to pay the extra $1500 and the lawyer implied he would not give us another child." Only $1500 medical and $1500 legal fees were declared in court. The couple did not think the costs were high. They paid from $12,000 to $15,000 for the first child.

Of the 131 adoptions examined in the study, 17, or 13% of the cases, were classified as legally questionable. As one would expect, this was associated with whether the couple was worried about the legalities ($p < .001$), whether cash was given to the intermediary ($p = .005$), and whether the adoption caused financial strain ($p = .016$).

When the data were examined to see if certain groups were more likely to be involved in legally questionable activities than others, some significant relationships were found.

Legally questionable activities were more likely to occur when the intermediary was a lawyer. Twenty-two percent of the adoptions arranged by lawyers seemed legally questionable, compared with only 4% of the adoptions arranged by doctors or other professionals.

Legally questionable activities were less likely to take place in states with strong controls on independent adoptions (consent statutes, requirements of investigation, etc.). No cases in California and Iowa were judged legally questionable, whereas in Pennsylvania, Florida and New York at least 20% of the adoptions seemed legally questionable.

Table 4-33
Legally Questionable Cases,
by Geographic Location

	Location	
	Iowa/California (N = 52)	Florida/ Pennsylvania/ New York (N = 79)
Legally Questionable	%	%
Yes	0	21.5
No	100.0	78.5
Chi-square = 11.02, df = 1, p<.001		

There is some indication (although not statistically significant) that interstate adoptions were more likely to be judged legally questionable than intrastate adoptions. Twenty-five percent of the interstate adoptions were judged legally questionable, compared with 10% of the adoptions within a state.

From the preceding two findings it appears that in areas where

Table 4-34
Legally Questionable Cases,
by Wife's Religion

	Wife's Religion	
	Jewish (N = 48)	Catholic/ Protestant/Other (N = 83)
Legally Questionable	%	%
Yes	29.2	3.6
No	70.8	96.4
Chi-square = 15.39, df = 1, p<.001		

adoptions are not strictly regulated (interstate and in states with weak statutes) the potential for abuse becomes a reality more often than in areas where strict laws are in effect.

In addition, Jewish couples in the study sample were significantly more likely to be involved in legally questionable adoptions than those of other religions.

This is probably a reflection of the greater scarcity of Jewish infants for adoption. Due to this scarcity, these couples may be forced to take larger legal risks than other couples in obtaining a child.

The age of the mother, the family income, the length of marriage, and whether there were other children in the household showed no relation to whether the adoption was judged legally questionable. It appears that young people are as likely to be involved in legally questionable activities as older people, high income couples as likely as those with low income, childless adopters as likely as those who have children.

From additional analysis on this variable, it appears that:

- Legally questionable placements take no less time to complete than other placements.

- Couples involved in legally questionable adoptions have a similar number of contacts with the child-placing intermediary as other couples.

- Couples involved in legally questionable adoptions have the same amount of information about the child as other couples, and are as satisfied with it.

- Couples involved in legally questionable adoptions are no more likely to worry about the child's physical or emotional condition or the biological mother's changing her mind or interfering with the child than other couples.

SUMMARY AND DISCUSSION

Although similar in age to couples adopting through agencies, the sample of independent adopters differed from their agency counterparts in some important ways: they were almost exclusively white; they were of higher socioeconomic status; they were better educated and were more likely to hold professional positions; and they were more likely to be Jewish.

There was great variation in the ways the couples located a child for adoption. The largest number of adopting couples (28%) found their children through attorneys with whom they had had no contact prior to adoption. Contrary to what is often presented as a reason for the continuance of independent adoptions — that the biological mother has a choice of who the adopting couple will be — only 5% of the couples found their children through direct contact with the biological mother and only 9% of the sample arranged for the adoption directly with her. Almost one-quarter of the adoptions were arranged between biological mothers living in one state and adoptive couples residing in another.

Placement of a child through independent means appears to take considerably less time than placement of a child through agencies. Half of the couples had a child placed with them within 6 months of approaching any intermediary. This short period is even more surprising when one recognizes that the children placed were, for the most part, healthy, white infants — the group least available for adoption through agencies.

Almost two-thirds of the couples reported having five or fewer contacts of any kind (the largest number were telephone contacts) with the intermediary. Only 17% of the adoptive couples reported a contact with the intermediary in their home. Given the nature and number of the contacts, it seems that the possibility of a child's being placed in an inappropriate home is greater in independent adoptions than in agency adoptions. This may constitute a risk to the child.

This same risk appears to continue after the child is placed. Almost half of the couples reported two or fewer contacts with the intermediary between the placement of the child and finalization. During this time only one-third of the couples reported discussion of the child with the intermediary. Thus, once a placement was made there was little, if any, followup to assure that the child was well cared for.

Not only did the number of contacts prior to placement indicate that the couples came under little scrutiny, but what was discussed during these contacts seemed to point to the risk of an inappropriate placement. Fewer than 30% of the adoptive couples reported talking about their life styles, their feelings about rearing a child not their own, etc. What was discussed most often was the child's background and legal procedures and fees. Even these were discussed with less than half of the adopting couples. It appears, then, that in independent adoptions basic information about the couple or the child may not be exchanged.

The data indicate that some couples come under more scrutiny than others. In cases where the adoptive couple was known to the intermediary prior to the adoption, the likelihood of discussion centering on the adopting couple diminished. It may be that these couples were not closely screened because the intermediary assumed that he had all the necessary information to make a sound placement, or that this information was not important in making such a placement.

The profession of the intermediary also seems to influence what is covered in the discussions prior to the placement of the child. Health and medical information was more likely to be transmitted to the adopting couple if the intermediary was a doctor, and procedural information was more likely to be transmitted if the intermediary was a lawyer. That the kind of information exchanged depends on the profession of the intermediary may also constitute a risk in independent adoptions.

The responses to questions concerning whether the adoptive couple had specific information about the biological parents and the child yielded some disturbing data. Almost 20% of the families reported that they had no information in each of the areas concerning the biological mother, and between 40% and 55% reported no information in each of the areas concerning the biological father. This can be considered a major problem in independent adoptions. The adopted child's need for information about his/her background in order to develop a sense of identity is well documented. It is obvious that obtaining accurate and complete medical information on the biological parents is necessary for both the adoptive couple and the child. That such information may not be available to the adoptive parents in independent adoptions constitutes a major risk.

Asked if they were satisfied with the background information they had, 18% of the sample said they were satisfied because they did not want information about the child. This group of adoptive parents did, in fact, get less information than the rest of the adopting couples. Not obtaining information and not acknowledging the need for it may indicate that these adoptive parents are denying that the child comes from a different background. This denial can have serious consequences for the child.

Almost half of the study couples were unaware of or unable to confront the fact that adopted children face a situation different from that of biological children. This lack of recognition that the adopted child faces problems about identity, as well as additional pressures in the community, can constitute a risk to the child adopted independently.

Over half of the sample of adoptive couples knew the identity of the biological mother. However, few were concerned about the possibility that the biological mother would interfere in the child's life. It is likely that, although the adoptive parents knew who the biological parents were, they were assured that the biological parents could not identify them.

Sixty percent of the couples reported that there was concern that the biological mother might change her mind before placement, and 45% of the couples reported this worry between placement and finalization. This concern was related to several factors, including the number of contacts with the intermediary. The association of this anxiety with a low incidence of contacts with the intermediary points to the importance of contact with the placing person about issues of concern.

Thirty-eight percent of the couples had no information about whether the biological father consented to the adoption. Lack of this information was more prevalent in states with weak consent statutes. It seems that only when the state has guaranteed the rights of the biological father in a strong statute do his rights become a topic of discussion and concern to the adoptive parents. This is reflected in the finding that, of the 29 couples who reported concern that the biological father might refuse to surrender the child, all but four were from states with strong statutes. That couples in states with weak consent statutes are unlikely to know that the status of the biological father constitutes a risk in independent adoptions, since the biological father's rights have been established by the Supreme Court.

Thirty-seven percent of the adoptive couples reported that there was concern about the child's physical condition prior to placement. This concern was more likely to be expressed by couples wanting more information about the child, a finding that once again points to the importance of information that couples adopting independently may not have.

The median cost of the adoption reported by the adoptive parents was $2223. However, 18% of the adoptions cost more than $4000. Twelve percent of the couples reported that cash was exchanged with the intermediary; 15% reported an attempt to increase the fee for the adoption after it had been set; and 20% felt that the cost of the adoption was not justified. Fifteen percent of the couples expressed concern that they were involved in legally questionable activities.

The study staff judged 13% of the total cases to be legally questionable. Legally questionable activity is more likely to occur in states with weaker adoption statutes, and interstate adoptions are more likely to involve legally questionable practices. From this, one can surmise that in the areas where adoptions are not strictly regulated through law (interstate and in states with weak statutes) the potential for abuse becomes reality more often than in areas where strict laws are in effect.

Finally, one-quarter of the couples indicated that the adoption caused them financial strain and one-fifth of the couples reported that they were worried about meeting the costs of the adoption. As expected, families with lower incomes were more likely to report this than families of better means. Since ability to pay is not a criterion for fees charged in an independent adoption, as it is in agency adoptions, some couples find themselves under financial pressure in completing an adoption.

REFERENCES

1. National Center for Health Statistics. *Monthly Vital Statistics Report*, Vol. 24, No. 11, Supplement 2, February 13, 1976.
2. For comparative data on couples adopting through agencies, see Trudy Bradley (Festinger), *An Exploration of Caseworkers' Perceptions of Adoptive Applicants*. New York: Child Welfare League of America, 1967.
3. Barbara Haring. *Adoption Statistics*. New York: Child Welfare League of America, May 1976, pp. 2, 6.
4. See, for example, Trudy Bradley (Festinger), *op cit.*, p. 62.
5. Barbara Haring, *op cit.*, p. 10.
6. California and Iowa — the new Florida statute had not been implemented at the time of the study.

5

The Adoptive Parents
Agency Experience and Their Feelings
About Adoption and the Adoption Process

To get a fuller picture of the experiences of the adoptive couples, they were asked about their contacts with social agencies, how they felt their adoptions had turned out, and their feelings about having adopted independently.

AGENCY CONTACTS REGARDING ADOPTION

The adoptive parents were asked if they had explored the possibility of adoption with a social agency in conjunction with their most recent decision to enlarge their families. A large majority (95) of the couples reported agency contacts.

Among the reasons cited by couples for not approaching an agency were: knowledge that there would be a long wait for a child or that intake was closed (N = 15); the couple did not feel they could meet agency requirements including age, religion, health, having other children, marital history, etc. (N = 7); not knowing about adoption agencies or what they did (N = 10); believing that agencies would not be helpful (N = 3); and previous negative experiences with agencies (N = 5).

Couples who had adopted independently prior to the adoption under study were less likely than other couples to approach a social agency (50% vs. 77%). It appears that having successfully adopted independently in the past, a couple is more likely to pursue only this route in subsequent adoptions.

Demographic variables did not differentiate between couples who did and did not approach social agencies. There were no differences among couples when the data were analyzed by geographic region, religion, income or whether there had been a history of divorce.

Over three-quarters of the 95 adoptive couples who approached social agencies felt that their applications were discouraged, and 22% were either told directly or by inference that they would be ineligible.

Those who felt they were discouraged (N = 70) from applying, explained most often that intake was closed or that the waiting list so long application seemed fruitless. This discouragement is not surprising when one considers how long these couples were told they would have to wait for a child. Fewer than 20% of the adoptive parents were told that the wait would be less than 3 years. Fifteen percent were told that it would be between 3 and 5 years, and 18% were told at least 5 years. The remaining couples — almost 50% of those who approached agencies — were told either that the wait would be indefinite or that the agency could not tell how long it would be.

In addition, 15% of the adoptive parents who felt discouraged by the agency cited agency requirements they did not feel they could meet. The requirements most often mentioned concerned age, religion or the presence of other children in the home.

Those who learned directly or by inference that they were not eligible to adopt a child through an agency (N = 20) most often said that they were above the age limit, that the agency did not place children with couples who already had children in the home, or that they had not been married long enough. Thus, agency requirements play a major role in couples' dropping the agency from consideration.

Couples from the Miami area were more likely than those in the other sample areas to have been told or led to believe that they would be ineligible to adopt (45% vs. 15%). This finding is consistent with findings from the agency questionnaire, in which agencies in the South had a greater number of eligibility requirements than agencies in other parts of the country.

In light of the pessimistic picture given to the adoptive parents and their feelings of discouragement, it is not surprising that over half (57%) of the couples who approached an agency never filed an application for adoption. Of those who did (N = 40) only one was rejected by the agency (for health reasons). Fifty-three percent (N = 21) were accepted, 20% withdrew their applications prior to a decision (primarily because a child became available independently) and 25% still had applications on file and were awaiting a decision.

Those couples who had been informed of the agency's decision regarding their application were asked about their experiences with the agency. Although not many respondents answered these questions (N = 22), interesting information about agencies was revealed.

Almost all of the 22 couples had to furnish references and information on medical and financial status. Ninety-five percent considered the demand for references appropriate, 90% thought the medical information request reasonable, and 90% saw furnishing the financial information requested as reasonable, although two couples felt uncomfortable about supplying this material. Eighty-five percent of the couples did not think agency demands on their time were excessive, although 30% felt that the number of forms was excessive.

The negative views expressed seemed to center on the quality of personal contact with the agency. Almost half of the couples felt that their worker asked too many personal questions (especially about their sex life and infertility), and 30% felt that they were treated in an impersonal way. However, 60% of the couples responding felt that the worker and agency were sensitive to their situations.

Of the couples whose applications were decided, most saw the agency and the worker as helpful in at least some areas. Fifty-five percent found the agency generally helpful, and an additional 20% saw it as helpful in some areas but not in others. Seventy percent of the couples regarded their workers as generally helpful, with 10% feeling they were helpful in some areas but not in others.

OPENNESS TO ADOPTION OF ATYPICAL CHILDREN

The adoptive parents who approached agencies were asked if they had discussed with their worker the possibility of adopting a child other than a normal white infant. Nearly two-thirds of the couples reported such discussions. In these cases, the discussions covered a wide variety of children, including children who were older, physically handicapped, emotionally disturbed, of minority ethnic background or having more than one of these characteristics. Of the couples with whom such adoption was discussed, 23% stated that they would have no reservations about the type of child, 15% said that although they had reservations, these children might be acceptable.

All of the adoptive couples were asked to indicate their feelings about adoption of nine specific types of child who might be available for adoption through agencies. The responses are presented in Table 5-1.

Table 5-1
Adoptive Parents' Feelings About Adopting Children Other Than White/Healthy Infants

Would Couple Adopt a:	Easily %	Minor Reservations %	Major Reservations %	Could Not Adopt %
Normal white child over 2	37	28	14	22
Normal white child over 6	8	16	28	48
White child with correctable handicap	38	34	12	17
White child with noncorrectable handicap	5	5	29	61
White child with mental illness in background	21	28	23	29
Normal black infant	8	5	13	74
Older black child	2	2	12	85
Infant of another ethnic group (Oriental, Chicano, Indian)	38	18	16	27
Older child of other ethnic group	8	12	14	66

On the whole, there was reluctance by most of the couples to adopt any child other than a healthy white infant. Fewer than 40% of the respondents said they could easily adopt any child described to them by the interviewer, and fewer than 10% could have easily adopted five of the nine different types described. Over 50% of the couples said they could not adopt four of the types described, and over 20% completely rejected four other types.

It is noteworthy that the closer the child described was to a normal white infant, the more accepting the adoptive parents were. Thus, 37% could have easily adopted a normal white child over 2, but only 8% could have easily adopted a normal white child over 6. Thirty-eight percent of the couples could have easily adopted an infant of another ethnic group, but only 8% could have easily adopted a black infant. Children with correctable handicaps were much more acceptable than children whose handicaps were not correctable.

To get an idea of what factors were associated with a couple's willingness to adopt a child other than a healthy white infant, a scale was constructed by taking a mean score of these nine items for each respondent. The respondents were then divided into three categories — high, medium and low acceptance — and cross-tabulations were run.

Significant relationships were found on three variables in relation to openness to adopting an atypical child. The lower the income, the greater the likelihood of accepting an atypical child.

Table 5-2
Acceptance of Atypical Child,
by Family Income

	Family Income		
Acceptance	Under $20,000 (N = 40) %	$20–30,000 (N = 49) %	Over $30,000 (N = 40) %
High	47.5	30.6	15.0
Medium/low	52.5	69.4	85.0
Chi-square = 9.88, df = 2, p<.01			

There was also a relationship between the wife's religion and the openness to adopting an atypical child. Families in which the wife was Jewish were less open to this possibility than couples of other religions.

Table 5-3
Acceptance of Atypical Child,
by Wife's Religion

	Religion			
Acceptance	Protestant (N = 45) %	Catholic (N = 32) %	Jewish (N = 48) %	Other (N = 5) %
High	46.7	31.3	16.7	20.0
Medium	26.7	43.8	33.3	60.0
Low	26.7	25.0	50.0	20.0
Chi-square = 14.8, df = 6, p<.05				

This relationship may help explain the greater involvement of Jewish couples in legally questionable activities reported previously. If Jewish couples are less willing to consider adopting an atypical child, the pressure to locate a normal white infant may be more severe, leading to greater willingness to involve themselves in legally questionable activities.

Geographic location was also related to the respondents' openness to adopting an atypical child. Respondents in Los Angeles and Iowa showed greater openness than couples in other areas.

Table 5-4
Acceptance of Atypical Child,
by Geographic Location

	Location	
Acceptance	Los Angeles/ Iowa (N = 52) %	New York/Philadelphia/ Miami (N = 78) %
High/Medium	76.9	57.7
Low	23.1	42.3
Chi-square = 4.28, df = 1, p < .05		

No relationship was found between the acceptance of an atypical child and the adoptive mother's age, the number of other children in the household, whether the couple had other adopted children, or whether they had adopted independently in the past.

AGENCY CONTACT CONCERNING
THE INDEPENDENT ADOPTION

The adoptive couples were asked if they had had contact with a social agency concerning their independent adoptions. More than 90% of the respondents said such contact had taken place. Of the 11 couples who reported no agency contact, six were couples whose adoptions had already been finalized.

Information about the number and nature of these contacts seems to confirm the data reported by the agencies — that there are fewer contacts with independent adopters, that the study takes less time than in an agency adoption, and that the criteria upon which a decision to approve the home is based are different for couples adopting independently.

The adoptive couples reported a median of 1.7 in-person contacts with the agency social worker, and over one-quarter of the adoptive couples (N = 33) had only one contact with the agency worker. Almost three-quarters of the adoptive couples reported only postplacement contact with the social agency. Since the timing of agency contact is determined by law, it is not surprising that there are sharp differences among the study sites as to when the initial contact took place.

Table 5-5
Timing of Initial Agency Contact,
by Geographic Region

Timing of First Contact	Geographic Region				
	Philadelphia (N = 23) %	Iowa (N = 23) %	Miami (N = 28) %	Los Angeles (N = 25) %	New York (N = 19) %
Preplacement	—	13.0	89.3	4.0	5.3
1–3 months postplacement	21.6	52.2	7.1	80.0	26.3
3 months or more post- placement	78.3	34.8	3.6	16.0	68.4
Chi-square = 108.83, df = 8, p<.001					

Since Florida is the only site in this study with an adoption statute requiring preplacement investigations, the finding that Florida couples were much more likely to be seen before placement than couples in other areas is not surprising. What is most revealing in this table concerns the other areas in this sample. Neither New York nor Pennsylvania law requires an investigation of the adoptive home. In both sites, an investigation is left to the discretion of the court and may not be ordered until a petition for finalization is filed. Thus, contact between social agency and adoptive couples in these states is delayed considerably. Sixty-eight percent of the couples in New York and 78% of the couples in Philadelphia reported no contact with a social agency until at least 3 months after the child was in the home. In contrast, the majority of the couples in Los Angeles and in Iowa (where agency study is mandated) reported that their first contact with agency personnel occurred within 3 months of placement.

All but one of the adoptive couples who had contact with agency personnel reported that at least one of the contacts took place in their home. Almost half of the couples also reported contact with a social worker at the agency office in addition to the home visits.

The adoptive parents tended to view the purpose of the agency contact in a legalistic way. The majority stated that the contact was to satisfy legal requirements — almost a formality. Considerably fewer reported that they discussed attitudes about adoption, or that the worker was there to ascertain the quality of parenting.

MEMBERSHIP IN ADOPTIVE PARENT ORGANIZATIONS

One-quarter of the sample were involved with adoptive parent organizations, either currently or in the past. For the most part, these couples lived in either New York or Philadelphia, a consequence of the method employed in locating the sample in these sites. (See Methodology.) Adoptive parent groups were seen as helpful by almost all those who were members. The benefit most often cited was that membership raises one's consciousness of adoption issues. Other benefits cited included meeting other adoptive couples facing similar issues, and enabling the children to meet other adoptees.

Given the consciousness-raising function, it is not surprising that members of such groups were more likely to be cognizant of the importance of background information and the special situations faced by an adopted child. A significant relationship was found between worry about having insufficient background information and membership in a group. Members of groups were more likely to be concerned about missing information (81% vs. 56%). Similarly, couples who were members of groups were more likely to recognize the special problems of rearing an adopted child (69% vs. 40%). In addition, in response to the

Table 5-6
Do Adopted Children Have Special Problems?
by Adoptive Parent Group Membership

Adopted Children Have Special Problems	Adoptive Parent Group Membership	
	No (N = 99) %	Yes (N = 32) %
No	41.4	15.6
Some yes, some no	9.1	12.5
Yes	49.5	71.9
Chi-square = 7.07, df = 2, p<.05		

question, "Do you think adopted children have any particular problems in growing up that other children do not have?" only 59% of the couples not members of groups thought adopted children had special problems, as compared with 84% of the group members.

ADOPTIVE PARENTS' VIEW OF THEIR EXPERIENCE

As a measure of satisfaction with the adoptive experience, the couples were asked how they would go about adopting another child. The responses reveal that the majority would adopt independently again, although some voiced reservations.

	%
Adopt independently: no reservations	49
some reservations	14
Either agency or independent: no reservations	12
Either agency or independent: reservations about independent	13
Prefer agency adoption	12
Other	1

Asked why they would prefer one type of adoption over another, the adoptive couples responded in the following ways (total is greater than 100% because of multiple responses):

	%
Independent adoptions: children available	33.6
are faster	9.9
good if intermediary is reputable	7.6
less complicated	3.8
the only way because of arbitrary agency requirements	3.8
better for children—no foster care	3.1
Would consider either route—whichever is faster or easier	13.7
Agency: affords more protection—safer	19.1
if children available	6.1
is less expensive	4.6
affords greater services—guidance, support	3.1
Other	7.6

The major advantage of independent over agency adoptions as perceived by the adoptive parents is the availability of children. Few of the adoptive couples expressed strong negative feelings about agencies. However, a substantial number of couples recognized that there are risks in independent adoptions and that agencies can diminish these risks.

This recognition of the risks was clearly expressed by the respondents when they were asked what they would tell friends who were considering adopting a child independently. Although 72% indicated that they would encourage this type of adoption, either because their experience was good or they recognized that this is a faster if not the only way to get a child, almost half the couples (N = 54) stated that one should know and trust the intermediary and avoid "shady" transactions; 10% would caution friends to make sure legal procedures are followed; and 9% would advise them to get all the information they could about the child. Almost 12% would tell friends that agencies are safer — that there are fewer risks.

Two of the risks mentioned in the preceding chapter were related to how the couple would proceed with another adoption. Couples who wanted additional information concerning their child were more likely to mention going through an agency than couples who did not want more information (44% vs. 29%). Also, couples who were worried about their ability to pay for the independent adoption were also more likely to mention agencies than couples who were not concerned about financing (56% vs. 32%). In addition, couples who approached social agencies about this adoption were more likely to mention the possibility of going to an agency for a subsequent adoption (41% vs. 26%).

Although some of the adoptive parents had reservations about independent adoption and some indicated that they would caution friends about the hazards, few had reservations about the end product of the process — their children. Fully 95% of the couples reported that their experience with the child had been extremely satisfying so far. Most of the couples (56%) said the adoption turned out much better than they had expected. Only two couples reported that the outcome was somewhat worse than expected. All but one of the couples felt that their child was progressing at least as well as other children, and 40% felt that the child was doing much better than others.

The positive attitude of the adoptive parents toward their children was confirmed in the global ratings of the interviewers, based on their observation of the home environment and their interaction with the adoptive parents. All but seven of the homes were rated average or above in terms of organization and appearance, and all but five were rated adequate in terms of light, space, furniture, etc. In all but two homes there was evidence of appropriate toys and play material. Only two of the children observed appeared to be not physically well cared for and only three of the mothers observed with their children were not considered warm and positive with them.

SUMMARY AND DISCUSSION

Prior to adopting independently, a large majority (70%) of the adoptive couples approached social agencies in their search for a child. More than three-fourths of these parents felt that their applications to adopt were discouraged. This was due primarily to the long wait they were told was necessary to get a healthy infant. Some couples were told the agency waiting list was closed. As a result, the couples perceived that the only way to adopt was independently.

One in six of the couples who approached agencies about adoption were discouraged from using these services because they could not meet agency requirements, which included age, religion or the presence of other children in the household. Although these requirements were more likely to have been reported in the southern region, they did occur elsewhere. It appears that at least some agencies continue to screen out couples on demographic characteristics. This effectively blocks the use of agencies by some couples.

Although such requirements and the closing of waiting lists may diminish the agencies' volume of work, they may be dysfunctional in other aspects. One-third of the couples who approached agencies never discussed the possibility of adopting a child other than a normal white infant. Although the data reveal resistance to adopting the most difficult-to-place children, many couples seemed amenable to adoption of preschool white children, white children with correctable handicaps and young children of other ethnic (although not racial) groups. By discouraging applicants early in the adoptive process, agencies may be losing adoptive parents for certain children waiting for adoptive homes.

With the adoptive couples' receiving a bleak picture from agencies about the possibility of adopting a child, it is not surprising that half of them did not file applications with agencies. Of those couples who completed agency home studies (N = 22), all but one was approved for adoption, which attests to the general high quality of independent homes as reported in the agency questionnaire.

The couples who completed home studies had generally positive experiences with the agencies. Few of the couples had negative feelings about the agency's requiring references, financial statements and medical information, or about the demands the agency made on their time. However, many couples felt that the worker asked too many personal questions, especially about their sex life and infertility. It seems that the emphasis on these areas is viewed as problematic by the adoptive couples, and may dispose them to turn to independent adoptions.

Almost all of the couples were seen in their homes by an agency worker about their plan to adopt independently. In states where a home study is mandated by law, the contacts took place more quickly and efficiently than in the areas where such contacts are left to the discretion of the court. By being able to evaluate the adoptive situation quickly, these states appear to offer better protection to the child. It is noteworthy that six of the couples whose adoptions had already been finalized were never seen by an agency representative. All six cases were in states where home study is not mandated by law. In these states there may be a real possibility of nonsupervision of the adoption — a risk to the child in independent placement.

The nature of the agency contacts reported by the adoptive parents appears to confirm agency reports that independent adoptive homes are evaluated on different criteria than homes approved for agency adoptions. A median of only 1.7 contacts were reported. The adoptive parents viewed these contacts as a necessary legal requirement and, for the most part, did not discuss adoption issues with the worker. One notes that all of the couples who knew the recommendation of the worker reported that they were approved for the adoption, and few reported that the worker had revealed any concerns.

One-quarter of the sample were members of adoptive parent groups. It appears that membership in such groups enhances the consciousness of the adoptive couples regarding their special situation and the special problems faced by adopted children. Such groups seem particularly important to independent adopters who, as reported in the last chapter, may not have the opportunity to talk about the issues concerning the adoption with anyone else.

The major advantage of independent adoption seen by the adoptive couples is that children are available and available quickly. However, over half of the adoptive couples recognized the risks involved in independent placements — especially the risks of involvement in legally questionable activities and of not obtaining sufficient information about the child. It may be concluded that these couples would like to see additional safeguards built into the independent adoption process.

6

The Biological Mothers

Interviews were completed with 115 biological mothers. On the average, these semistructured interviews took 1¾ hours, although five ran as long as 3 hours. For the most part, the interviewers felt that the participants were candid and open about their experiences. Interviewers rated only 5% of the mothers as showing any hesitancy in their responses.

The principal areas covered were: the biological mother's relationship with the intermediary; the risks she encountered; the services she received; and her experience with agencies.

THE SAMPLE

The biological mothers in this accidental sample[1] were found to be only

Table 6-1
Age of Biological Mother

	Interviewees %	Agency Clientele %
Under 18	40	45
18 – 21	29	31
21 – 24	16	18
25 or more	16	6

slightly older at the time of the birth of their child than unmarried mothers being served in agencies.[1] Forty percent of the women in the sample were less than 18 years old at the time they gave birth and 12% were under the age of 15.

At the time of the interview the women were older, of course, with 20% under the age of 18, 30% between 18 and 21, 26% between 21 and 24, and 24% age 25 or older.

If father's occupation is taken as an indicator, the data reveal that the biological mothers interviewed came from all socioeconomic strata:

	%
Professional	17
Manager/proprietor	14
Clerical/sales/crafts	34
Operative	10
Service/laborer/farm	14
Not employed/not present	10

At the time of the interview less than two-thirds of the respondents had finished high school and only four had completed college.

Table 6-2
Educational Level of Biological Mothers

	%
Elementary	3
Some high school	32
High school graduate	29
Business/technical	5
Some college	29
College graduate	3

Only 9% (N = 10) of the biological mothers were married when they became pregnant, but many married subsequently. At the time of the interview, 40% of the respondents reported that they had been or were currently married.

All but seven of the biological mothers were white (94%); the seven nonwhite mothers included two blacks, three Chicanos, one Oriental and one "other."

Almost two-thirds of the women (N = 72) lived with either their parents or relatives during their pregnancies. Most of the others lived

independently, either by themselves (N = 17), with friends (N = 12), or
with a man (N = 8). Only two of the women lived in maternity residences
or foster care. As one might expect, given the age and living arrangements
of the biological mothers, 85% reported that their parents knew about
their pregnancy. This was more often true among the younger women,
with only two mothers under the age of 18 reporting that their parents did
not know about the pregnancy.

THE RELATIONSHIP WITH THE INTERMEDIARY

Just as most of the adoptive parents reported that they obtained their
children through intermediaries, over 90% of the biological mothers
placed their children with the help of an intermediary. Only 10 made
arrangements for the adoption directly with the adoptive couples, and
only five of these knew the adoptive couples for any period of time prior
to the placement.

Of the 105 nondirect placements, 60% were facilitated by lawyers,
30% by doctors and 10% by members of other professions. These figures
are similar to those for the child-placing intermediaries reported by the
adoptive parents. As with the adoptive couples, many of the biological
parents had contact with more than one facilitator; more than one-third
(N = 38) reported that they were referred from one intermediary to
another for help in arranging the adoption.

Less than 20% (N = 19) of the biological parents knew the
child-placing intermediary prior to becoming pregnant. Most of them
came to know about the intermediaries through other professionals
(doctors, clergy, social workers, etc.) (N = 35), friends (N = 25) and
relatives (N = 15).

Thirty percent (N = 32) of the biological mothers were approached
by the intermediary and offered help. Six of the women who knew the
facilitator prior to pregnancy and 26 of those who did not were
approached and offered assistance in arranging an adoption. Some of the
circumstances described by the biological mothers were:

> "(The intermediary) was a friend of the guidance counselor. She told
> him about me and he telephoned."

> "The doctor asked me what I planned to do about the baby. When I
> said I was considering adoption he told me he knew several couples
> who were seeking to adopt an infant."

The biological mother went to a clinic for medical care only. The clinic then approached her by offering to help with the adoption. They referred her to _____, who told her that she had the names of many families who wanted to adopt. She gave the biological mother the name of one adoption agency, but told her nothing about it. With the help of _____ she selected a family from those presented to her on a list.

Most of the women (86%) considered one or more plans other than adoption for the child when they found out they were pregnant. The alternatives considered were keeping the child and rearing it with the help of family (N = 62); having an abortion (N = 43); marrying the father and keeping the child (N = 25); and placing the child in foster care (N = 9).

Although most of the women thought about other ways of handling the situation, only 40% reported that the facilitator discussed alternatives with them. Such discussions were more likely to take place if the intermediary was not a lawyer.

Table 6-3
Discussion of Alternatives,
by Profession of Intermediary

	Intermediary's Profession		
Alternatives Discussed	**Lawyer (N = 63)** %	**Doctor (N = 32)** %	**Other (N = 10)** %
No	68.3	53.1	30.0
Yes	31.7	46.9	70.0
Chi-square = 6.17, df = 2, p<.05			

With so many women considering alternatives when they found out they were pregnant, and fewer than half discussing these options with the intermediary, it is not surprising that doubts about adoption continued throughout the pregnancy for many of the respondents. Almost two-thirds of the women (64%) reported such doubts. Of these 67 women, only 25 discussed their doubts with the intermediary. Thirteen who did have such discussions reported that the intermediary did not try to persuade them and left the decision in their hands, while 11 said the intermediary attempted to influence their decision by discouraging discussion, pointing out the positives of adoption and the negatives of alternatives. Only one mother was referred for counseling. One-fifth (N = 13) of the women with continuing doubts felt that the intermediary placed pressure on them to surrender the child. Some facilitators pointed out that the child had been promised to an adoptive couple; others alluded to difficulties that would occur if the biological mother changed her mind; still others discouraged the use of alternatives.

As a summary measure of the nature of the relationship between the biological mothers and the facilitators, the women were asked: "Did you feel that the intermediary had your interests at heart or do you feel that he/she was more interested in arranging the adoption?" Fifty-six percent of the biological mothers felt that their interests were primary, 13% felt that both their interests and facilitating the adoption were involved, and 31% felt that the intermediary's primary interest was in arranging the adoption.

The 72 women who thought that the intermediary had their interests at heart, either as sole factor or coupled with interest in arranging the adoption, cited the following reasons for feeling this way: the inter- mediaries were kind and sympathetic (N = 45); they did not pressure the mothers to relinquish their children (N = 21); they took time to talk with them (N = 14); the intermediaries were known or were friends (N = 8); and alternatives were discussed (N = 7). The 46 biological mothers who felt that the adoption was of primary concern or was of concern along with the mother's best interest mentioned the following as reasons: the intermediaries were brusque and businesslike (N = 9); their job was arranging adoptions and they wanted her to sign papers (N = 9); the facilitators were the adoptive couple's friends and looking out for their interests (N = 8); intermediaries did what the biological mother's parents wanted, not what the mother wanted (N = 6); and there was no discussion about alternatives and/or there were threats about the results of a change in mind (N = 6).

Four variables were found to be related to the biological mother's perception of her relationship with the facilitator, including: geographic location, the profession of the intermediary, whether the intermediary was known before the pregnancy, and whether alternatives were discussed.

The majority of the women in New York, Philadelphia and Miami felt that the interest of the intermediary was focused upon arranging the adoption.

Table 6-4
Perception of the Nature of Relationship With
the Intermediary, by Location

	Location				
Interest	Los Angeles (N = 21) %	Iowa (N = 21) %	Miami (N = 24) %	Philadelphia (N = 23) %	New York (N = 16) %
Biological mother	91.3	66.7	45.8	38.1	31.3
Arranging adoption/ both arranging and biological mother	8.7	33.3	54.2	61.9	68.7

Chi-square = 20.3, df - 4, p<.001

Lawyer intermediaries were seen as concerned with completing the adoption significantly more often than intermediaries of other professions.

Table 6-5
Perception of the Nature of the Relationship With
the Intermediary, by Intermediary's Profession

Interest	Lawyer (N = 63) %	Doctor/Other (N = 42) %
Biological mother	44.4	73.8
Biological mother and arranging adoption	15.9	9.5
Arranging adoption	39.7	16.7

Chi-square = 9.0, df = 2, p<.02

Facilitators who discussed alternatives with their clients were perceived as having the best interest of the mother as their primary concern significantly more often than those who did not discuss alternatives (77% vs. 44%). In addition, intermediaries who were known prior to pregnancy were also more likely to be perceived as having the mother's interests at heart than those who were not previously known (79% vs. 51%).

BACKGROUND INFORMATION

Through a series of structured questions, the biological mothers were asked whether specific areas of information about themselves and the biological father were discussed directly with the intermediary or the adoptive couple. As is apparent from Table 6-6, information about the mother was reported as given to the intermediary much more frequently than information about the father or the relationship between the mother and father.

Table 6-6
Information Discussed With the Intermediary
(N = 115)

		Yes/Already Knew %
Biological mother:	Family background	85
	Health/medical	87
	Education	87
	Occupation	83
Biological father:	Family background	72
	Health/medical	74
	Education	70
	Occupation	76
Reasons biological parents could not care for child		78
Biological parents' feelings for each other		61

In addition to the topics listed in the table, some biological mothers also mentioned discussing: religion (N = 15); hobbies/talents (N = 9); use of drugs/alcohol (N =5); and their preferences for an adoptive couple (N = 5).

These data are consistent, in part, with the data furnished by the adoptive couples — 13% to 18% of the biological mothers reported not discussing basic information about themselves, as compared with the 16% to 20% of the adoptive couples who reported not receiving such information (Table 4-15). However, the biological mothers reported giving information about the biological father and their relationship with him much more frequently than the adoptive couples acknowledged receiving such information. This may indicate that the intermediary does not share such information with the adoptive parents.

A scale was constructed from the items reported in Table 6-6 of the overall amount of information shared with the intermediary. Using this scale, we found differences among geographic regions that are consistent with the information supplied by the adoptive couples. Adoptive couples in Philadelphia and Iowa reported getting less information than other couples. The biological mothers in these two sites reported sharing less information than biological mothers in other areas.

Table 6-7
Amount of Information Shared With Intermediary,
by Location

Amount of Information	Location				
	Philadelphia (N = 21) %	Iowa (N = 24) %	New York (N = 17) %	Miami (N = 25) %	Los Angeles (N = 24) %
High/Medium	47.6	58.3	70.6	92.0	91.7
Low	52.4	41.7	29.4	8.0	8.3
Chi-square = 17.9, df = 4, p<.01					

The amount of information shared is also related to the biological mother's feeling that the intermediary had her best interest at heart. Women who felt that their interests were primary were more likely to have shared extensive information than those who felt that the intermediary was more concerned about arranging the adoption (46% vs. 22%).

KNOWLEDGE OF ADOPTIVE COUPLE'S IDENTITY

Contrary to the assurances that may have been given to the adoptive parents, almost one-third of the biological parents (32%) placing their children through intermediaries knew the identity of the adoptive parents. This situation is most prevalent in Los Angeles, where "open" adoptions are more accepted than in the other areas.

The biological mother was also more likely to know the identity of the adoptive parents if the facilitator was not a lawyer. Twenty-four percent of the women relinquishing through lawyers knew the adoptive couple's identity, compared with 46% of those relinquishing through doctors or other intermediaries.

Table 6-8
Knowledge of Adoptive Couple's Identity, by Location

Know Adoptive Couple's Identity	Location				
	Miami (N = 24) %	Philadelphia (N = 21) %	Iowa (N = 21) %	New York (N = 16) %	Los Angeles (N = 23) %
No	100.0	95.2	76.2	62.5	4.3
Yes	0	4.8	23.8	37.5	95.7
Chi-square = 61.8, df = 4, p<.001					

Of the 34 mothers who said they knew the identity of the adoptive couple, the majority (24) knew how to get in touch with them and nine of the mothers had direct contact with them. Many (N = 44) of the mothers reported that the adoptive couple's names were on the consents that they signed.

RAMIFICATIONS OF BIOLOGICAL MOTHER'S CHANGING HER MIND

The biological mothers were asked whether they had discussed with the intermediary or the adopting couple what would happen if the mothers changed their minds about surrendering prior to signing a consent. Forty percent (N = 46) of the mothers reported having such discussions. Asked what they were told would happen if they reversed their decision, more than half of these women (N = 25) said they were informed that they had this right. However, some were told that all compensation (medical care, housing costs, etc.) would have to be paid back (N =9) or that there would be legal problems (N = 5). In addition, five women were told that the adoptive couples would be upset, and three were told that they did not have the right to change their minds.

Those women who did not have discussions about changing their minds (N = 69) were asked what they thought would have happened if they had decided against relinquishing the child. Three mothers thought that the intermediary would be supportive, and 13 said they knew they would get their child (back). Thirteen of the women stated that they would not have considered changing their minds, and therefore did not speculate upon the facilitator's response. Six women said they knew they would have to repay the compensation, three thought there would be trouble, 11 stated that the adoptive couple would be upset, and nine thought the intermediary would be angry.

Discussion of this topic was more likely to occur with younger women. Fifty-four percent of the women under 18 at the time of the birth of their child reported discussing a change of mind, as compared with 35% of the women between 18 and 24, and 17% of the women over 25. One possible explanation is that the intermediaries believe that younger women are more likely to change their minds.

RAMIFICATIONS OF ADOPTIVE PARENTS' CHANGING THEIR MINDS

One-quarter of the biological parents (N = 29) had discussions about what would happen if the adoptive couple decided they did not want the child. Asked what they were told, 20 of these women said they were assured either that the couple would not change their minds or that other adoptive parents would be found. However, the other nine were told they would have to plan for the child if the adoptive parents decided not to adopt.

The 86 women who did not discuss this possibility with the intermediary were asked what they thought might happen if the adoptive parents reversed their decision. The majority (60%) thought that the adopters would not change their minds or that other adoptive couples would be found. But 26 women believed they would have to plan for the child themselves, and most of these thought they would probably keep the child. Five women did not know what would happen.

RAMIFICATIONS OF CHILD'S BEING BORN WITH PROBLEMS

The mothers were asked if they had discussed with the facilitator the consequences of the child's being born with a physical or developmental problem. Over one-quarter of the women who placed through an intermediary (N = 27) reported that such discussions took place. About half (N = 13) were told either that the adoptive parents would keep the child or that the intermediary would take responsibility for planning. However, nine were informed that the child would be returned to them for planning, and two were told that they might become responsible for the child.

The 77 biological mothers who did not discuss this were asked what they thought might happen if the child were born with a problem. Twelve women said they did not know, and 24 thought that the adoptive couple would keep the child or the intermediary would help plan for it. However, 36 women thought that the child would become their responsibility and that they would have to plan for it either alone or with the help of a social agency.

INVOLVEMENT OF THE BIOLOGICAL FATHER

Eighty-five percent of the biological mothers reported that the biological fathers knew about the pregnancies. However, only 40% of the mothers said the biological father was involved in the decision to surrender the child for adoption. No geographic differences occurred on whether the father knew about the pregnancy. However, there were regional differences in the involvement of the biological father in the decision to surrender. It may be recalled that the adoptive parents in Iowa and Los Angeles were more likely to have information about whether the father consented to the adoption (Table 4-24). Similarly, the biological mothers in these regions were more likely to report that the fathers were involved.

Table 6-9
Involvement of Biological Father,
by Location

	Location				
Biological Father Involved	Iowa (N = 25) %	Los Angeles (N = 25) %	Miami (N = 25) %	Philadelphia (N = 22) %	New York (N = 18) %
No	40.0	52.0	60.0	72.7	83.3
Yes	60.0	48.0	40.0	27.3	16.7

Chi-square = 10.4, df = 4, $p < .05$

Once again, we find that involvement of the biological father was more likely in states with strong consent statutes.

THE SURRENDER

The biological mothers were queried about the circumstances under which the surrender was taken and their feelings about this process. As expected, the great majority (89%) of the women signed consents after the birth of the child. Most did so while still in the hospital, although some reported signing at a social agency, in the lawyer's office or in court. Thirteen mothers said they signed consent papers before birth, and four of these mothers also reported signing papers after the birth of their child.

Asked about any anxieties in signing the consent, more than half (53%) of the mothers reported that elements in the surrender process upset them. Many told of feelings that might be expected in an emotionally charged situation. Twelve women expressed their discomfort in general terms — that it was an emotional situation and difficult to go through. Some (N = 15) were more specific: they were troubled because the decision was irrevocable, and they would never know about or see their child. However, some women voiced feelings that appeared directly related to the way in which the procedure was handled: 12 said they did not want to sign the papers; 12 said the matter was carried out in a cold, impersonal way, without their being able to discuss it; seven said they felt pressured into signing by the intermediary or by their own parents; and three said that at the time their physical condition was such that they did not know what was happening.

Biological mothers who had been approached by intermediaries and offered help were more likely to be distressed by the surrender. Sixty-eight percent of the women who were approached reported being ill at ease, compared with only 45% of the women who approached an intermediary and asked for help. The proportion of women troubled by the surrender procedure ranged from 80% in Iowa to 33% in Los Angeles.

The biological mothers were asked directly if they felt anyone had placed pressure on them to sign the surrender papers. Almost 20% of the women (N = 21) responded in the affirmative. Six felt pressured by the intermediary, five by their parents, and five by both. In addition, three women said they were put under pressure by the adoptive couple, one by both the adoptive couple and her own parents, and one by her boyfriend. The same geographic differences emerged on this variable as on the mothers' being upset by the surrender procedures. Thirty-two percent of the women in Iowa felt pressured, compared with only 4% of the women in Los Angeles.

DISCUSSION OF CONCERNS

A large proportion (85%) of the biological mothers reported that they wished to talk with someone about the decision to surrender their child and/or other personal problems they were facing during pregnancy. The specific areas of concern were:

	% *
Help with decision/discussion of alternatives	73
Own emotional problems/confusion/depression	28
Relationship/problems with parents	13
Relationship with bio-father	5
Information about adoptive couple	12
Preparation for child's birth	7
Other	9

*Percentages total greater than 100% because of multiple responses.

Although most of the biological mothers wanted to discuss their decision to place the child for adoption, many were aware of emotional stress and interpersonal problems and wanted help in coping with these difficulties.

Of the 98 women who wanted to talk with someone about their decision to surrender or other problems, all but 10 reported that discussions about these issues took place. The 88 women reported discussing their concerns with one or more of the following: friend (N = 42); parents or relatives (N = 34); the intermediary (N = 26); social worker, psychologist or school personnel (N = 26); biological father (N = 14). Thus, only 26 talked with someone trained to counsel persons under stress. It is apparent that many of the women spoke only with persons directly involved in the adoption.

Younger women (under 18) were more likely to have talked about their concerns with a professional than older women (48% vs. 20%). This is probably because of the greater availability of school personnel (included as professionals) to the younger women.

THE PROVISION OF SERVICES

It is generally thought that financial aid from the adoptive parents is a strong inducement to mothers to choose independent adoption. The biological mothers were asked how they managed during their pregnancy, how they coped with their medical, housing and living needs, and whether they received help in meeting these expenses.

For the most part, the women obtained medical care from private physicians. Two-thirds reported this as their only source of medical care, and an additional 10% received medical care first through a clinic and later from private physicians. Only 18% used clinics throughout their pregnancy. The other mothers received either no prenatal care (3%) or received care through other means (3%). Few of the women (6%) reported having any problems in obtaining medical care.

Eighty-six percent (N = 99) of the biological mothers received help in paying their medical expenses, usually (N = 77) from the adoptive couples directly or through the intermediaries. Only 12 women reported that their medical expenses were met through public assistance. The rest were helped either by parents or the biological father. Thus, of the 115 mothers interviewed, two-thirds received help from the adoptive couple with medical expenses. This is somewhat lower than the 85% of the adoptive couples who reported paying such expenses.

As mentioned earlier, the majority of the respondents in this sample (63%) lived with either parents or relatives during their pregnancy. The rest lived either independently (15%), with friends (11%), or with the child's father (7%). Few (2%) used agency services such as maternity homes or foster care.

The living situations of 30% of the mothers changed after the mothers became pregnant. Some women living independently moved home and some moved from home to another living situation. However, few (3%) of the mothers interviewed had any practical problems in obtaining housing.

With so many of the women living at home, it is not surprising that only 28 received help in meeting housing expenses. Of these women, only seven received help from the adoptive parents. The others were helped by parents (N = 9), the biological father (N = 6), public assistance (N = 3) or other sources (N = 3). Thus, only 6% of the mothers said they received help in housing from the adoptive couples — again less than the 15% of the adoptive couples who reported providing help in this area.

Fourteen percent of the mothers reported encountering problems in meeting other living expenses. Thirty-one percent received help with such expenses, usually from their own parents (N = 10), the biological father (N = 6), or public assistance (N = 8). Only 10% of the total group of biological mothers (N = 12) were assisted with living expenses by the adoptive couple.

Eleven percent (N = 13) of the women were helped by the adoptive couples with other expenses such as transportation, legal fees, dental bills, etc., prior to the birth of the child. In addition, 13% (N = 15) obtained financial aid from the adoptive parents after the child was surrendered, usually for additional medical fees, although a few women (N = 8) received money for clothes, living expenses and housing.

An effort to determine the total cash value of the assistance from the adoptive couple proved fruitless because few of the biological mothers knew the costs of their medical care and other expenses. In all, 81 women (71%) reported receiving some help from the intermediary or adoptive couple. There were no differences in whether financial help was received from this source between older and younger women; those living at home and on their own; those from different parts of the country; those who were approached by the intermediary and those who were not; those who knew the intermediary previously and those who did not; or those who placed through lawyers and through other intermediaries.

The women who received financial help from the adoptive couple were approached by the intermediary and those who were not; those who decide about plans for the child. Forty percent of these mothers (N = 33) said the presence of aid influenced their decision:

> It was a big reason for leaving the agency and seeking an independent adoption. She was receiving unemployment compensation but the agency told her the only way to receive medical assistance was to go off unemployment compensation and apply for welfare. This meant a cut in income, concern about the regularity of the checks. She waited for hours at public welfare — found it so depressing and degrading that she gave up and went to a lawyer.

> Her parents made a big issue out of the $2000 they would be liable for in hospital costs if the expense was not met by the adoptive couple.

> "It took a lot off my mind. I don't know if I would have kept the baby if they hadn't paid. . . . I might have still released the child."

> She had no money to pay the medical bills and it was an important factor that entered her decision.

In all, 29% of the total sample stated that the provision of financial aid was influential in their decision to relinquish their child independently.

AGENCY EXPERIENCE

In exploring the decision of the biological mothers to place their child without the help of a social agency, the interviewers asked: 1) whether the biological mothers had knowledge of social agencies; 2) whether they had contact with agencies and, if so, the nature of the contact and their feelings about it; 3) their perceptions of the helpfulness of agencies; and 4) the perceived blockages to the use of agencies.

Almost half of the biological mothers did not know about a specific social agency that could help them in planning for their child. Included were 18 women who did not know about the existence of social agencies, and 39 women who knew of their existence but did not know of a specific agency that could help. With little more than half of the women knowing of a specific social agency, it is not surprising that only 35% (N = 41) stated that it was ever suggested that they go to a social agency for help, and that only 29% (N = 33) actually went.

Unless the biological mothers came into contact with professionals other than the intermediary during their pregnancy, the likelihood of referral to a social agency was small. Of the 41 mothers who reported that social agencies were suggested to them, 22 said the suggestion came from school, hospital or other professional personnel. Only eight mothers received this suggestion from the intermediary, six from their parents, and five from other sources, such as the biological father or friends. The 82 women who did not approach a social agency were asked their reasons for not doing so. The results are shown in Table 6-10.

Table 6-10
Reasons Biological Mothers Did Not Approach
Social Agencies*
(N = 81)

	%
No need—involved with intermediary	33
Did not know about agency/never thought about using them	26
Thought agencies impersonal/uncaring	11
Independent more private/fewer hassles and questions	11
Parents/intermediary would not allow/discouraged	9
Agencies do not allow mothers to choose adoptive couple	9
Knew intermediary	7
Agencies place children in foster care	6
Previous bad experience with agency	5

* Percentages total greater than 100% because of multiple responses.

As can be seen, the major reasons cited were that the mothers were already involved with an intermediary or did not know about agencies. However, some women cited negative aspects of agencies that deterred them from asking for service. These included that agencies are impersonal, are less private, and might place their child in foster care before adoptive placement; and that the mother had previous negative experiences with agencies. Despite these objections raised by some, asked if they thought agencies might have been helpful had they approached them, 62% of the women responded affirmatively, 23% did not know and only 15% responded negatively.

The majority of the 33 women who did approach agencies reported that the contact was helpful, at least in certain areas. Five mothers felt the agency was very helpful, 17 found it somewhat helpful and 11 thought the experience was not helpful at all. Those women citing positive aspects of the experience most often mentioned that the worker was warm and understanding (N = 12), that he/she explained options (N = 11), that concrete services such as housing or medical care were provided (N = 6), or that the worker explained adoption procedures carefully (N = 2).

The women who said the agencies were either somewhat or not at all helpful (N = 28) gave reasons including: their relationship with the worker (judgmental, insensitive, unconcerned, condescending) (N = 9); the agency could not provide services such as medical care, money (N = 6); counseling was excessive or of a type that was not useful (N = 5); the agency refused service (N = 3); or the agency would not tell her about the adoptive couple (N = 3).

The women who had contact with agencies were asked why they chose to place the child without the agency's help. The reasons cited included: financial/medical needs could not be met in an acceptable way (N = 11); they did not like/trust worker (N = 8); they did not know who the adoptive couple would be and would never see the child (N = 8); and they did not want the child to go into foster care (N = 4). In addition, five mothers said they liked the agency but preferred to adopt independently for a variety of reasons, and four mothers stated that they would have continued with an agency but their parents interfered.

FACTORS IN AGENCY SERVICES DISCOURAGING THEIR USE

In anticipation that some mothers would feel that the agency's way of providing help with medical, financial and housing needs would not be acceptable, the questionnaire included specific items on these topics. All mothers were asked how they thought the agency would help in these areas, and whether the way this help was provided would be acceptable to them.

In regard to medical care, 7% of the women did not think the agency could help, 41% thought that help would be provided through a clinic, 20% were aware that the agency would help but did not know how, and 31% were not sure if the agency could help in this area. When this variable was analyzed by whether such help would be acceptable, 75% of the women who did not know how the agency would provide help believed service would be satisfactory, compared with only 41% of the women who thought the agency would provide medical service through a clinic.

Similar differences were also found with respect to financial and housing assistance. Women who thought the agency could help financially but did not know how were more likely to say that agency services would be satisfactory than women who thought that help would be provided through public assistance. Regarding housing, women who did not know the specific way the agency could help, or thought that the agency would pay their rent were more likely to perceive agency services as satisfactory than women who thought the agency could help only through placing them in foster or maternity homes.

Through the agency questionnaire (Chapter 3) the investigators confirmed that most agencies were able to provide services in these areas, either directly or through referral. However, medical care would be provided through clinics and financial aid through public assistance, and few agencies could provide services that would allow the mother to live independently. From the mothers' reports, these forms of assistance seem the least acceptable to women who relinquished their children independently for adoption.

Many agencies also reported that the involvement of other parties in rendering services to the unmarried mother might deter her use of agency services. This seems to be confirmed in the data furnished by the biological mothers. Each mother was asked if notification of the child's father, a state agency and/or her parents would deter her from going to an agency. Table 6-11 presents the results.

The table shows that more than one-fourth of the mothers believed that notification to parents, father or state agency would deter them from using agency services. In addition, seven mothers said the requirement to notify their parents had, in fact, been a deterrent to the use of the agency

Table 6-11
Notification as a Deterrent to Biological Mother
(N = 115)

	Deter	
Notification of:	Yes %	No %
Parents	44	56
Child's father	36	64
State agency	26	74

services; 12 mothers reported that the requirement to notify the child's father had deterred them; and six reported that the requirement to notify a state agency had had a similar effect.

Many mothers also said the likelihood of their child's spending a brief time in foster care prior to adoptive placement would deter their use of agency services. Over two-thirds of the mothers (N = 77) said this would stop them from going to an agency and 28 reported that this was a deterrent to their use of agencies.

To assess the mothers' perceptions of agency services, statements were read to the mothers to which they responded on a scale from "strongly agree" to "strongly disagree." The items and results are in Table 6-12.

The table shows that the large majority of the biological mothers saw agencies as helpful in counseling (Item 12) and planning (Item 5) and saw these services as useful and available to all who need them (Item 8). In addition, about three-fourths of the mothers thought social workers were concerned about their individual clients (Item 3) and protected their privacy (Item 6). The major negative perceptions of agencies stem from the way concrete services are provided (Items 4 and 7), the perceived "red tape" and waiting in agencies (Item 9) and the probing into sensitive areas of the mother's personal life (Item 1).

The items in Table 6-12 were highly intercorrelated.[2] To get a summary measure of agency image, an index was constructed by reversing the negative items and computing a mean score for the nine items. The mothers were then divided into three approximately equal groups — poor, fair, and good agency image.

Women who felt they had little control over the placement of the child were more favorably disposed to agencies than women who consciously chose the independent route. Thus, women living at home

Table 6-12
Perceptions of Agency Services

	Strongly Agree %	Agree %	Disagree %	Strongly Disagree %	Total Negative Image %
1. Agency social workers are often nosy. The ask too many questions that are not really their business.	10	27	43	20	37
2. Social workers in agencies give helpful advice.	19	66	10	5	15
3. Social workers are concerned about the people who come to them for help. They really care about them as individuals.	24	50	16	10	26
4. Agencies won't help people financially. All they do is send you to welfare.	15	32	46	7	47
5. Social agencies really help mothers plan for their children. They are useful for people who need help.	19	68	8	5	13
6. One of the big problems in going to an agency is that your privacy is not protected. Your situation becomes known to others in the community.	5	17	54	24	22
7. The way agencies help with medical care is not enough. They only send you to clinics.	12	43	38	5	55
8. Agencies help all people — not just the poor or people on welfare.	20	63	11	5	16
9. Agencies help you as soon as you ask. They don't make you wait.	11	40	43	7	50

with parents, who might have had pressure placed on them to relinquish independently, were more likely to have a good image of agencies than women living independently (42% vs. 19%). Similarly, women who felt pressure to relinquish their child either from the intermediary or others were also more favorably disposed toward agencies (52% vs. 28%).

Finally, women who knew the intermediary prior to their pregnancies were also more favorably disposed to agencies than those who consciously sought out an intermediary to help in placing the child (62% vs. 26%).

The biological mothers who had contact with agency personnel about the independent adoption were more likely to have a positive image of agency services. In areas where an agency contact with the biological mother who is relinquishing independently is mandated (Iowa and Los Angeles), the women were more likely to have good images of agencies.

Table 6-13
Agency Image, by Location

	Location				
Agency Image	Iowa (N = 25) %	Los Angeles (N = 25) %	Miami (N = 25) %	Philadelphia (N = 22) %	New York (N = 18) %
Poor/fair	44.0	60.0	72.0	81.8	88.9
Good	56.0	40.0	28.0	18.2	11.1
Chi-square - 13.5, df = 4, p<.01					

Although the single mandated contact between agency personnel and the biological mother appears to enhance the mother's feelings about agencies, ongoing agency counseling and services appear to have a polarizing effect. Of the women who reported speaking with someone about their concerns (N = 88) those who spoke with professionals were

Table 6-14
Agency Image, by Whether Biological Mother
Talked to Professional

	Talked to Professionals	
Agency Image	Yes (N = 27) %	No (N = 61) %
Poor	48.1	36.1
Fair	14.8	42.6
Good	37.0	21.3
Chi-square = 6.7, df = 2, p<.05		

more likely to have either good or poor images, compared with the women who did not have such contact.

THE BIOLOGICAL PARENTS' VIEW OF THEIR EXPERIENCE

As a summary measure, the biological mothers were asked: "In thinking over your experience in arranging an adoption, did things go better than expected, as well as could be expected, or not as well as expected?" Most of the women said the procedure had gone either better than expected (37%) or as well as expected (44%). However, for almost one in five of the women (18%) the experience did not go so well as anticipated.

The reasons cited by at least five women for feeling that the process had gone better than expected were: there were no problems, everything went smoothly ($N = 20$); they were treated well ($N = 19$); they received good information on the adoptive couple and were confident they would be good parents ($N = 7$); their privacy was protected ($N = 6$).

Women who stated that the process had gone as well as expected also said that everything went smoothly ($N = 16$); that they were well cared for ($N = 9$); and that they received good information ($N = 8$). They also said there was no pressure on them ($N = 4$) and that the experience was not so traumatic as expected ($N = 6$). However, within this group, four women said they expected the experience to be bad and it was, and an additional four women said matters proceeded all right but it was a cold, impersonal experience.

The reasons cited by at least three women who stated that the experience did not go so well as expected were: they felt that others made decisions for them and their feelings were not considered ($N = 8$); they were pressured into relinquishing ($N = 6$); they did not like the adoptive couple chosen ($N = 4$); and the intermediary lied to them ($N = 3$).

As expected, women who were bothered about signing the consent, who felt they were pressured into signing, and who felt that the intermediary was more interested in arranging the adoption than in them as individuals were significantly more likely to feel that the process did not go so well as expected. (27% vs. 7%, 57% vs. 10%, 38% vs. 8%, respectively.) On the other hand, women who received medical assistance through the intermediary were more likely to report that the experience was better than expected, than those who did not receive such help (43% vs. 0%). There were no differences on this outcome measure by geographic region, age, education, the profession of the facilitator or whom the biological mother was living with.

As a second summary measure, the biological mothers were asked what they would advise a friend in the same position to do. Sixteen percent of the respondents (N = 18) said they would not advise their friends; half would advise friends to do the same as they had done; one-third would advise their friends to do differently.

Of the women who would advise their friends to do the same, each of the following reasons were mentioned by at least five: the experience was positive/all went well (general statement) (N = 19); independent adoptions are more personal (N = 10); woman trusted her intermediary (N = 10); full or better picture of the adoptive couple provided (N = 9); the stigma of going to an agency is avoided (N = 6); and it is easier or less bureaucratic (N = 5).

When the women were asked what they would advise their friends to do differently, each of the following alternatives were mentioned by at least two women: go to an agency to avoid what they had experienced with the intermediary (N = 16); keep their child (N = 10); make sure they could trust the intermediary (N = 5); get counseling (N = 2).

From the foregoing it appears that one-third of the sample was dissatisfied with at least some aspect of the independent adoption. Women who were bothered about signing the surrender papers, who felt that pressure was exerted on them to sign and who felt that the intermediary was more interested in arranging the adoption were more likely to advise friends not to do as they had done (52% vs. 26%, 85% vs. 29%, 65% vs. 19%, respectively). On the other hand, women who received help with medical expenses or expenses other than housing and living expenses were more likely to report that they would advise their friends to do the same as they had done (66% vs. 17% and 68% vs. 42%, respectively).

SUMMARY AND DISCUSSION

The biological mothers in the sample were similar in age, at the time they gave birth, to unmarried mothers receiving services through agencies. Forty percent were under the age of 18. They represented all socioeconomic strata, with over 30% coming from homes where the fathers were employed in professional, managerial or proprietary occupations. At the time of the study somewhat more than one-third had gone beyond high school. Less than 10% were married at the time they became pregnant, although 40% reported being married subsequently. With few exceptions, the mothers interviewed were white (94%).

As in the case of the adoptive parents' sample, few of the biological mothers reported making plans directly with the adoptive couples. For the most part the adoptions were arranged by a facilitator, usually a lawyer, rarely known to the biological mother prior to her contact about the adoption. Over one-third of the mothers had contact with more than one intermediary in the process of placing the child. Almost 30% reported that the intermediary approached them and offered help.

The great majority of the women (86%) considered plans other than adoption and almost two-thirds reported that during their pregnancies they had doubts about relinquishment. Yet, only 40% of the women discussed alternatives to adoption and fewer than half of the women with doubts discussed these with the intermediary. In addition, many of the women (85%) stated that they had had the desire to talk with someone about their decision to surrender or about other personal problems. Yet of these 98 women only 26 reported discussing these concerns with someone who was trained to counsel persons under stress (that is, with a social worker, psychologist, school counselor). It appears, then, that many of the biological mothers did not receive help in considering alternatives and were not able to discuss personal problems with a disinterested party. This lack of counseling is likely to be a major risk in independent adoptions for the biological mothers.

Almost one-third of the mothers felt that the intermediary's primary concern was in arranging the adoption. Reasons cited for this included the manner in which the biological mother was treated (cold, impersonal, etc.); that pressure was exerted to relinquish the child (either by the intermediary or the woman's parents); that her desires were not taken into account; and that discussion about alternatives was discouraged. Many of these same complaints were voiced elsewhere in the interview by women who were troubled about signing the consent (53% of the sample), women who felt that the adoption process did not go as well as expected (18% of the sample), and those who would advise friends to proceed differently (33% of the sample). From these findings it appears that in about one-third of the cases the needs and rights of the biological mother were subjugated to the desire of her parents or the needs of the adoptive couples, who were the intermediary's primary clients. This has often been cited as a risk to the biological mother in independent adoptions and speaks strongly to her need for involvement of a disinterested party.

From 13% to 30% of the biological mothers reported that in particular areas they did not give the facilitator basic information about themselves or the biological father. The consequences of this for the adoptive parents and the child were discussed earlier. The biological mothers reported furnishing more information about the biological father than the adoptive couples reported receiving. This may indicate that the intermediary does not give all the information to the adoptive couples, a factor that may be an additional problem in independent adoptions.

Despite guarantees of confidentiality given to the adoptive couples, 41% of the mothers reported that the couples' names were on the consent the mothers signed. Thirty-two percent reported knowing the identity of the adoptive couple and 21% said they knew how to contact the couple. It appears that the possibility of the biological mother's interfering in the child's life is greater in independent adoptions than in agency adoptions, where the identity of the adoptive couple is, under most circumstances, kept from the biological mother.

The ability to provide for a child under all circumstances after relinquishment is often cited in the literature as an advantage of agency over independent adoptions. This is because many child welfare agencies provide not only adoption, but many other specialized services for children in need. It has been noted that in independent adoptions, if the child cannot be placed in the home originally designated, the biological mother may have to plan for the child without the help of the intermediary.

Two areas of inquiry in the biological mothers' interviews seem to confirm the literature in this area. More than one-third of the biological mothers were either told directly or believed that they would have to plan for their child if the adoptive couple changed their view and decided not to adopt. This situation held true for even a greater number of women if the child were born with a physical or developmental problem. This is an additional risk for the biological mother who chooses independent adoption, since, having prepared herself to relinquish the child, she may face the need to make alternative arrangements.

The data also indicate that the mother's right to change her mind prior to signing surrender papers may be abrogated in independent adoptions. Eight mothers were told either that they did not have this right or that there would be legal problems if they exercised it. Of those who did not discuss a change of mind with the intermediary, many believed there would be consequences in terms of discomforting or angering the intermediary and/or adoptive couple. Fear of such consequences could dissuade the mother from pursuing this option. And in fact, once involved with a facilitator, many of the biological mothers were discouraged from even considering exercising their right not to relinquish their child. This is less likely to happen in an agency, where the mother is encouraged to explore her feelings about relinquishment and plan for it in a way that is both realistic and meets her needs.

A related deterrent to a change of mind for some women was that the provision of services (medical, financial, housing, etc.) was connected to their relinquishment of the child. Some biological mothers were told they would have to repay all financial assistance received from the adoptive couple if they decided not to relinquish. Linking financial assistance to relinquishment places economic pressure on the mother not to exercise her options.

There is some evidence that the rights of the biological fathers may also be abrogated in independent adoptions. Although 85% of the biological fathers knew of the pregnancy, only 40% were involved in the decision to surrender. In states where strong consent statutes are in effect, the biological fathers were more likely to be involved. Not involving the biological father may leave the adoption open to challenge by him and thus constitute a risk for the adoptive couple and the child.

Two-thirds of the mothers received financial assistance from the adoptive couple for medical costs. Few received help from this source for housing (6%), living expenses during the pregnancy (10%), living expenses after the pregnancy (13%) or other expenses (11%). In all cases, the proportion of women who reported receiving help in these areas is lower than the proportion of adoptive couples who reported providing such assistance. Forty percent of the women who received help from the intermediary (29% of the total sample) stated that the aid received was important in their decision to surrender the child independently. It appears that the extent to which services are provided and the type of assistance available influence some biological mothers in their decision to relinquish independently.

This supposition is confirmed by data gathered from the biological mothers regarding agency services. More than half of the women who thought agencies would send them to clinics for medical care found such assistance unacceptable. The type of housing and financial services available and the manner in which they might be provided through agencies were also considered undesirable. In addition, the items receiving the highest negative response on a scale concerned with agency image were items reflecting the way in which concrete services were provided. It appears, then, that a major deterrent to the use of agencies is the biological mother's perception of the manner in which concrete services are provided.

Another factor affecting the use of agencies by these mothers is the apparent lack of knowledge about the availability of specific agencies. Eighteen women did not know of the existence of social agencies and 39 women did not know of a specific agency that could help. Without such knowledge, one would expect a mother to seek help in planning from those she knows are able to provide such help.

Many of the women also reported that involvement of other parties (parents, biological father, state) would also deter them from using agency services. The absence of such mandated involvement or its avoidance may make independent adoptions more attractive to some women.

The biological mother's knowledge that her child may spend some time in foster care pending evaluation and adoptive placement was an additional factor in the avoidance of agencies. This appears to be a major consideration for the biological parents who are consciously seeking a permanent home for their child.

Other factors cited by the mothers as deterrents to their use of agency services were: that there was no choice of the family to which the child would go; that agencies would be less caring; and that they would be asked personal, embarrassing questions.

Although some mothers who did go to social agencies felt that the relationship with the worker was not satisfactory or that the counseling was not useful, the majority of the women who approached social agencies (66%) reported that agency contact was helpful in at least some areas. The reasons most often given for a positive experience were the relationship with the worker and the fact that options were presented and discussed.

NOTES

1. Data on the age of unmarried mothers served by agencies were collected through the agency questionnaire.
2. Of the 36 possible correlations, 23 were significant at the .001 level, six at the .01 level, three at the .05 level, and four were not significant. Three items were significantly correlated with all other items, five items were significantly correlated with all but one other item and one item was correlated with all but three other items.

7

The Facilitators

A semistructured interview form was used to conduct a total of 75 interviews with lawyers, doctors or other persons involved in facilitating the placement of children for adoption without the use of a social agency. Fifteen interviews were conducted in each of the study sites.

The interview schedule, which took about 1½ hours to complete, covered six areas of information: 1) the nature and extent of the facilitators' involvement in the adoption field; 2) practice with biological parents; 3) practice with adoptive parents; 4) direct knowledge of risks involved in independent adoptions; 5) knowledge of "adoptions for profit" and their recommended solutions for this problem; and 6) perceptions of the advantages of independent and agency adoptions.

THE FACILITATORS' INVOLVEMENT IN THE ADOPTION FIELD

There was an overrepresentation of attorneys and an underrepresentation of physicians in the interview sample. Almost 90% (67) of the facilitators interviewed were attorneys, compared with 53% of the child-placing intermediaries in the adoptions covered in the adoptive parent phase and 60% in the biological parent phase. This is due to the greater visibility of lawyers engaged in adoption work and the method of selecting the samples, in which the first 15 facilitators in each site whose cooperation was obtained became part of the sample. There was also some indication that lawyers were more willing to grant interviews. Of the eight other respondents, six were physicians and two were clergymen.

Adoption is only a small part of the total practice of the majority of the intermediaries interviewed. Almost half (47%) of the respondents reported helping to facilitate no more than two adoptions in the last year, with an additional 24% facilitating between three and five adoptions. Only 5% of the intermediaries reported facilitating as many as 25 adoptions in the last year.

The relatively small number of adoptions facilitated by the intermediaries is reflected in the number of couples awaiting children with whom they were currently involved. Over one-third (37%) of the intermediaries were not currently involved with any families, and an additional 27% were involved with five or fewer couples. Only 16% of the intermediaries were involved with more than 25 couples. As is noted throughout this chapter, the reports of intermediaries with large and small adoption practices (as measured either by the number of adoptions completed in the last year or the number of families the facilitator is currently working with toward adoption) differed in many respects.

Just as the agencies reported a decrease in adoptions, most of the intermediaries (64%) indicated that the volume of adoptions in which they were involved was declining. Only 16% reported an increase in the volume of their adoption work, and 20% said the amount had remained constant.

Interstate adoptions accounted for much of the work of the intermediaries. More than one-fourth reported that at least half of the adoptions they facilitated during the last year were interstate, and 18% indicated that this was the only type of adoption in which they were involved. Only one-third of the intermediaries were involved in no interstate placement during the year prior to the interview.

The majority (72%) of the lawyers interviewed represent only the adoptive parents in an adoption proceeding. All but one of the remaining lawyers represent both the adoptive and biological parents. When the lawyers who represent only the adoptive parents were asked who represented the biological mother, the majority (56%) said she did not have representation and an additional 30% said this usually was the case, although occasionally the mother had her own attorney.

THE FACILITATOR AND THE BIOLOGICAL PARENT

Confirming the data reported by the biological parents, most of the intermediaries had not known the biological mother prior to the contact about the adoption. Almost 60% knew none of the biological parents prior to the adoption contact, and another 29% were previously acquainted with fewer than half of the biological mothers they helped.

The data supplied by the intermediaries as to how the biological parents happened to come to them is similar to the responses of the biological parents:

Source of Referral	%
Other intermediaries	78
Former clients	29
Adoptive parents	20
Friends	14
Other professionals	14
Word of mouth	14
Clinics	9
Known prior to pregnancy	7
Other	5

As the table shows, most of the biological mothers were referred through other intermediaries — doctors, lawyers and clergy — while some came through friends or former clients. One source of referral reported by the intermediaries but not by the biological mothers was the adoptive couples. This occurred when the adoptive couple and the biological mother had located each other either independently or through another intermediary, and then approached a respondent lawyer for legal work.

Over three-fourths believed that by the time biological mothers came to them they were committed to adoption. Only 11% were of the opinion that most of the mothers had doubts about this plan. Although the sample of nonlawyers is too small to allow statistical testing, it should be noted that 83% of the lawyers felt that the biological mothers were usually committed to adoption, compared with only 25% of the intermediaries of other professions.

Over one-third of the intermediaries never talked to the biological mothers about alternatives to adoption. Of the 44 intermediaries who did discuss alternatives, only half discussed all the possibilities; the rest had such discussions only when the biological mothers expressed doubts, and many mentioned only certain alternatives, such as keeping the child.

The responses indicate that facilitators currently working with couples toward the placement of a child are more likely to discuss alternatives with the mothers than intermediaries who may occasionally facilitate an adoption but are not currently working with couples toward this end.

With so many of the intermediaries verbalizing their belief in the biological parents' commitment to adoption, it is not surprising that fewer than half (46%) suggested that a biological mother go to a social agency for help in planning for her child. Of the 31 intermediaries who made this suggestion, only seven did so as a matter of routine. The rest suggested this only if the biological parent was hesitant about adoption or when there was a factor in the child's background that made him/her more difficult to place, e.g., mixed racial heritage, mental retardation in family, etc.

Of the 37 intermediaries who never suggested the possibility of going to a social agency to the biological parents, many (17) indicated they believe there is no need for this because the biological mothers are committed to adoption or specifically to independent adoption. However, among the other reasons mentioned for not making such a suggestion are: the adoptive parents are their clients and this might jeopardize the adoption (five); and the intermediary does not deal with personal matters — only with legal issues (four).

Table 7-1
Suggest Going to Social Agency, by Number
of Families Currently Awaiting a Child

Suggest Social Agency	Families Currently Waiting	
	0 - 5 (N - 42) %	6 or More (N - 27) %
No	64.3	37.0
Yes	35.7	63.0
Chi-square = 3.87, df = 1, p<.05		

Whether the facilitator suggests going to a social agency was also related to the size of the facilitator's practice. Intermediaries with large adoption practices were more likely to suggest that the biological mother go to an agency than those with smaller practices.

Information Elicited From the Biological Parents

The intermediaries were asked: "What background information about the (biological) mother and her family and the (biological) father and his family do you routinely elicit from the surrendering parents?" The responses are reported in Table 7-2.

Table 7-2
Percentage of Facilitators Routinely Eliciting
Information About the Biological Parents

	%
Bio-Mother:	
Medical history	85
Parents' medical history	74
Education	72
Occupation	49
Reason for surrender	46
Feelings about bio-father	32
Type of home desired for child	32
Bio-Father:	
Medical history	66
Parents' medical history	60
Education	60
Occupation	41
Reason for surrender	37
Feelings about bio-mother	27
Type of home desired for child	25

In addition to the foregoing, some intermediaries routinely elicited other information from the biological parents, including:

	%
Physical characteristics	34
Drug use	31
Ethnicity/race	29
Religious preference	25
Family background	24
Personality characteristics	18
Talents/hobbies	13

Although more than half of the intermediaries routinely requested information concerning the medical history and education of both the biological mother and father, fewer than half collected other types of information. More information was collected about the biological mother than the biological father, a finding supported by the data collected from the biological parents' sample.

An index of the amount of information routinely elicited was constructed by taking an average score for the 14 items in Table 7-2. The intermediaries were divided into two groups — those high and those low on the amount of information elicited. Intermediaries who had completed relatively few adoptions in the last year were more likely to be found in the low group.

Table 7-3
Amount of Information Elicited, by Number
of Adoptions Completed in Last Year

	Adoptions Completed	
	5 or fewer (N - 47) %	6 or more (N = 21) %
Information Elicited		
High	42.6	71.4
Low	57.4	28.6
Chi-square = 3.76, df = 1, p<.05		

Provision of Services

The intermediaries also reported that the biological mothers with whom they had contact usually lived at home with their parents. Only 15% indicated that biological mothers most often lived independently, with 10% reporting other living arrangements as the norm.

Almost two-thirds of the intermediaries stated that help from parents was the primary source of support for biological mothers during pregnancy. Nineteen percent gave employment and 11% named the adoptive couple as the primary means of support, with less than 5% of the intermediaries mentioning public assistance as the primary support. Also similar to the findings from the biological parents' sample, 95% of the facilitators stated that the biological mothers involved in independent adoptions usually obtained medical care through private physicians.

The intermediaries were asked the frequency with which adoptive couples helped meet expenses incurred by the biological mother. The results are in Table 7-4.

Table 7-4
Report of the Facilitator as to the Proportion of Biological
Mothers Receiving Assistance From Adoptive Couples
for Medical, Living and Housing Costs

	All %	Most %	Some %	None %
Medical expenses	72	19	7	1
Housing costs	4	7	32	56
Living expenses during pregnancy	3	7	35	55
Living expenses after pregnancy	1	7	24	68

As the table shows, the large majority of the intermediaries (72%) reported that all the biological mothers with whom they had contact received payment for medical expenses from the adoptive couples. In contrast, fewer than half stated that any received help with housing or living expenses.

The larger the facilitator's practice, the more likely he or she was to report that at least some of the biological mothers received help from the adoptive couples with housing and living expenses. For example, 75% of the intermediaries currently working with more than 25 families stated that at least some of their mothers received help with housing during pregnancy, compared with 38% of the intermediaries currently working with fewer than 25 couples (p<.05).

Almost half (43%) of the intermediaries listed other expenses that were paid by the adoptive couple when necessary. Most often mentioned were legal fees for the biological mother, transportation, clothing, medicine, dental care and school costs. Once again, facilitators with larger adoption practices (more than 25 waiting families) were more likely to report that adoptive couples provided assistance with other expenses than were intermediaries with smaller ongoing practices (p.<.05). There were also geographic differences. Over two-thirds of the intermediaries in New York and Los Angeles reported that such assistance was provided, as compared with an average of 35% in the other sites (p<.01).

The facilitators were asked about the cost of the total assistance package provided to the biological mothers. There were wide variations in the minimum and maximum amounts listed. Ten percent of the facilitators stated that biological mothers might receive no financial assistance from the adoptive couples, while 12% reported that they would receive at least $2000 for medical expenses, housing, etc. Similarly, 10%

reported the maximum as under $1000, while 21% reported more than $2500 as a maximum and 7% stated that a biological mother may receive more than $3500 for medical expenses, housing, living costs, etc.

The maximum compensation likely to be received by a biological mother was found to be related to geographic location, with New York's intermediaries reporting the largest maximum compensation.

Table 7-5
Maximum Compensation to Biological Mother, by Location

	Location		
	Philadelphia/ Iowa (N = 29)	Miami/ Los Angeles (N = 25)	New York (N = 14)
Maximum Compensation	%	%	%
Under $1500	65.5	36.0	14.3
$1500 or more	34.5	64.0	85.7
Chi-square = 11.1, df - 2, p<.01			

The higher maximums in New York and Los Angeles are consistent with the facilitators' report of more frequent provision in these locales of assistance to the biological mother for legal fees, transportation, clothing, etc.

The intermediaries were asked if they thought this assistance influenced the biological mother to relinquish her child independently. Over half of them (57%) did not believe this to be the case, while one-third thought it was and 10% were not sure. This finding is consistent with the 40% of the biological mothers who received assistance and said

Table 7-6
Compensation Influencing Decision, by Location

	Location		
	Philadelphia/ Iowa (N = 29)	Miami/ Los Angeles (N = 26)	New York (N = 14)
Compensation Influencing Decision	%	%	%
No/Not sure	80.6	69.2	42.9
Yes	19.4	30.8	57.1
Chi-square = 6.79, df = 2, p<.05			

such help influenced the decision to place their children independently. In areas where maximum compensation tended to be high, the intermediaries were more likely to feel that the compensation influenced the decision.

Biological Father's Consent

The lawyers in the sample were asked if they were required to obtain consent for the adoption or a termination of rights from the biological father. Almost four-fifths stated that this was the case. In only one site (Iowa) did all the lawyers report that this was a requirement. Five lawyers in Miami (33%), four in New York (29%), three in Philadelphia (21%) and two in Los Angeles (14%) said they were not required to obtain the biological father's consent or the termination of his rights. For the most part, the lawyers who obtained consent seemed to follow standard procedures such as: taking written consents if the biological father was known and willing (81%); taking court action if indicated (37%); placing notices or ads (21%); and allowing an investigating agency to handle this aspect (10%). However, 6% of the lawyers told the biological mothers to state that the biological father was unknown when this was not the case, so that consent need not be sought. An additional 4% said they felt that the biological father should not be involved or that he should not have rights, and therefore they did not involve him.

Advantages of Independent Adoption for the Biological Mother, as Seen by Facilitators

As to why they believed biological mothers chose independent rather than agency adoption, at least 10% of the facilitators mentioned that independent adoptions were:

	% *
More personal/more trust or better rapport with intermediary	43
Greater privacy/more confidential	34
Greater benefits/money	33
Fewer hassles/fewer questions to answer	30
Has choice of family/more information about family	27
Chance/system to which they were referred	23
Child placed directly/no foster care	13

*Percentages total more than 100 because of multiple responses.

It appears that the intermediaries see the major attraction of independent adoption stemming from the nature of the relationship. Such adoptions are seen as more personal, more confidential and less probing or threatening. Other attractions included the type of benefits provided to the biological mother and the belief that she may have more control over the placement of her child. However, almost one-quarter of the respondents believed that biological mothers came to them for help by chance and were just as likely to approach an agency.

The facilitators also cited factors they felt discouraged biological mothers from using agencies, including: the impersonal nature of the relationship and the fact that the biological mother may have to deal with more than one person to get what she needs (27%); the red tape or bureaucratic hassle she may go through to get service (26%); her lack of control in the placement or in the choice of families (20%); being asked embarrassing personal questions (17%); agency failure to guarantee privacy and confidentiality (15%); the likelihood that the child will go into foster care (12%); the judgmental attitudes of agencies (11%); and the failure to provide in an acceptable way the services a biological mother might need (private physician, etc.) (10%).

THE FACILITATOR AND THE ADOPTIVE PARENTS

Three primary referral sources through which adoptive parents came to them for help were reported by the facilitators. The first is through clients, with 41% of the facilitators stating that adoptive couples located them through former clients and 23% reporting current clients as a source of referral for prospective adoptive parents. The second is through other intermediaries, with 31% reporting referrals from doctors, 23% from attorneys and 7% from clergy. The third route is less formal, with 32% of the intermediaries receiving referrals through "word of mouth" and 20% stating that the adoptive parents were personal friends. In addition 15% of the intermediaries mentioned that they obtained clients through sources such as hospitals, clinics, adoption agencies, etc.

Asked about the usual period of time between a couple's approaching them for help and a child's being placed, intermediaries tended to report a longer interval between inquiry and placement than the adoptive couples did. Thirty-three percent said they were usually able to place a child within 6 months, compared with 62% of the adoptive parents who reported this period between approaching the child-placing intermediary and placement. Sixteen percent of the intermediaries estimated placement within 6 to 12 months, 37% saw the time span as 1 to 2 years, and 15% reported more than 2 years as the usual time. Intermediaries with larger adoption practices reported longer periods between inquiry and placement than those with smaller practices.

Table 7-7
Length of Time Between Inquiry and Placement, by
Number of Families Currently Awaiting a Child

	Families Currently Waiting	
	5 or fewer (N = 30)	6 or more (N = 22)
Length of Time	%	%
Less than 6 year	63.3	27.3
1 year or more	36.7	72.7
Chi-square = 5.24, df = 1, p<.05		

Despite the longer time reported between inquiry and placement, the number of contacts reported by the facilitators with the adoptive couples is remarkably similar to the number reported by the sample of adoptive parents. Twenty-seven percent of the intermediaries have no more than two contacts with the adoptive parents, 31% have three or four contacts, 16% have five to seven contacts and only 20% have more than seven contacts of any kind with the adoptive couple.

Facilitators who completed a small number of adoptions over the last year were likely to have had a greater number of contacts with the adoptive couples than those who facilitated a larger number of adoptions.

Table 7-8
Number of Contacts With Adoptive Couples, by
Number of Adoptions Completed in Last Year

	Adoptions Completed	
	5 or fewer (N = 31)	6 or more (N = 20)
Contacts	%	%
1 – 4	32.3	75.0
5 or more	67.7	25.0
Chi-square = 7.25, df = 1, p<.01		

The data in Tables 7-7 and 7-8 appear to contradict the information supplied by the adoptive parents. From those data, it was found that couples who had longer periods of time between inquiry and placement were more likely to have had a larger number of contacts with the intermediary. From Table 7-7 and 7-8 we find that intermediaries with smaller practices place children faster but also have more contact with the adoptive couples. One can speculate that the reason is that intermediaries who arrange only occasional adoptions are arranging them for friends or acquaintances. They are likely to have more contact with personal friends than intermediaries arranging adoptions for couples they do not know.

Information Elicited From and Shared With the Adoptive Parents

Similar to the questions asked in other phases of the study, the facilitators were asked what they usually discussed with the adoptive couples prior to the placement of the child. As is shown in Table 7-9, the only topics discussed by more than 50% of the intermediaries were the legal aspects of the adoption, the adoptive parents' finances and the biological parents' medical history.

Intermediaries with larger, ongoing adoption practices were significantly more likely to discuss the adoptive couple's health, financial situation and attitudes toward parenting than intermediaries with smaller, more sporadic adoption practices. Those with larger practices were also more likely than other facilitators to score high on a scale constructed to measure the amount of information transmitted between the adoptive couples and facilitators. These findings are consistent with the adoptive parents' reports, if one assumes that intermediaries with smaller practices are more likely to be arranging adoptions for friends or acquaintances. In the analysis of the adoptive parent data it was found that more information was likely to be discussed if the intermediary was not previously known.

Forty-three percent of the intermediaries share all information about the biological parents with the adoptive couple, 53% share some information and 4% share none. Those who share only some information ($N = 38$) were asked what was withheld. Although half share all but the identity of the biological parents ($N = 19$), the others limit the information to: health and race ($N = 5$); information specifically asked for by the adoptive couples ($N = 3$); information that would not put the biological parents in a bad light and cause the adoptive parents to question their decision to adopt ($N = 3$); or a combination of these replies ($N = 8$). It thus appears that 19 intermediaries share only limited or

Table 7-9
Topics of Discussion With the Adoptive Parents

	%*
Adoptive Parents	
Finances	61
Ability to provide for child	50
Health	47
Reasons for wanting to adopt	45
Attitudes toward parenting	34
Marital history	25
Religion	21
Ethnic background	16
Problems in rearing adopted child	15
Presence of other children	10
Biological Parents	
Medical history	53
Family background	50
Reason for surrendering	22
Legal Aspects of Adoption	66
Costs of Adoption	50

*Percentages total more than 100 because of multiple responses.

positive information with the adoptive couples and three share no information at all.

Only 49% of the facilitators routinely discuss with the adopting couple ways of handling the subject of adoption with the child as he/she grows up. Most of these advise the adoptive parents to tell the child about his adopted status at an early age or when appropriate. However, two of the intermediaries tell the parents not to reveal the adoptive status to the child and two others tell parents that this should be revealed only when the child is an adolescent.

Almost all (97%) of the intermediaries reported that they have contact with the adoptive parents after finalization of the adoption. However, this contact is usually not related to the child's progress or the adoption. The contact is either social or concerned with other professional business. Only 13% of the intermediaries mentioned that the child was a focus of concern in contacts with the adoptive parents after finalization.

Attempts to Screen the Adoptive Couples

In an attempt to determine what, if any, criteria were used by the facilitators in placing a child independently we asked: "Do you attempt, in any way, to screen the couples with whom you help to place a child?" Over one-quarter of the intermediaries responded that no attempt was made to screen adoptive applicants. Those who do screen (N = 53) were asked what criteria they used. The results are presented in Table 7-10.

Table 7-10
Factors Used in Screening Adoptive Couples

	%[*]
Finances/socioeconomic indicators	42
Nature of marital couple's relationship/ marital stability	30
Gut reaction/feeling couple is moral	30
Emotional maturity of parties	26
Motivation for adoption	26
Meet minimum standards for court	15
Health	13
Age	11

*Percentages total more than 100 because of multiple responses.

Factors such as ability to parent, personal references, and the desires of the biological mother were mentioned by fewer than 10% of the intermediaries.

It is clear that the intermediaries who screen adoptive couples do not use standard criteria. No single criterion was mentioned by as many as half of the intermediaries. Many appear to base their decision solely on socioeconomic factors or "gut" reactions, rather than on such factors as motivation for adoption, ability to parent, etc. Since few of the intermediaries said that they request references, there is little corroboration of their impressions of the couple.

Differences again emerge between intermediaries with large and small adoption practices on whether they attempt to screen couples. All of the facilitators currently working with more than 25 couples attempt to screen the couples who come to them, compared with only 52% of the intermediaries who were not working with any couples (p.<.05).

Costs to the Adoptive Parents

Questions were asked about minimum and maximum costs to the adoptive parents for medical fees, housing, maintenance and legal expenses of the biological mother, court costs and other adoption-related expenses. These figures were added together to produce the minimum and maximum total costs for the adoption, reported in Table 7-11.

Table 7-11
Minimum and Maximum Costs of the Adoption
to the Adoptive Parents

	Minimum %	Maximum %
Under $1000	13	5
$1000 - 1499	28	8
$1500 - 1999	30	27
$2000 - 2499	9	15
$2500 - 2999	8	10
$3000 - 3999	8	16
$4000 - 4999	3	5
$5000 +	2	15

The median minimum cost reported by facilitators was $1637, while the median maximum cost was $2372. These figures do not differ substantially from the median of $2223 reported by the adoptive couples.

There were significant regional differences in maximum costs, with intermediaries in Miami and New York reporting higher maximum costs than intermediaries in other locations.

Table 7-12
Maximum Costs of Adoption, by Location

	Location				
Costs	Iowa (N = 12) %	Philadelphia (N = 14) %	Los Angeles (N = 15) %	New York (N = 14) %	Miami (N = 12) %
Under $2500	83.3	63.3	60.0	35.7	25.0
$2500 or more	16.7	35.7	40.0	64.3	75.0
Chi-square = 10.90, df = 4, $p < .05$					

The same relationship held true when minimum costs were analysed by geographic region.

Advantages of Independent Adoptions for the Adoptive Parents, as Seen by Facilitators

The facilitators were queried as to what they thought were the major reasons adoptive parents chose independent rather than agency adoptions. The two reasons most often cited concerned the availability of children — 56% stating that healthy white infants were available through this channel and 48% stating that placements could be accomplished faster through the independent route. Other advantages, mentioned by substantially fewer intermediaries, included: more individualization and personal relations with the child-placing intermediary (25%); fewer bureaucratic restrictions (12%); and greater privacy (11%).

The problems in agency practices and procedures cited by the facilitators were consistent with their view of the advantages of independent adoptions. Included were: long or closed waiting lists (51%); the impersonal nature of agency relationships (27%); agency requirements that facilitators do not have (age, religion, etc.) (24%); and agency intrusion into the couple's personal life (13%).

THE RISK FACTORS

Similar to the procedure followed in the agency questionnaire, the facilitators were asked if they had *direct* knowledge of possible risks in independent adoptions and, if they did, to cite the most recent case in which they had been involved or that had come to their attention. Not unexpectedly, it was found that intermediaries with large adoption practices were more likely to be aware of cases entailing risks.

The first risk explored concerned confidentiality and difficulties arising because adoptive and biological parents were known to each other. Almost half of the intermediaries (46%) reported that they had been involved in cases where the identity of one party in the adoption was known to the other party, and 13 of the intermediaries said this is true in at least 25% of the adoptions they facilitate.

A total of 20% of the intermediaries reported that they knew of a case in which difficulties arose because the parties were known to each other. Typical of the cases mentioned were:

> Three years after finalization the biological mother went to the adoptive parents' home and asked to see the child. They refused, so the biological mother went to the child's school and met her there. The parents felt hassled by the biological mother and moved to a different city.

> An older couple adopted from a 19-year-old biological mother and a 26-year-old biological father. The biological father drank and when he was drunk he sought out the adoptive couple, wanting to see the child.

> Two weeks after the child was placed the biological mother wanted the child back. (She) went to the adoptive couple and asked for $1000 additional compensation. Lawyer told the adoptive couple not to pay.

The second risk was related to the permanence of the placement. As mentioned earlier, the adoptive parents are contracting with the intermediary for a normal child. They are under no obligation to accept a child born with a physical handicap.

More than half (56%) of the intermediaries reported knowledge of complications in an adoption because the child was born with a physical problem. In many of these cases, especially when the condition was serious, the child was returned to the biological mother for planning or care. Confirming the agency reports, it appears that it is in these situations that social agencies may become involved in planning, along with the mother, for the child. Typical of cases in which the adoptive couple chose not to accept the child are:

> There was a young couple with a small income waiting for a child. The baby was born with a heart murmur. They were fearful of the risk and declined the child. The intermediary referred the biological mother to a doctor, who informed her of the baby's problem. She was referred to the county, which placed the child.

> If something is wrong with the baby he usually sends the biological mother to a private agency. In one case the child was placed in a home for the retarded. In another, where the child had visual problems, the agency placed the child, whose condition was surgically corrected.

> In one case the child's breathing was delayed at birth and there was some risk of brain damage, although the baby appeared to be fine. Original couple did not take the baby. He (the intermediary) located an attorney in (another state) who placed the baby with a medical doctor willing to accept the risk.

As one might expect, knowledge of such cases is related to the size of the adoption practice of the intermediary. Twenty-nine percent of the facilitators currently working with no prospective adoptive couples, 63% of those working with between one and 25 adoptive couples, and 100% of the intermediaries working with more than 25 couples had knowledge of complications in an adoption because of a child's physical problem (p. < .05).

The intermediaries were also asked if they had knowledge of a case in which there was a custody dispute between the biological and adoptive parents prior to the finalization of the adoption. Forty-four percent of the respondents had such knowledge.

Knowledge of such occurrences was found to be related to the number of adoptions completed in the last year — 63% of the intermediaries completing three or more adoptions had knowledge of such cases, compared with 23% of those completing two or fewer adoptions (p. < .05). There were also geographic differences, with intermediaries in Los Angeles and New York the most likely to know of such cases and the Iowa facilitators the least likely (p. < .05).

Regardless of the outcome of such cases, there is emotional trauma for all the parties. The cases reported by the intermediaries include:

The biological mother went to court to obtain custody of her twins before the adoption was finalized. She was awarded custody by the court.

Six months after the child was placed the mother wanted the child back. A private investigator was hired. He found that the biological father had a criminal record and was alcoholic. The adoptive parents won.

After the consent was signed the biological mother changed her mind and went to another attorney. A conference was held with the biological mother, her attorney and the judge. It was decided that she was within her rights and that she was able to rear the child. She was granted custody and the attorney returned the fee paid by the adoptive parents. The attorney prepares the adoptive couples for this possibility and they are made to understand that this is a risk they must take.

The biological mother changed her mind after the child was placed in an adoptive home in Canada. She sought another lawyer to represent her, but after 2 years the case has not been resolved.

Almost one-third (32%) of the facilitators reported knowing of cases where the biological mother was in need of counseling but not receiving it. Several respondents said almost all the biological mothers are in need of counseling. Intermediaries reporting knowledge of this risk are more likely to suggest that the biological mother go to an agency than intermediaries who do not report such knowledge (50% vs. 16%). Typical of the cases cited by the facilitators on this point were:

> The bio-mother did not face reality . . . couldn't hold a job. She had had a previous child whom she kept and doted upon him. "In my opinion she was suffering from a little mental illness." Actually a lot of biological mothers could use counseling. Many seem confused and sad. They show their insecurity and their hesitancy. Some don't ask questions they should be asking about the adoptive couples.

> "A biological mother I worked with was very ambivalent — seemed confused. She was only 15. Her father was dictating what she should do. He seemed immoral and asked for more money after she delivered the child. If the adoptive parents wouldn't pay he threatened to 'sell' the child to some else. With a father like this, the girl needed counseling for sure."

> "Most girls can use counseling. I observe this when they come to the office to sign the papers. Giving up an infant is a major decision and counseling can help."

> "The mother was firm about adoption all along. She was going to a school for unwed mothers. One month after delivery her mother told me she was extremely depressed. I felt she needed supportive counseling. Usually nobody, especially the adoptive parents or the biological grandparents, want her to get counseling because they don't want her to change her mind about the adoption."

More than one in five of the intermediaries (21%) stated that they had knowledge of cases in which a critical factor in the child's background was not revealed by the biological mother because she feared that the adoption might be jeopardized. Case examples include:

> The mother had syphilis and the child was born damaged. The mother revealed this after the child was adopted.

> The biological mother lied about the bio-father's race. Mother said he was Caucasian. The adoptive parents gave the child to a friend 2 to 3 months after the child was placed with them but before the adoption was finalized.

> After the birth the pediatrician suspected that the baby was interracial. The lawyer confronted the mother with this. She admitted the biological father was black and kept the baby.

> Very often the biological mother doesn't talk. He (the intermediary) places the child anyway. You can always find a home for a child.

Another risk explored with the facilitators was the possibility of the child's being left in legal "limbo" because the adoption process was not completed. Approximately 15% of the respondents knew of such cases. Once again, intermediaries currently working with more than 25 families were more likely to have such knowledge than intermediaries with smaller practices (42% vs. 10%). Some of the cases reported include:

> The biological mother disappeared. The lawyer never filed abandonment in court. The adoptive parents never pressed the lawyer — didn't want to rock the boat. So the child is in limbo.

> "I have been involved in one. The judge refused to approve the adoption because the adoptive parents had a criminal record. He granted legal custody and 7 years later finally approved the adoption."

> The biological mother put the adoptive parents' name on the birth certificate. Couple never went to court because they paid so much money for the baby. "I've heard of 20 such cases in the last 5 years."

> "This is a 'pseudo-adoption.' The bio-mother agrees to put the name of the adoptive parents on the birth certificate. There are no legal proceedings. The one bio-mother I represented was approached by a lawyer who suggested this plan."

LEGALLY QUESTIONABLE ACTIVITIES

The final risk explored with the facilitators concerned adoptions for profit. Although a question regarding their own practices in this area would not have yielded reliable results and would have caused a substantial amount of stress in the interview situation, we did ask if the intermediaries knew "of cases in which adoptive parents have paid or been asked to pay fees substantially above the reasonable and customary cost of the services involved." Almost half (45%) of the intermediaries reported knowing of such instances either directly or through hearsay. Many cited cases in which $10,000 or more was the figure, and a number cited cases where the costs would have been $50,000. The following examples were typical:

> "I have heard second-hand rumors which have not been verified. Many of my clients talk of this. I have heard of couples being asked $10,000, $25,000 and $50,000, predominantly on the East Coast."

> "One of my nurses became pregnant and decided to place for adoption." After delivery she told him she arranged to place the child through a New York attorney because she would receive $10,000 for the baby. "I can only assume that the adoptive parents were asked to pay fees above the customary costs."

> Clients tell him they have been offered babies for payment of $8000-$40,000.

> "A family came to me for a second adoption. Four years ago they had gotten a baby from Miami. Paid $7000. I also know several N.Y. lawyers who overcharge."

> "I know a biological mother who was offered $5000, plus 7 to 9 months during pregnancy in a luxury hotel."

> On two occasions he received offers of a baby for $9000 and $10,000. He refused to place the children but he believes that if such offers were made someone may well have accepted and in turn offered them to adoptive parents at high prices.

Intermediaries in New York and Philadelphia were more likely to be aware of such practices than those in the other sites (60% vs. 36%).

The facilitators were also asked how much of the independent adoption activity in their area they believed was "for profit." Although the majority (59%) thought there was almost no "for-profit" activity in their area, about 10% felt that most or nearly all independent adoptions were of this type. Again, intermediaries in New York and Philadelphia, where the laws governing adoption tend to be weaker, were found more likely to report a greater percentage of independent adoptions as "for profit" (68% vs. 27%).

A third question concerning this problem was whether the intermediaries believe" . . . there are organized rings of doctors, lawyers, hospital personnel, abortion clinics, etc., that specialize in such (illegal) activities." Over half of the facilitators (56%) reported that they thought such organized activities existed. Respondents in New York and Philadelphia were again more likely to believe that such rings exist (75% vs. 47%).

Of the 37 facilitators who responded positively to the question about organized "for-profit" activities, eight had direct knowledge of these activities. Two case examples are:

> "A young woman who was known to me went for counseling at a midwestern abortion clinic. She kept receiving offers of money from an attorney in this city to place her baby for adoption with him. His law firm turned over her complaint and documentation to the Bar Association." Doesn't know if any disciplinary action followed.

> "I know someone who paid $25,000 for a child. She said her doctor and lawyer were involved in a ring and that they had many babies available."

Despite the findings that 45% of the intermediaries had direct knowledge of "for-profit" activities, that 41% felt that at least a minority of the independent adoptions in their area were "for profit" and that 56% felt that organized "baby-selling" rings existed, there were only 22% of the intermediaries who thought that weaknesses in the law allowed adoptions for profit to continue.

The specific weaknesses in the law mentioned by at least two facilitators included: the permissibility of third-party placements, rather than restriction of adoptions to agencies; the complexity of the law, making it easy to circumvent; the unrealistic requirements of the law, which encourage irregularities; lack of a specific prohibition of adoptions for profit; penalties for violations not great enough to serve as a deterrent; and absence of a requirement to report fees to the court.

More than one-third of the facilitators (38%) thought that there were problems in the enforcement of the law that allowed such activities to continue. Although a number of the respondents simply mentioned that the existing laws were not enforced, some mentioned specific reasons for this, including: information about fees is not collected from the three parties involved and, when it is, the testimony is not corroborated; adoption has a low priority and is seen as a "noncrime;" and enforcement manpower is not available.

As a final question concerning adoptions for profit, respondents were asked what they thought should be done to eliminate such activity. Eleven intermediaries said the problem did not exist, and therefore nothing had to be done; eight felt that there was no hope of eliminating this practice while a shortage of infants remained; and five said they did not know what should be done. The rest cited a diversity of needed steps. Suggestions made by more than five intermediaries included: changing or tightening current laws, including setting legal limits on fees (N = 14); stricter supervision of independent adoption by professional organizations (N = 8); stricter penalties for violations of the law (N = 8); greater monitoring of independent adoption activities (N = 8); outlawing of independent adoptions (N = 6); and stricter supervision of independent adoptions by the court (N = 6). From the preceding, it appears that a large majority of the facilitators see a need for stronger laws, greater monitoring of placements and adoption practices, and stricter penalties for violators.

AREAS OF COOPERATION

Almost two-thirds of the facilitators believed that there were areas in which they and social agencies could cooperate. The specific areas of cooperation mentioned included: agencies and facilitators sharing resources and exchanging lists of available children and waiting couples (N = 13); agencies providing counseling for biological mothers and adoptive couples engaged in independent adoption (N = 11); agencies doing home studies on adoptive couples prior to placement (N = 7); and agencies placing children not acceptable to adoptive couples because of physical or other problems (N = 3). It appears that some facilitators see the agencies' involvement in independent placement as a way of dimishing risks that might be present.

ADVANTAGES OF INDEPENDENT AND AGENCY ADOPTIONS, AS SEEN BY FACILITATORS

The final questions asked of the intermediaries concerned their perceptions of the advantages of independent and of agency adoptions.

The advantages of independent adoptions were seen as relating to the length of time it takes to have a child placed, and the nature of the relationship between intermediary and client. Over 40% of the facilitators mentioned that children were available through independent adoption or that the wait for a child was shorter. This is consistent with the data provided by the adoptive couples. The nature of the relationship between the adoptive parents and the intermediary was seen as an advantage because of such characteristics as: more personal — greater trust in the intermediary and being able to deal with an individual rather than an agency (45%); greater privacy and confidentiality because fewer persons are involved (16%); less degrading because a judgment as to suitability is not being passed (7%); and less intrusive because fewer personal questions are asked (5%).

In addition to the foregoing, facilitators mentioned advantages of independent adoptions that relate to aspects of agency practice. Included are: the independent parties have greater choice of adoptive home or child to accept (20%); the child is placed directly in an adoptive home rather than spending time in foster care (20%); procedures are simpler in independent adoptions — less red tape (11%); the biological mother gets better benefits in independent adoptions (medical care, housing, etc.) (8%); and there are fewer requirements (age, religion, etc.) (7%).

All of the advantages of agency adoptions mentioned by the intermediaries centered on the reduction of risks in independent adoptions. These included:

	%*
More thorough home study	27
Counseling for adoptive and biological parents	22
Bio-mother cannot reclaim child	15
Parties not known to each other	12
Less expensive	10
Greater choice of adoptive couple for child	10
Resources for hard-to-place children	5
Other protection (greater information, postplacement services, etc.)	18

*Percentages total more than 100 because of multiple responses.

SUMMARY AND DISCUSSION

The facilitators interviewed were mostly attorneys. Physicians and other intermediaries were underrepresented. For most, adoptions were only a small part of their practice, with only 16% reporting that they were currently working with more than 25 prospective adoptive couples and only 24% facilitating more than five adoptions during the last year. A large part of their adoption practice appears to involve interstate placements, with 25% of the respondents reporting that at least half of their placements were of this nature.

The facilitators' comments on the intermediary role with the biological parents seemed to confirm some of the suspected risks of independent adoptions. The biological mothers tend to be without legal representation, since the adoptive couples are the facilitators' clients. Even in cases where the lawyer says he is representing both parties, there is an obvious conflict of interest — the best plan for the biological mother may conflict with the adoptive couple's interest in obtaining a child. Without representation, the legal rights of the biological mother may not be protected. She may, in fact, be open to pressure from the intermediary.

The biological mothers are viewed as being committed to adoption as the best plan for the child. Only 11% of the intermediaries felt that the biological mothers have doubts about this plan. With this perception, it is not surprising that over one-third of the intermediaries never discuss alternatives to the adoption with the biological mother, and an additional one-third discuss only certain alternatives or discuss alternatives only under specific circumstances. It appears that many of the biological mothers who place their children through an intermediary may not have knowledge of or ever discuss alternatives to the adoption.

Less than half of the facilitators questioned ever suggest that the biological mother go to a social agency and only seven do so routinely. The rest suggest a social agency only when the adoption may be in jeopardy, as when the biological mother is hesitant about the adoption or there is a possibility that the child will have a characteristic that makes him or her hard to place. Five of the intermediaries who never refer biological mothers to agencies gave as the reason that the adoptive parents are their clients and such a referral may place the adoption in jeopardy. Such data suggest that the primary concern of some facilitators are the desires of the adoptive parents, not the well-being of the biological mother. If it appears that the adoption will go smoothly and a normal white infant will become available, few of the respondents suggest that a biological mother go to a social agency to clarify any conflicts that she might have.

The data also confirm that significant information about the biological parents may not be collected. Although over 50% of the intermediaries reported eliciting information about medical history and education of the biological parents, fewer than half mentioned collecting information in any other area. It is apparent that these intermediaries cannot share important information with the adoptive parents, a factor that could have serious consequences for these parents and for their children.

It is noteworthy that facilitators with larger adoption practices tend to discuss alternatives, refer to agencies, and collect more complete background information on the biological parents more often than do intermediaries with smaller practices. Apparently facilitators with greater adoption experience are more cognizant of the issues in adoption practice and recognize the need for service and information. Thus, it seems that risks are more often incurred by biological mothers who arrange adoptions through facilitators with small or sporadic adoption practices. The facilitators confirmed much of the data supplied by the biological mothers in their interviews, lending the results greater reliability. Biological mothers are primarily young, living at home and being supported by their parents. The principal assistance offered to them is payment for medical care, although some receive housing costs and living expenses. Many intermediaries believe the provision of such assistance influences a biological mother's decision to surrender her child. This is more likely to be true in areas where the compensation to the biological mother is higher, a finding that shows that at least some mothers may be deciding to place their children on the basis of economic need, rather than in the child's or their own best interest.

Almost 20% of the intermediaries were not aware of the provisions in their state concerning the *Stanley vs. Illinois* decision, which guarantees the biological father some rights in the placement of the child. In only one area were all the respondents familiar with these provisions. Some intermediaries consciously tried to avoid involvement of the biological father by having the biological mother report that he was unknown, and some simply did not involve him at all, even if known. It appears that in at least some cases the rights of the biological father are abrogated.

The facilitators confirmed that the adoptive parents come to them for help through a variety of routes, including referrals from other intermediaries and personal friendship. Although the facilitators reported a longer time between contact with the adoptive parents and placement of a child than the adoptive parents did, they did not report a greater number of contacts during this period. The possible ramifications of the slight contact were discussed previously.

Intermediaries arranging adoptions for friends (those with smaller practices) tended to have greater contact with the adoptive couples. However, they were less likely to discuss important information such as the adoptive couple's health, financial status and attitudes toward parenting an adopted child. These findings are consistent with the information elicited from the adoptive parents. The consequences for the child were discussed previously.

Importantly, 22 of the intermediaries said they share either no information or very limited information with the adoptive parents about the child's biological heritage. This can be viewed as a major risk in independent adoptions, since the family will not have important information to share with the child.

Fewer than half of the facilitators said they discuss with adoptive parents ways of handling the subject of adoption with the child. Of those who do, a number said they tell the parents not to reveal the adoption to the child. It appears that many couples may not have the opportunity to talk about this crucial subject, and that some who do are given damaging and faulty advice.

Over one-quarter of the intermediaries in the sample make no attempt to screen couples with whom they place a child. Those who do screen tend to base their decisions on financial indicators and "gut reactions" to the couples. Few base their decisions on references, the health of the couples, their motivation for adoption, etc. Thus the possibility of a child's being placed in a home that does not meet his or her emotional and physical needs is greater in independent adoptions than in agency adoptions. Again, facilitators with more experience in adoption tended to screen more often than facilitators with small practices.

The costs of the adoption reported by the intermediaries is closely similar to those reported by the adoptive couples. Adoption costs were found to be related to geographic region, with costs highest in Miami and New York and lowest in Iowa.

Other possible risks in independent adoption identified by the study staff and substantiated in the agency questionnaire were confirmed by the facilitators. Over half of the facilitators knew of cases in which complications arose because the child was born with a physical problem. Forty-four percent knew of custody disputes in independent adoptions, and 32% knew of instances where the biological mother was in need of counseling and not receiving it. Moreover, 21% had direct knowledge of cases where a critical factor in the child's background was not revealed, 20% knew of difficulties arising because the biological and adoptive parents were known to each other, and 15% knew of cases where the child was left in legal "limbo." This last included cases of "pseudo-adoption" in which the biological mother checked into the hospital under the adoptive mother's name, negating the need for any formal adoption proceeding. In such instances, there are no controls on the adoption. Intermediaries with larger practices were more likely to have direct knowledge of these identified risks.

In addition, almost half of the intermediaries were aware of cases in which the adoptive couple had paid or had been asked to pay high fees to adopt. About 40% of the facilitators felt that at least a minority of the independent adoptions in their areas were "for profit" and 56% felt that there were organized rings of doctors, lawyers, clinics, hospitals, etc., arranging "for-profit" adoptions. Such knowledge was more likely to be reported by intermediaries in New York and Philadelphia, where the laws and regulations governing independent adoptions are weaker. The primary solutions to this problem were seen as changing and tightening laws within the state, stricter monitoring and supervision of such placements by professional and judicial groups, and stricter penalties for those who violate the law.

The facilitators seemed to acknowledge some of the risks in independent adoption by suggesting that agency-facilitator cooperation can take place by the agency's providing counseling, conducting home studies, and planning for hard-to-place children. In addition, they said agency adoptions include a more thorough home study, offer counseling to the various parties, etc., and provide a more secure environment during the initial months of placement.

8

The Laws
on Adoptive Placement

INTRODUCTION

Adoption is a state-created judicial procedure whereby a child is permanently placed with a new parent or parents when the birth parents, for whatever reason, are no longer willing or able to fulfill their parental duties or assume their rights over their child. This chapter focuses on those points in the adoptive placement procedure most often open to risks and abuses that may defeat the goals of the state in facilitating adoptions. Included is a review of state laws and regulations concerned with: 1) birth parent consent; 2) the placement of children for adoption; 3) the placement study conducted by the state or its agent; 4) fees and compensation involved in the adoption; 5) penalty provisions for violations of the adoption statute; and 6) the finality provisions of the various state laws. We have found it especially important to highlight the significance and consequences of independent (as opposed to state-licensed adoption agency) placements and the particular problems inherent in independent placements over and above those generally found in the adoption process.

CONSENT TO ADOPTION

Before a child may be adopted the consent of the biological parents is

The information upon which this chapter is based was obtained in 1976.

required in all instances unless they have voluntarily relinquished their child, or the courts have terminated the parents' rights in the child due to abuse or neglect, or have determined that waiver of the consent requirement would be in the best interests of the child. The biological parents may give consent directly to the adoptive parents or may relinquish their parental rights to the social agency, in which case the consent must be obtained from the agency.

No matter how the adoptive placement is made, whether by agency, parent or independent third party, all 50 states require that some form of consent be filed with the petition for adoption. The consent assures the court that the biological parent is giving up his or her child voluntarily and understands the implication of consenting to the adoption — that the parent-child relationship will be completely and permanently severed. Furthermore, consent affords protection to the prospective adoptive parents as a legal guarantee of the child's availability. However, the amount of protection afforded in consent provisions varies in each state, depending on the procedure of consent and the flexibility of the withdrawal-of-consent statutes.

Consent Requirements

If the biological parents are living and their parental rights in their child have not been terminated, the requirement of a parent's consent depends on the status of the parent in relation to the child. In every state both parents of a legitimate child must execute a consent to an adoption. In addition, every state requires that mothers of children born out of wedlock give their consent to adoption unless parental rights have been terminated. Historically only the mother had to consent to an adoption. Typically, in the past the father of an illegitimate child did not have to assent to the adoption of his child, nor was he given the opportunity to challenge the proposed adoption. But the status of the father of the illegitimate child has changed markedly since the United States Supreme Court decision in *Stanley v. Illinois*.[1]

Since *Stanley*, the father of an illegitimate child must be afforded the right to notice of any adoption, custody or termination proceeding concerning the child. Since the court did not indicate the form or extent of the notice required, nor clarify the extent of the putative father's role in such proceedings, the state courts and legislatures have differed in their interpretation of *Stanley*.

Currently the legislation in 16 states (Georgia, Idaho, Kansas, Massachusetts, Mississippi, Missouri, New Jersey, New York, Oklahoma,

Oregon, Pennsylvania, South Carolina, Texas, Vermont, West Virginia and Wyoming) does not provide for the consent of the father to the adoption of his illegitimate child. Of these states, Georgia[2] and Wyoming[3] in their regulations instruct field staff workers to seek out the putative father and obtain his consent to the adoption, or document unsuccessful attempts to find the father, although this is not legislatively mandated.

The Supreme Court of Pennsylvania, in *Adoption of Walker*,[4] struck down that state's consent statute as unconstitutional since it required for an adoption the consent only of the unwed mother and not of the father. The Pennsylvania legislature, however, has not yet amended its statute.

New York has attempted to meet the requirements of *Stanley*, without amending the existing legislation, by rather tenuous judicial construction. In *Doe v. Department of Social Services*[5] the New York Supreme Court interpreted a statute similar to that considered in *Stanley* as follows:

> Section 111(3), Domestic Relations Law (Adoption) expressly provides for the mother's consent only if the child is born out of wedlock. In view of *Stanley*, there must now be read into that statute, and it must be so construed, that the mother's exclusive or sole consent suffices only where there has been no formal or unequivocal acknowledgment or recognition of paternity by the father. It is not that the father's consent is now necessary as a condition precedent to adoption, but rather that he be served with "notice," ergo, according the father an opportunity, if he is so advised, to present facts for the court's consideration in determining what is in the best interests of the child.[6]

In *In re Adoption of Malpica-Orsini*[7] the New York Court of Appeals again upheld against challenge the constitutionality of Section 111(3) of the New York Domestic Relations Law.[8] Recently the Surrogate's Court of Kings County, New York, reiterated the New York stance on the issue of consent to adoption by fathers of children born out of wedlock in *In re David and Denise*.[9] The court once again declared that a putative father has the right to be heard at adoption proceedings, but that his consent to the adoption is not a legal necessity.

In Texas, the state's Supreme Court in the decision *In re K*[9] held that the father of an illegitimate child has the right to notice of a proceeding to terminate parental rights, but not the right due to the father of a child born in wedlock, and that as such his consent to an adoption of his child is not legally necessary.

Idaho[10] requires only the consent of the mother of an illegitimate child to her child's adoption. Legislation[11] proposed in 1976 would have required termination of the biological father's rights before a child would be legally available for adoption. However, the legislation never got off the ground. As it now stands, the father of an illegitimate child can "adopt" his child simply "by publicly acknowledging it as his own, receiving it as such . . . into his family and otherwise treating it as if it were a legitimate child . . ." This procedure results in the legitimation and adoption of the child by his father, and under these circumstances, a father's consent to his child's adoption by others would probably be required.

Currently, legislation[12] has been proposed in Massachusetts, New Jersey, Oklahoma and West Virginia to meet the notice requirements of *Stanley*. Yet if such legislation is enacted it does not necessarily follow that the consent of the father of an illegitimate child will be required by those states. New York and Texas have both declared that notice must be provided, but both have likewise determined that the putative father's consent to his child's adoption is not required.

Twenty-three states (Alabama, Alaska, Arizona, Arkansas, Colorado, Connecticut, Florida, Hawaii, Indiana, Kentucky, Louisiana, Maine, Maryland, Minnesota, Nebraska, Nevada, New Hampshire, New Mexico, North Carolina, North Dakota, Ohio, South Dakota and Tennessee) have legislation that requires the unwed father's consent to his child's adoption if the father has established or acknowledged paternity, or the child has been legitimated. The procedure to be followed varies slightly in each state; some states have additional requirements.

Ten states (California, Delaware, Illinois, Michigan, Montana, Rhode Island, Utah, Virginia, Washington and Wisconsin) have legislation placing the unwed father in much the same position with regard to the consent requirement as the unwed mother. However, even among this group of states there exists some variation in the legislative approach to requiring the consent of the putative father to the adoption.

It is evident that the unwed father's consent is required only in certain somewhat limited circumstances. In the vast majority of the states the burden is placed upon the father to assert his paternal interest in his child before his parental rights in that child will be guaranteed by the state. A balance is thus struck between the necessity of giving the unwed father an opportunity to be a parent to his child and the need to facilitate placement of the child.

Consent by Other Than Biological Parents

Twelve states (Indiana, Kentucky, Michigan, Minnesota, New Hampshire, Oklahoma, Pennsylvania, Rhode Island, Vermont, Washington, West Virginia and Wisconsin) require additional consent when a minor parent is giving up a child for adoption.

Of this group, Kentucky, Washington and Wisconsin require[13] that a guardian *ad litem* be appointed to consent to an adoption when minor parents are consenting. West Virginia requires judicial approval.

Indiana,[14] New Hampshire[15] and Vermont[16] require the consent both of the minor parent and of his/her parents whenever the court deems it advisable. It is not required in all cases.

Michigan[17] requires the consent of the minor's parents to the release of their grandchild if the minor has not been emancipated. In other words, the consent of the grandparents would not be required if their daughter is married.

Minnesota,[18] Oklahoma,[19] Pennsylvania,[20] and Rhode Island[21] require a concurring consent from the parents of a minor who is giving up a child for adoption.

Georgia[22] by statute, does not require grandparents' consent to their grandchild's adoption when their child is relinquishing parental rights. However, that state's Social Service Manual[23] instructs that such consents would be desirable.

Connecticut[24] requires that a guardian *ad litem* be appointed to consent to the termination of a minor's parental rights in a child. The guardian *ad litem*, however, need not consent to the adoption.

Despite the protection afforded by requiring consent from the parents of minors who are relinquishing their children, the vast majority of states do not require such consents, and the national trend is toward abolishing this requirement.

Termination of Parental Rights

Parents who can no longer provide for the needs of their children may give up their parental rights and duties by executing a release, relinquishment or surrender, which transfers those rights and duties to a state welfare department or agency. In some cases the state may find it necessary to terminate parental rights when a child has been abandoned, abused or neglected by parents, and the care and custody of the child then becomes the responsibility of the state welfare department or an agency. All 50 states have procedures whereby the biological parent's rights may be terminated or voluntarily relinquished, and the need for parental consent to the adoption obviated. Whether parental rights have been severed voluntarily or involuntarily, the court also steps into the picture to help in determining the future of the child. With the termination of biological parental rights, the state department, agency or the court (through a court-appointed guardian) substitutes for the biological parents and must either execute or withhold a consent to an adoption.

Under Iowa's new Adoption Act,[25] which took effect on January 1, 1977, parental rights must be terminated before a petition for adoption may be filed. As a result, no parental consent to an adoption is required. Instead, the consent must be executed by a court-appointed "guardian."

By terminating parental rights, the court can be assured that the interests of the child, the natural parents and any adopting parents will be protected. The parent-child relationship must be permanently severed prior to the filing of the adoption petition, and full parental rights and duties are vested in the welfare department, agency or guardian, all under the scrutiny of the court. It is then the responsibility of all concerned to act in the best interests of the child when deciding whether to execute or withhold consent to an adoption, without the interference of the natural parents, since their rights have been terminated.

Form of Consent

All of the states, with the exception of Alabama, Louisiana and Pennsylvania, have statutory provisions requiring written consents to adoptions. Louisiana,[26] in its case law, requires that consents be both written and notarized.

In addition to these three states, eight states (Connecticut, Hawaii, North Carolina, Oregon, Rhode Island, South Carolina, Texas and Vermont) do not require statutorily that consents be witnessed, verified or notarized.

Time of Consent

To help prevent the biological parent's decision to consent to a child's adoption from being hasty and unreflective, a small group of states, (Alaska, Arizona, Florida, Illinois, Indiana, Massachusetts, Mississippi, Nevada, New Hampshire, New Mexico, North Dakota and Virginia) have provisions that delay the execution of consents until after the birth of the child. The remaining states make no provision in their law about when a consent may be obtained.

Alaska,[27] Florida,[28] Indiana,[29] Nevada,[30] New Mexico[32] and North Dakota[32] require the biological parents to execute consents at any time after the birth of their child. Although delaying the consent to an adoption until after the delivery of the child helps to ensure that the parent actually wishes to take such action, this may not be sufficient to guarantee thoughtful decision making. Parents may make a hasty decision (due to the physical and psychological effects of childbirth or pressure placed on them by other parties) that does not accurately reflect their later feelings.

Arizona,[33] Illinois,[34] Mississippi,[35] and New Hampshire[36] require a 3-day period after the delivery of the child before a consent may be given. Massachusetts[37] requires a 4-day lapse after the birth of the child before consent may be given. In Virginia[38] a consent may not be executed until 10 days after the birth of the child.

It is interesting to note that consent to the adoption of a child may not be given in Great Britain until 6 weeks after the birth of the child,[39] in marked contrast to the predominant statutory approach in this country.

Withdrawal of Consent

Except where there has been a judicial process to terminate parental rights prior to adoption, the adoption proceeding necessarily involves an adversary relationship between the biological parents of the child and the prospective adoptive parents. Even when the biological parents cooperate fully with procedure, the adopting parents are their legal opponents in that they are seeking to terminate the child's relationship with its birth parents and to claim the child as their own.

This adversary relationship becomes serious — and often bitter — when biological parents change their minds about the adoption and try to formally withdraw their consent to surrender the child for adoption. Whether the reason for withdrawal is based on serious consideration, legal grounds or pure whim, this act by the consenting parent involves all parties in a conflict that usually must be resolved by the courts.

If the petition for withdrawal is made after the child has already been placed with the prospective parents, the situation is complex and difficult. Even if there has been no placement (or surrender) at the time the consenting parent seeks to revoke, the best interests of the child are often in question because the parent, at least for some time, desired to give the child away — a fact that in some instances could be a consideration in determining the fitness of the biological parent.[40]

In addition to the conflicting interests of the biological and adoptive parents, the state has a legitimate interest both in furthering the best interests of the child and in completing the adoption proceedings once the crucial decisions have been reached. These interests often conflict with each other. Most states have attempted to deal with this problem at least in part by enacting statutory requirements and limitations for revocation of consent. Such statutes generally make consent revocable within a stipulated time period, in specific circumstances (which usually put the validity of the consent in doubt), or by the court's decision that withdrawal is in the best interests of the child. Even if the withdrawal appears to be clearly valid under the statute, the final decision to allow or deny withdrawal is left to the state courts, which frequently base their decisions on what is best for the child.

Five states (Kansas, Massachusetts, Michigan, Nevada and New York) have statutes that forbid withdrawal of consent in certain circumstances. The Kansas[41] statute provides that when consent is given before a notary, it is revocable only if the petitioner can prove that it was not freely and voluntarily given. However, if consent is given before and acknowledged by a judge, it is absolutely irrevocable. The Kansas courts have upheld this strict legislative mandate.

Massachusetts[42] adoption law makes consent final and irrevocable when it is executed "in accordance with the law." The Massachusetts courts, however, have tempered this language with their interpretations of the statute. In the case of *In re Revocation of Appointment of Guardian*,[43] the Supreme Judicial Court considered a consent valid and irrevocable where: a) the state agency representative had explained the consequences of the surrender and consent to the mother; b) the mother had clear knowledge that the state agency would rely at once on her surrender and consent; c) the agency did in fact rely on the surrender and consent, as did the prospective adoptive parents with whom the child was placed. In *In re Child*,[44] the Massachusetts Appeals Court held that consent cannot be valid unless it is given voluntarily and with full understanding, and that it cannot be withdrawn without the approval of the probate judge. The court added that the fundamental factor in such approval or disapproval by the probate judge should be the welfare of the child.

The Michigan law[45] makes the consent irrevocable once the child has been placed with the prospective adoptive parents. In Nevada,[46] consent to a specific adoption, i.e., where the parents are consenting to an adoption of their child by a particular couple, is irrevocable.

In New York,[47] consent to adoption is required only in private, that is, independent, placements, since agency placements must be preceded by the surrender of parental rights. The New York adoption statute has a rather complicated set of provisions for revocation, conditioned on the type of consent given. Normally, consent to a private placement is irrevocable. However, the consent agreement itself may stipulate certain conditions wherein revocation is valid, such as within a certain time limit. In *In re Emanual T.*,[48] however, the statute was interpreted to infer that in any case, the court may take whatever action is necessary to protect the interests of the child, even if such action contravenes the terms of the consent.

Ten states (Alaska, Georgia, Louisiana, Maryland, Mississippi, North Carolina, Pennsylvania, Tennessee, Texas and Virginia) have statutes that give effect to withdrawals made under any circumstances, with certain limitations. Under Alaska[49] law, withdrawal of consent may be made for any reason, but not after the entry of a decree of adoption. If the withdrawal is made within 10 days of the giving of consent, all that must be done to make it effective is to give notice to the party in whose favor the consent was executed. After this 10-day period, however, the court becomes involved in the action. Notice must be given to the party that received the consent, and a hearing is held to determine if such withdrawal would be in the best interests of the child. The Georgia[50] statute provides that consent given freely and voluntarily "may not be revoked by the parents as a matter of right." The State Department of Human Resources, however, has interpreted this law in its regulation[51] to conform to the holding of the Georgia Supreme Court in *Duncan v. Harden.*[52] In that case, the court held that withdrawal of consent was allowable "prior to final adoption for good and sufficient cause," and a mother who had signed the consent under circumstances that amounted to severe mental anguish, duress and undue influence was allowed to withdraw the consent.

Louisiana,[53] Maryland,[54] North Carolina,[55] Pennsylvania,[56] Tennessee[57] and Texas[58] all have statutes that make consent revocable for any reason prior to the entry of an interlocutory (temporary) or final decree of adoption. After that point, the consent becomes absolutely irrevocable. In *Lange v. Cole,*[59] the Louisiana Appeals Court held that a withdrawal *after* the interlocutory decree will prevent the final adoption only if the biological parent can show that the adoptive parents are unfit, or that the adoption in some other way would not be in the best interests of the child. The court also held that valid consent was implied where the biological mother was served with the petition for adoption and failed to appear to contest the matter, rendering formal, notarized consent unnecessary.

Under Pennsylvania law, consent may be withdrawn under any and all circumstances up to the entry of the final decree. The Pennsylvania Supreme Court has indicated, however, that the biological parents may not be so free to change their minds as the statute might imply. In *In re Stone's Adoption,*[60] the court held that "such consents, if given voluntarily and intelligently, may be considered on the question of abandonment; standing alone such consents are not sufficient to establish abandonment, but they are evidence of a willingness at the time (of the consents) to surrender the care and support of the child." Thus, the liberality of the withdrawal statute could conceivably be circumvented by a judicial finding of abandonment (which obviates the necessity for consent), which may be based in part on the fact that the parent at one time intended to give up the child.

The Mississippi[61] statute provides for an unconditional right of withdrawal within 6 months of the entry of the action. Furthermore, this statute allows for withdrawal of consent if jurisdictional defects arise during the adoption proceedings.

Virginia's[62] consent statute allows withdrawal under any circumstances prior to the filing of the adoption petition. After that point, the standard for revocation becomes a showing of "good cause" by the revoking party, which leaves the court to determine whether to allow the request.

Ten states (Alabama, Arizona, Florida, Illinois, Kansas, Missouri, New Hampshire, New Mexico, Washington and West Virginia) have statutes that allow consent to be withdrawn where it was obtained by duress, fraud or incapacity. There is some variation among these states, e.g., some allow withdrawal for fraud alone, others for fraud or duress, or duress alone.

In 17 states (Alabama, Alaska, Arizona, Arkansas, California, Delaware, Hawaii, Indiana, Minnesota, Montana, New Hampshire, North Dakota, Ohio, Oklahoma, South Carolina, Wisconsin and Wyoming), the law contains a "catch-all" provision that allows the judge to make virtually any decision having to do with consent, notice or withdrawal requirements based on the best interests of the child rather than any specific statutory criteria. Thus the "best interests of the child" doctrine has been codified to some extent by these state legislatures. The language of the statutes of these states are nearly identical in almost every case. The Minnesota[63] law, a typical one, reads as follows: "After a petition has been filed, the consent to the adoption may be withdrawn only upon order of the court after written findings that such withdrawal is for the best interest of the child."

The Arkansas Supreme Court has given a noteworthy interpretation to that state's statute. In *Martin v. Ford*[64] and *Bradford v. Fitzgerald*,[65] the court held that where consent is not withdrawn until after the entry of an interlocutory decree, a presumption is raised that it would not be in the best interests of the child to deny the adoption petition at that point. This presumption must then be overcome by the biological parents if their withdrawal is to be effective.

The Oklahoma[66] adoption statute requires a petition for withdrawal to be filed within 30 days of the execution of consent; the court may then order the withdrawal to take effect if it is in the best interests of the child. Consent is irrevocable under the law after the entry of an interlocutory decree. In the case of *In re Adoption of Graces*[67] the court held that, in view of the continued existence of the statute making adoption decrees generally subject to attack within a year from the entry of the final decree, the biological parents of an adopted child were entitled to be heard, within this time period, on their petition to withdraw consent and set aside the adoption decree. Thus, in spite of explicit statutory language to the contrary, the best interests doctrine extends all the way up to a year after the adoption decree is entered.

Wisconsin[68] law makes consent irrevocable after the entry of the final adoption order. In *In re Adoption of Morrison*,[69] the Wisconsin Supreme Court interpreted that statute to mean that there is no absolute right of withdrawal prior to the entry of the order, but rather that it is a matter of judicial discretion, with the best interests of the child as the controlling factor.

Under Ohio[70] law, consent is irrevocable after the entry of an interlocutory or final decree. A withdrawal made prior to the entry of such a decree will be given effect only if the court finds, after a hearing, that it would be in the best interests of the child to do so.

Twelve states (Colorado, Connecticut, Idaho, Kentucky, Maine, Nebraska, New Jersey, Oregon, Rhode Island, South Dakota, Vermont and Virginia) have no statutory provisions concerning withdrawal of consent. In these states, the courts are left to deal with the problems of revocation and make the law in this area, case by case. Some of them (Connecticut, Kentucky, New Jersey, Oregon and South Dakota) seem, through their case law, to favor the doctrine of "best interests of the child."

The Supreme Court of Maine has taken a hard line against withdrawals. In *In re David*,[71] the court held that ". . . the execution of the surrender-release is, when all statutory requirements have been met, a completed act of solemn import, irrevocable by the mother, which can be set aside only by judicial action on the basis of fraud, duress, mistake or incapacity."

In *Batton v. Massar*,[72] the Supreme Court of Colorada inferred the legislative intent on the question of revocation by looking at other sections of the adoption law. It held that a mother's voluntary consent to adoption could not be voided merely by a showing that she did not realize the seriousness and finality of the consent, in the absence of fraud, duress, coercion or other equitable ground for avoiding a legal obligation. This holding was justified by a reading of the adoption laws as a whole, which not only stressed the finality of the adoption once a decree is entered, but provided that the minority of a biological parent is not a bar to such parent's consent.

The Rhode Island Supreme Court, in *In re Adoption of a Minor Child*,[73] held that withdrawal of consent falls within the coverage of the state proceeding subject to attack within a year of its entry or commencement. Such an attack can succeed for such reasons as mistake, fraud, duress, jurisdictional defects or "any other reason justifying relief from the operation of the judgment." Therefore, a petition to withdraw consent must be decided by a judge using standard principles of equity.

The Utah Supreme Court has applied contract principles to the area of consent to adoption. In *In re Adoption of F.*,[74] it was held that if the biological parent freely and voluntarily signs a consent to adoption, ". . . it is binding the same as any other contract. It is, of course, true that if no rights or interests of third parties have intervened, the courts are quite liberal in permitting the withdrawal of such a consent." But where the child has already been placed or prospective adoptive parents have in some other way relied on the natural parent's consent, ". . . a parent who has voluntarily given consent cannot simply arbitrarily change her mind and withdraw it. Such a duly executed agreement can be avoided only on a showing that it was not entered into voluntarily but was induced through duress or undue influence, or under some misrepresentation or deception, or other ground which would justify release from the obligations of any contract."

From the foregoing discussion, it is obvious that there may be risks to the various parties in the adoption process. Because independent adoptions focus on the provision of a child to an adoptive couple, these risks are likely to be heightened. For example, if the father's consent is required by law, and this would slow down the placement process, the facilitator may counsel a biological mother to say that she did not know who the biological father was, thus eliminating the need for his consent.

Analysis of State Adoption Statutes and Regulations: Consent to Adoption

Consent Requirements
1. Consent by parent(s) of legitimate child
2. Consent by mother of illegitimate child
3. Consent by father of illegitimate child
4. Consent by father of illegitimate child if paternity established or child legitimated
5. Consent by parents of minor consenting to adoption of child
6. Consent by other when parental rights have been terminated or relinquished

Form of Consent
1. Written
2. Witnessed, verified or notarized

Time of Consent
1. Predelivery
2. Postdelivery

Withdrawal of Consent
1. For any reason, with certain limitations
2. Due to fraud, duress or incapacity
3. Within a time limitation of the child's birth
4. When in the best interest of the child

Key: Required — x Not required — o No relevant provision — –
Allowed — w Prohitited — z

State	Consent Requirements						Form		Time		Withdrawal			
	1	2	3	4	5	6	1	2	1	2	1	2	3	4
Alabama	x	x		x	–	x	–	–	–	–		w		w
Alaska	x	x		x	–	x	x	x	z	x			w	w
Arizona	x	x		x	o	x	x	x	z	x		w		w
Arkansas	x	x		x	o	x	x	x	–	–				w
California	x	x	–		o	x	x	x	–	–				w

State	1	2	3	4	5	6	7	8	9	10	11	12	13	14
Colorado			w		i	i	x	x	x	o	x		x	x
Connecticut				i	i	i	i	x	x	x	x		x	x
Delaware	w				i	i	x	x	x	o		x	x	x
Florida			w		x	n	x	x	x	i	x		x	x
Georgia				w	i	i	x	x	x	o		o	x	x
Hawaii	w				i	i	i	x	x	o	x		x	x
Idaho		w		i	i	i	x	x	x	o		o	x	x
Illinois		w	w		x	z⁵	x	x	x	o		x	x	x
Indiana	w				x	n	x	x	x	x	x		x	x
Iowa	w		w		i	i	x	x	x	i	i	i	i	i¹
Kansas				z⁶	i	i	x	x	x	o		o	x	x
Kentucky				i	i	i	x	x	x	x³	x		x	x
Louisiana				w	i	i	i	i	x	i	x		x	x
Maine				i	i	i	x	x	x	i	x		x	x
Maryland				w	i	i	x	n	x	o			x	x
Massachusetts				z	x	n	x	x	x	i	x		x	x
Michigan			w	n	i	i	x	x	x	x		o	x	x
Minnesota					i	i	x	x	x	x		x	x	x
Mississippi				w	x	n	x	x	x	i			x	x
Missouri	w				i	i	x	x	x	o	x	o	x	x
Montana				i	i	i	x	x	x	o	x	o	x	x
Nebraska				n	i	i	x	x	x	i	x		x	x
Nevada	w		w	n	x	n	x	x	x	o	x	x	x	x
New Hampshire				i	x	n	x	x	x	x			x	x
New Jersey				i	i	i	x	x	x	o	x		x	x
New Mexico	w		w		x	n	x	x	x	i		o	x	x

New York	x	x	o		o	x	x	-	-	N	w
North Carolina	x	x	o		o	x	x	-	-	w	w
North Dakota	x	x	-	x	-	x	x	N	x		w
Ohio	x	x	o	x	o	x	x	-	-		
Oklahoma	x	x	o		x	x	x	-	-	-	
Oregon	x	x	o²		-	x	x	-	-	w	
Pennsylvania	x	x	x		x	x	-	-	-	-	
Rhode Island	x	x	x		x	x	-	-	-		w
South Carolina	x	x	o		o	x	x	-	-	-	
South Dakota	x	x	-	x	-	x	x	-	-	w	
Tennessee	x	x	x	x	o	x	x	-	-	w	
Texas	x	x	o		-	x	x	-	-	-	
Utah	x	x	x		o	x	x	x	-	-	
Vermont	x	x	o		x	x	x	-	-	w	
Virginia	x	x	x	x	o³	x	x	N	x	w	w
Washington	x	x	x		x⁴	x	x	-	-	w	w
West Virginia	x	x	x		x³	x	x	-	-	w	w
Wisconsin	x	x	x		x³	x	x	x	-		w
Wyoming	x	x	o		o	x	x	-	-		w

[1] Parental rights must be terminated in all instances; appointed guardian must consent.
[2] Pennsylvania Supreme Court found statute unconstitutional in 1976.
[3] Guardian ad litem must be appointed to give consent.
[4] Judicial approval required.
[5] The father may consent before the birth.
[6] Prohibited if given before a judge.

Many states do not specify when a consent may be taken from a biological mother. Thus, pressure to relinquish a child may be exerted and a consent signed before the biological mother has had time to consider the decision adequately. Although the mother can attempt to withdraw her consent, she must prove (in some states) that fraud or duress was involved. Most states determine such cases on the "best interests of the child" doctrine. As was stated, the best interests of the child may be in question simply because a consent was signed at some point. The courts have great latitude in this area.

PLACEMENT FOR ADOPTION

One of the most critical points in the adoption process is the placement of the available child with the prospective adoptive parents. Such placements are accomplished in various ways. Some adoptive couples seek children through social service agencies, friends, relatives, physicians and lawyers. At times, physicians and lawyers seek out unwed women to supply babies to their clients, bypassing the adoption agency route. At times, the entire adoption process may be eliminated by arranging an adoption in which birth certificates are altered and petitions for adoptions never filed.

The states vary as to the procedure to be followed in adoptive placement. Certain states have enacted legislation that limits placement activity to licensed agencies and state welfare departments. At times, states, in modifying their statutory framework to eliminate potential abuses in the adoptive placement process, have created unforeseen loopholes. Other states do not place restrictions on the adoptive placement, but have strict regulations with respect to compensation that may be sought by or offered to a party who has arranged an adoptive placement. In some instances, states have not enforced existing laws designed to prevent such abuses. Although each state's approach to adoptive placement is somewhat distinct, there are certain aspects to which most state laws have addressed themselves.

Form of Placement

Placement by State Welfare Department or Licensed Adoption Agency

When a child's biological parents have died or their parental rights and duties have either been voluntarily surrendered (relinquished or released) or involuntarily terminated by court action, the care and custody of the child are often transferred to a licensed adoption agency or state welfare department. The chief goal of such an agency is to find a permanent home for the child by locating a suitable adoptive home.

Within the context of the state department or licensed agency placement, many risks associated with the adoption process may be eliminated. When parental rights have been voluntarily or involuntarily terminated by a court, the biological parent need not be involved. The relinquishment or the involuntary termination has, at this stage, already been established in the courts. There is much less chance that the biological parents have been forced or persuaded under duress to give up their child — there is no point in a doctor or lawyer, acting in behalf of a client eager to adopt, exerting pressure on a mother to make a decision when this cannot lead to an independent placement. All placement fees and costs must be reported and are strictly regulated under state licensing statutes — the profit motive in adoptions is eliminated. Further protection may be afforded to the child in that the agency's placement decision may be based upon the suitability factor alone, rather than necessity or monetary gain. The agency can monitor the child's development within the prospective adoptive home, and the prospective adoptive parents are offered greater protection since the legal availability of the child has been established.

Of course, legislation prohibiting or restricting independent adoptions will be effective only if the state enforces the law, and if the law provides officials with noncompliance penalties strict enough to act as deterrents.

Although all 50 states have provisions that allow adoptive placements to be made by licensed agencies or state welfare department, only six states (Connecticut, Delaware, Georgia, Massachusetts, Michigan and Minnesota) absolutely prohibit the placement of a child for adoption by other means, except in the case of the biological parent who places a child with a stepparent or close relative. By law these states forbid independent placements, but they still occur in Georgia because of a lack of enforcement. The provisions of the laws that bar independent placements vary somewhat from state to state.

*Placement by Biological Parents With Stepparent or
Close Relatives*

All the states allow the biological parents to place their child with stepparents or close relatives, usually up to the third degree of consanguinity or affinity. The theory behind this is that many of the risk factors normally associated with independent placements are not evident in placements with relatives. The family members are known to each other, and the child bears some relationship to his prospective adoptive parents. It is also expected that the biological parents will be somewhat protected within the familial context, since it is less likely that fraud and duress will occur among family members. In such a relationship it would be difficult to take the child and run. Furthermore, the danger of profit making is practically obviated: there would be little or no opportunity for a third-party intermediary to make money on such placements. Intrafamily adoptions also may strengthen the preexisting family unit.

Placement by Biological Parents With Prospective Adoptive Parents

All placements other than those made by licensed or authorized placement agencies or those with stepparents or close relatives are considered independent placements. However, states often distinguish between placements made by a parent and those arranged by an intermediary. Fourteen states (Alabama, California, Maine, Maryland, Missouri, Nebraska, Nevada, New Jersey, North Dakota, Ohio, Oregon, Rhode Island, Tennessee and Wisconsin) have statutes that allow parents to place their child with any prospective adoptive parents without the intervention of an intermediary. The purpose of such legislation is to prevent profit making by intermediaries while still allowing maximum flexibility in arranging placements. Unfortunately, this goal has not usually been achieved in these states. Often, intermediaries do come into the picture and circumvent the purpose of the laws. They act as intermediaries in the guise of agents who arrange adoptive placements on behalf of the biological parents. Abuses in terms of possibly exorbitant fees may therefore surface just as easily in this situation as in states that allow any type of placement to take place. Once again, although this group of states in general has developed the same basic approach with regard to biological parent placements, each state has some unique features in its placement statute.

Placement by Independent Third-Party Intermediary

A majority of the states allow adoptive placements to be arranged by an intermediary. In a few instances, states have enacted statutes specifically to allow such practices; but in the majority of states, independent placements through intermediaries are taking place because of unforeseen loopholes in the laws.

The risks inherent in third-party independent placements are well known. Those most cited by opponents of independent adoptions are: 1) potential profit making, 2) poor placements, 3) failure to provide proper notification to the biological father of a child born out of wedlock, 4) pressures exerted by intermediaries upon parents, and 5) the uncertainty with which prospective adoptive parents may be plagued. Some states, while allowing intermediaries to place children, have attempted to eliminate the abuses most often encountered, and a variety of alternative approaches to adoptive placement have developed.

Under Iowa's new Termination of Parental Rights — Adoption Act,[75] custody of a child may be transferred by the biological parents by having a third party accept a release of custody, whereupon that person becomes the custodian of the child. Among those specifically enumerated as able to accept a release is "a person making an independent placement."[76] To monitor carefully any possible abuses in the arrangement of the placement, a full accounting[77] of all expenditures must be presented to the court. The only expenditures permitted are for necessary services provided biological parents in connection with the birth and for the usual and necessary fees to those who assisted in placing the child, commensurate with the services rendered.

In Indiana,[78] no child may be placed in a proposed adoptive home without prior written approval of the placement by a licensed agency or public welfare department. The approval of the placement must be filed along with the petition for adoption.

Arizona[79] has a somewhat similar procedure. In that state, a person must be certified by a court officer, agency or a division of the State Department of Social Services as acceptable to adopt children before a petition to adopt a child may be brought. A decision is then made as to the suitability of the child's placement with the applicant. In this way, both Indiana and Arizona protect the best interests of the child while allowing an independent placement to be made.

Kentucky's[80] placement statute presents an interesting scheme. No petition for adoption may be filed unless the child has been placed by a licensed agency or the welfare department, with the exception of stepparent or close relative placements. "Private persons,"[81] however, are allowed to place or receive a child for adoptive placement by making written application to the state secretary for permission to do so. When such an application has been filed, the secretary's office investigates the suitability and the circumstances of the placement. This allows the scrutiny necessary to prevent abuses.

Under the Florida Adoption Act,[82] placements by intermediaries are readily acknowledged and accepted. As designated in the legislative intent, one of the basic safeguards provided by the act is that:

> "all expenditures by intermediaries placing, and persons independently adopting, a minor are reported to the court and become a permanent record in the file of the adoption proceedings."[83]

Emphasis is here placed upon monitoring rather than prohibiting such placements. An affidavit must be filed[84] by the adoptive parents and the intermediary containing a full accounting of all disbursements and receipts in connection with adoption. Further protection is afforded by requiring the intermediary to report intent to place a child for adoption prior to the placement.[85] An investigation is made into the suitability of the placement.

The New York[86] placement laws place no limitation upon any party to participate in the process of adoptive placement. Private independent placements are specifically provided for within the statutory scheme. An affidavit must be attached to the petition indicating how lawful custody of the child was obtained. Specific provision is also made for placement of children from foreign nations who are being privately placed.[87] Under this provision, extensive background information is required. There must be documentary evidence that the child has been orphaned or has parents incapable of providing for the child, and that the child has been irrevocably released for immigration and adoption purposes. These precautions in intercountry adoption cases should promote the permanency of the placement and eliminate some risk factors.

The Pennsylvania "Adoption Act"[88] allows for the independent placement of children for adoption through an "intermediary." The procedure is under the strict scrutiny of the court. "Intermediary" is defined as "any person or persons, or agency acting between the parent or parents and the proposed adoptive parents in arranging an adoption placement."[89] When a child under 18 years of age has been in the exclusive care of an adult who has filed a report of intention to adopt, the parents of the child may petition the court for permission to relinquish forever all parental rights to their child.[90] The adult having care of the child must file a separate consent to accept the custody of the child. This provision allows for independent placement. Every person having or retaining possession, custody or control of any child, for the purpose or with the intention of adopting, must report to the court in which the petition for adoption will be filed. A report of the intermediary is also required.[91] Furthermore, the court must require a disclosure of all costs and fees of any type paid or to be paid to any person or institution in connection with the adoption, including the fees of any intermediary.[92]

In New Mexico,[93] no petition for adoption may be granted unless the child has been placed in the home of the proposed adopting parents by the public health and social services department, the appropriate authority in another state, or a licensed child placement agency. This requirement does not exist, however, when the child is sought to be adopted by a stepparent or a relative. In addition, the requirement does not exist in placements with sponsors at baptism or confirmation, a person named in a deceased parent's will, or adoptions arranged through nationally recognized religious organizations. The court may waive the restriction prior to the actual placement of the adoptive child upon giving the department 30 days' notice. The department is afforded opportunity to challenge the court's action.

A prime example of legislation that seems to prohibit independent placements, yet in fact allows them, exists in Colorado. Under the Colorado[94] placement statute, no placement of any child for adoption purposes can be made except by the court, county social service department, a licensed agency, or an individual in whom guardianship of the person of the child has been placed by the court. Guardianship of the person of the child may be transferred, upon termination of parental rights, to

> "an individual of good moral character, if such individual shall have
> had the child living in his home for a year or more."[95]

As a result of this provision, a child simply has to be placed within the home of the prospective adoptive parents that the biological parents or their intermediary have selected. Independent placements can be easily carried through by this device.

Notification of Placement

Some of the abuses that may arise in adoptive placements may be reduced by requiring that the courts or the welfare division be notified of an intended adoptive placement prior to allowing a petition for adoption to be filed. This would be particularly helpful in independent placements, where the notification and study requirement may disclose abuses before the child is placed and before the petition may be filed.

Four states (Arizona, Maryland, Pennsylvania and Wisconsin) require that the courts be notified concerning a placement before a petition to adopt may be filed. Six states (Florida, Indiana, Kentucky, Nevada, Rhode Island and Virginia) require that such notice be given to the state welfare department. Often, the requirement exists only in limited circumstances, as when an independent placement is contemplated. Some of the statutory schemes present interesting alternatives.

In Arizona,[96] the court must be notified in order that an agency be appointed to investigate the prospective adoptive parents, the child to be placed, and the suitability of the placement. Upon the recommendation of the agency, the parents wishing to adopt may or may not be certified as fit to adopt. Certification is required before an adoption petition may be filed. Although independent placements are allowed, the certification requirement guarantees agency involvement at a relatively early stage.

Maryland[97] takes a slightly different approach. In that state, when a nonrelative placement by a parent or grandparent is contemplated, the consent of the court to the placement must be sought prior to placement and pending final action of the adoption petition.

Pennsylvania[98] requires that a report of intention to adopt must be given to the court in which the petition for adoption is to be filed. When the placement is through an intermediary, detailed information must be provided concerning the circumstances of the placement and the intermediary. Less detail is required when the placement has been made by an agency, and no such report is necessary when a child is placed with close relatives.

In Wisconsin,[99] written approval of the court is required for independent placements arranged by parents or guardians. Such reports serve to monitor independent parent placements.

Nevada[100] requires written notice of the proposed placement from the prospective adoptive parents, the person recommending the placement, or a licensed agency. Investigations must then be made except in the case of placement by licensed agencies, where notice is sufficient. Relatives adopting a child within the third degree of consanguinity need not give such a notice to the welfare division. Once again, this procedure gives the state a chance to check possible abuses. In Florida,[101] an intermediary must report to the state, prior to the placement, his intent to place a child for adoption. A study is then made to determine whether the adoptive home is suitable.

Analysis of State Adoption Statutes and Regulations:
Placement For Adoption

Form of Placement
1. Placement by state welfare department or licensed adoption agency
2. Placement by biological parent(s) with stepparent or close relative
3. Placement by biological parent(s) or relatives directly with prospective adoptive parents
4. Placement by independent third-party intermediary

Notification of Placement
1. Notification of adoptive placement to court prior to filing adoption petition
2. Notification of adoptive placement to welfare department or agency prior to filing petition for adoption

Key: Required — x   Not required — o   No relevant provision — –
Allowed — w   Prohibited — z

State	Form of Placement				Notification	
	1	2	3	4	1	2
Alabama	w	w	w	z	–	–
Alaska	w	w	w	–	–	–
Arizona	w	w	w	w^3	x	–
Arkansas	w	w	w	–	–	–
California	w	w	w	z	–	–
Colorado	w	w	w	w	–	–
Connecticut	x^1	w	z	z	–	–
Delaware	x	w	z	z	–	–
Florida	w	w	w	w	–	x
Georgia	w	w	z	z	–	–
Hawaii	w	–	–	–	–	–
Idaho	w	–	–	–	–	–
Illinois	w	w	w	w	–	–
Indiana	w	w	w	w^3	–	x
Iowa	w	w	w	w	–	–
Kansas	w	w	w	w	–	–
Kentucky	w	w	w^2	w^2	–	x
Louisiana	w	w	w	w^4	–	–
Maine	w	w	w	z	–	–
Maryland	w	w	w	z	x	–
Massachusetts	x	w	z	z	–	–

Michigan	x	w	z	z	–	–
Minnesota	x[1]	w	z	z	–	–
Mississippi	w	–	–	–	–	–
Missouri	w	w	w	z	–	–
Montana	w	–	–	–	–	–
Nebraska	w	w	w	z	–	–
Nevada	w	w	w	z	–	x
New Hampshire	w	w	w	w	–	–
New Jersey	w	w	w	z	–	–
New Mexico	x[1]	w	z	z	–	–
New York	w	w	w	w	–	–
North Carolina	w	w	w	w	–	–
North Dakota	w	w	w	z	–	–
Ohio	w	w	w	z	–	–
Oklahoma	w	–	–	–	–	–
Oregon	w	w	w	z	–	–
Pennsylvania	w	w	w	w	x	–
Rhode Island	w	w	w	z	–	x
South Carolina	w	–	–	–	–	–
South Dakota	w	w	w	–	–	–
Tennessee	w	w	w	z	–	–
Texas	w	w	w	–	–	–
Utah	w	w	w	w	–	–
Vermont	w	w	w	w	–	–
Virginia	w	–	–	–	–	x
Washington	w	w	w	–	–	–
West Virginia	w	–	–	–	–	–
Wisconsin	w	w	w[5]	z	x	–
Wyoming	w	–	–	–	–	–

[1] Agency placement requirement may be waived.

[2] State department approval required prior to placement.

[3] Agency or court approval required prior to placement.

[4] Adoption Act has been construed to permit such placements.

[5] Preplacement court approval required.

Although the prohibition of independent adoptive placements provides maximum opportunity to eliminate risks and abuses in the placement scheme, alternative legislation that allows, yet carefully and judiciously monitors, independent placements should not be overlooked. In addition, analysis of the laws regulating placements must contain one caution. No matter how clear, precise and prohibitive the enacted legislation may be, it will be totally ineffective if it is not enforced or if the deterrent provided is insufficient to assure compliance.

SOCIAL STUDY PROVISIONS

Some form of inquiry into the circumstances of an adoption is required in every state. No adoption is legal without a court decree, and judges generally need more than the petition setting forth basic facts in order to make reasoned decisions. The additional input can take several forms, including oral testimony of the parties and private interviews between the judge and child. The most common form, however, is an investigation or social study of the child, the prospective adoptive parents and the environment that they create together.

The home study is extremely important. Aside from oral testimony of the parties, which tends to be self-serving, the social study is the only means by which the judge can get a sense of what the adoptive child's new life style will be if the adoption is allowed. It is hoped that the study information will be objective and professionally prepared, so that at the final hearing on the adoption petition, the petition will be evaluated with the best interests of the child in mind.

The general legal significance of the social study is that it may give the judge and state authorities information that indicates whether the placement, adoption and child care laws of the state are being complied with by the various parties in the adoption. This factor is particularly important in cases where a state office or adoption agency is not involved in the application and placement processes, since independent placements can be effected with little or no attention. In those cases, the social study will be the first and perhaps only look that the court will have at the proposed adoptive situation. If a placement violated the laws of the state, the social study would be crucial in bringing this to the attention of the judge.

Generally, the adoptive social study is conducted by a state adoption worker or a social worker employed by the licensed adoption agency handling the placement. Most state laws either stipulate the party responsible for conducting the investigation, or give the presiding judge the right to designate a person. In such situations a judge may employ a state or court employee, licensed agency representative or an individual guardian *ad litem* (such as an attorney) to conduct the home study.

Since an important factor in a judge's decision to allow or deny an adoption petition is the degree and success of adjustment by the child to the adoptive home and family, almost every state requires that a social study be made after the placement of the child. In most of these states, this is the only investigation provided for by law, and is usually required after the adoption petition is filed. This timing factor presumably stems from the assumption of state legislatures that the placing agency will make an evaluation on its own before the placement (whether this is true in an independent adoption and whether the intermediary is in a position to make this judgment are questionable) and from the consideration that a fair and complete evaluation of the proposed adoption cannot be made until the child has been living in the adoptive home for some time.

The legal role of the social study (in giving an indication to the court whether the state placement laws are being complied with) suggests that there is a valid place for a preplacement social study. Such studies are always done in agency placements, although they may not be required by law. Although obviously not sufficient for the purpose of making a final recommendation on an adoption petition, such studies would serve the more limited purposes of first, protecting the child from a potentially detrimental placement situation, and second, allowing the placement agency to make better matches between qualified families and adoptive children.

In spite of these considerations, only seven states have adoption laws providing for preplacement social studies (Iowa, Kentucky, Florida, Nevada, New Hampshire, Virginia and Washington). The requirements of these statutes are triggered by different circumstances, but the effect of all is to protect the child from the potential dangers of independent placement, where trained state or agency personnel are not involved.

The Virginia adoption law makes a preplacement investigation mandatory only on licensed child-placing agencies, and does not mention unlicensed private placements in the preplacement section. Ironically, this seems to assume that a licensed agency must be ordered to make an investigation prior to a placement and that nothing can be done about unlicensed placements at the preplacement stage. It certainly seems more logical for a state legislature to assume that a licensed agency will automatically make its own preplacement investigation, while for unlicensed private placements there should be mandatory investigations prior to the placement.

In light of the legal significance and presumed legislative intent of preplacement social studies, it is suggested that such a legal requirement provides an important element of protection in licensed as well as independent placements for adoption. Of the seven states that require such investigations, the Washington law seems to afford the highest degree of legal protection to the adoptive child. The Virginia statute, on the other hand, leaves the largest gap in the preplacement stage by not requiring such an investigation in unlicensed private placements, thereby allowing the most room for abuses in independent adoptions.

As mentioned earlier, every state requires some form of social study after the child has been living in the adoptive home for some time, with certain exceptions in special situations, noted later. This postplacement study requirement is triggered by the filing of the adoption petition, at which point the court must (or may) order a qualified person to conduct an investigation.

The contents of the postplacement social study are largely left up to the individual or agency making the study, anticipating that the investigator will fill in the outline according to state regulations, agency policy and the specific facts of each case. The typical adoptive social study verifies the allegations of the petition and contains all basic information about the child and its biological parents, the petitioners and their home and family life. A state statute of this general type is the California[102] law, which requires the state Department of Health or adoption agency

> . . . to investigate the proposed adoption and to submit to the court a full report of the facts disclosed by its inquiry with a recommendation regarding the granting of the petition within 180 days after the filing of the petition.

As usual in almost every state, California Department of Health regulations[103] provide more specific guidelines for the contents of the investigation.

New York[104] law requires that an investigation be made by a "disinterested person" or by an authorized agency, appointed by the court. The investigator must verify the allegations of the adoption petition and inquire into such factors as family and medical history of both the child and petitioners, property and income of the petitioners, any compensation paid for the placement of the child, whether petitioners have ever been involved in a child neglect proceeding, and social, religious and emotional characteristics of the adoptive family. The provision that a "disinterested party" may complete a home study is likely to be a risk in independent adoptions. The person appointed to make such a study may not be trained or qualified to make judgments regarding psychological characteristics of the adoptive couple or the quality of care the child is likely to receive.

Although private placements are legal in New York, there is no preplacement requirement in the state's adoption law. However, the statute does provide that if the findings of the investigation give the judge cause for concern, he may order a hearing where the petitioners must show cause why the child should not be removed from the home. Consequently, such a private placement may be terminated before the petitioners get to the adoption hearing stage.

Ohio's[105] adoption law requires an investigation to be conducted by the court-appointed "next friend" of the child, who may be the county welfare department, an authorized agency, the state department, or some qualified person. The report must include, in addition to any specific information requested by the court, the physical and mental status of the child and petitioner, family backgrounds, reasons for the separation between the child and its biological parents, the biological parents' attitude toward the proposed adoption, the circumstances under which the placement was made, the suitability of the proposed adoption, and the child's attitude toward the adoption. The "next friend" must also make a recommendation to the court based on his findings. The petitioners must pay the costs of the investigation.

The Pennsylvania[106] adoption statute is unique in that it requires two postplacement investigations. Pennsylvania allows independent placements by intermediaries and requires a first report to be filed by the intermediary within 30 days after the placement of the child.[107] This report must set forth the circumstances surrounding the placement and detailed information concerning the child and the prospective adoptive parents. Upon receipt of this report, the court must order an investigation into the placement already made, to be carried out by a child care agency or other qualified party. Such investigation and report are presumably required for the purpose of monitoring compliance with child placement laws and standards. From an equity standpoint, however, it seems that a more effective means of preventing abusive placements would be to require these reports before a proposed placement is made.

The second investigation required by Pennsylvania law is triggered by the filing of the adoption petition. The court must appoint a qualified agency or person "to verify the statements of the petition and such other facts that will give the court full knowledge of the desirability of the proposed adoption." The court may rely on the earlier investigation (which is also required in agency placements, though in less detail) if it considers it sufficiently informative.

An interesting fact that emerges from the Social Study Provisions chart is that only 30 states, or 60%, require the person or agency conducting the social study to include in the report a recommendation in favor of or against the proposed adoption. Although there is no state law that makes an agency's recommendation binding on the court hearing the adoption petition, it must be presumed that a court has substantial confidence in the person or agency it appoints to conduct the social study, and therefore that the investigator's recommendation will have considerable, if not presumptive, influence on the judge's decision.

From a legal standpoint, therefore, the presence or absence of a recommendation requirement in a state social study provision can have great significance. In states that require it, the judge's decision will undoubtedly be influenced by the values and adoption standards of the person or agency making the social study. Conceivably, an adoption agency's standards that might be considered arbitrary or unreasonable could be given effect in the form of such a recommendation without being overtly stated. Where a recommendation is not included in the social study, on the other hand, the judge's decision would tend to be based on more objective input from the social study, and, consequently, more heavily on his own perception of the case. This may or may not be desirable.

Waiver provisions of some sort are included in almost every state adoption law. They allow for waiver of the social study in one or more of the following circumstances: 1) when the placement is made by the court or a licensed agency, on the presumption that such a placement will have already been investigated and evaluated by qualified persons; 2) stepparent adoptions, where one biological parent is still living with the child and the "placement" presumably does not involve a radical change in the child's home environment; 3) adoptions by close relatives (usually defined as within three or four degrees of consanguinity), where again the presumption is that the child is not confronted with a totally new or strange environment; 4) at the descretion of the court, in cases where particular facts obviate the necessity for the social study.

Under present adoptions laws, eight states provide for waiver of the social study in cases involving placement by the court or a licensed agency. Eighteen states allow waiver in stepparent adoptions, 10 in adoptions by close relatives, and 17 states permit the court to waive the social study requirement at its own discretion. This may be a risk in independent adoptions, since there would then be no scrutiny of the adoptive placements.

Thirteen states (Arkansas, Georgia, Idaho, Indiana, Kentucky, Michigan, New York, North Carolina, Ohio, Oregon, Pennsylvania,

Analysis of State Adoption Statutes and Regulations:
Social Study Provisions

Provisions

1. Preplacement investigation
2. Postplacement investigation
3. Recommendation included in social study
4. Recommendation not included in social study
5. Waiver of social study — court or agency placement
6. Waiver of social study — adoption by stepparent
7. Waiver of social study — adoption by close relative
8. Waiver of social study — discretion of court

Key: Required — x Allowed — w No relevant provision — –

State	1	2	3	4	5	6	7	8
Alabama		x		x				
Alaska		x	x		w	w	w	w
Arizona		x	x			w	w	w
Arkansas		x	x		–			
California		x	x		w	w		
Colorado		x	x		w			
Connecticut		x	x					w
Delaware		x	x					w
Florida	x¹	x	x			w	w	

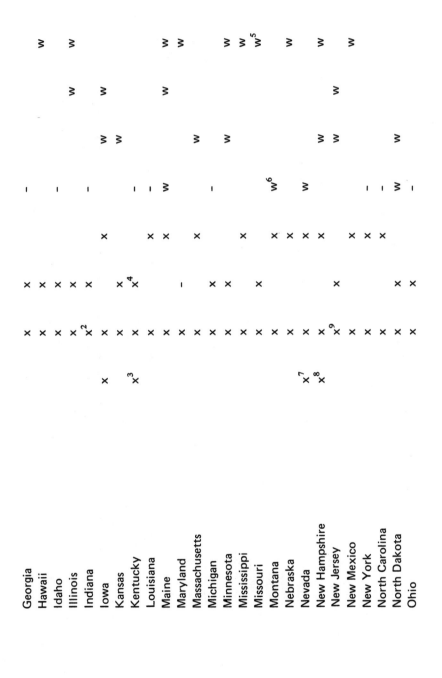

Oklahoma		x	x			w	
Oregon		x[10]	x		-		w
Pennsylvania		x[11]	x	x	-		
Rhode Island		x	x	x		w	
South Carolina		x	x	x			w
South Dakota		x	x[12]		-		
Tennessee		x	x			w	w
Texas		x	x	x	-		
Utah		x	x		w	w	
Vermont		x	x			w	w
Virginia	x	x		x		w	w
Washington	x	x	x			w	
West Virginia		x	x	x			w
Wisconsin		x	x	w			
Wyoming		x	x	x			w

[1] Required in private intermediary placements involving persons other than relatives or stepparents.

[2] Although a preplacement investigation is not required by law, the law states that no private, nonrelative placement may be made without the prior approval of a licensed agency or county department of welfare.

[3] Required in private placements.

[4] A formal recommendation is required in the preplacement report in private placements; the postplacement report must state whether the adoption is in the best interests of the child and whether the child is suitable for adoption.

[5] House Bill 1278 (1976), passed by both houses of the Missouri Legislature, gives the court the power to waive the investigation in stepparent adoptions and when all parents involved have given their consent to the adoption or custody transfer.

[6] Section 61-209 (1975) provides that the investigation may be waived only if the state Department of Social Services chooses to do so.

Footnotes continued

[7] The investigation is ordered upon notice of a proposed placement by other than a licensed agency; the placement may be enjoined or prohibited if found to violate any part of the state adoption law.

[8] Required in all cases other than relative adoptions and adoptions through an agency.

[9] If it appears that the placement in question was not made in accordance with the law and the child has been living in the home for less than 6 months, the child may be declared a ward of the court and a preliminary investigation is made at that point to determine the advisability of continuing the placement.

[10] The social study is mandatory only when the state department or a licensed agency gives the consent to adoption following termination of parental rights; in other cases the Children's Services Division may submit a report to the judge if it wishes to do so.

[11] In cases of private placement by a third party, the intermediary must file with the court a report on the parties involved and the details of his involvement in the placement.

[12] The report is forwarded to the state Division of Child Welfare, which approves the report and makes a recommendation to the court therefrom.

South Dakota and Texas) have no waiver provisions in their adoption laws. Presumably this means that in those states no adoption may be approved without some kind of investigation submitted to the court. Whether or not this is so in all cases, the legal significance of the absence of any waiver provision is that no adoption will be approved without some objective, informational input. Even in the most noncontroversial adoptive placements, such information could lead a court to a more thorough investigation of the petitioners or placement agent. The effect, therefore, should be added protection against placements or adoptions that are not in the child's best interests.

FEES AND COMPENSATION

Among the adoption law provisions that fall under the heading of "protective," those relating to fees and compensation can be most effective. Nevertheless, many state legislatures have not established controls over adoption compensation for the protection of the concerned parties. Even if a state's legislative policy permits independent placements, the state can discourage exploitation and abuse of the practice by placing restrictions on the fees that may be collected by intermediaries and by requiring that all such fees be reported to the court for its approval. Many financially secure childless couples are willing to pay large sums to obtain a child, and reports of exorbitant fees charged by so-called "baby brokers" are commonplace. Restrictions on the payment and receipt of placement and other fees, then, serve to protect both innocent parents and children.

A review of state adoption and child welfare laws indicates that less than half the states (21) have no provisions relating to fees charged in connection with adoption.[108] The presumption with regard to these states is that the legislatures have not perceived (or been alerted to) the risks inherent in not placing restrictions on the financial aspects of adoption.

Seven states (Alabama, Arkansas, Connecticut, Indiana, Louisiana, Texas and Washington) have statutes that deal only with agency fees and court costs. These laws are largely procedural rather than restrictive in nature; they usually say that the petitioners may be required to pay the "reasonable" agency and court costs incurred in the adoption process.

The Connecticut[109] law, which is typical, provides:

> For any report (social study) under this section the court of probate
> may assess against the adopting parent or parents a reasonable fee

covering the cost and expenses of making such investigation, which fee shall be paid to the state or to the child-placing agency making the investigation . . .

The effect of such statutes in regard to independent adoptions is negligible. Even though some of these seven states outlaw independent placements and therefore, arguably, do not need to restrict fees, the presence of restrictive legislation would serve to add impact and an extra degree of protection against violators of child-placing laws.

The remaining 22 states have statutes dealing in some way with fees and compensation that can be used to regulate or discourage the giving and receiving of compensation for child placement. These statutes fall into three classifications, largely according to the state's policy on independent placements.

The first type of restrictive compensation statute requires that the adoption petition or investigation contain an itemized report of all expenditures charged and paid in connection with the adoption, or that such expenditures be reported to the state welfare department. The expenditures must then be approved by the court or state department before proceeding with action on the adoption petition. Nine states (Alaska, California, Florida, Iowa, Michigan, New York, North Dakota, Oklahoma and Pennsylvania) have this type of statute. Most of these states allow some form of independent placement for adoption, so this statutory requirement does not have the effect of prohibiting or discouraging the payment of any placement-related fees whatsoever.

The California[110] statute, a particularly explicit one in this category, provides:

> The petitioners in any proceeding seeking the adoption of a minor child shall file with the court a full accounting report of all disbursements of anything of value made or agreed to be made by them or on their behalf in connection with the birth of the child, the placement of the child with the petitioners, any medical or hospital care received by the natural mother of the child or by the child in connection with its birth, any other expenses of either natural parent of the child, or the adoption. The accounting report shall be under penalty of perjury and shall be submitted to the court on or before the date set by the court for the hearing on the adoption petition, unless an extension of time is granted by the courts.

> The accounting report shall be itemized in detail and shall show the services relating to the adoption or to the placement of the child

for adoption which were received by the petitioners, by either natural parent of the child, by the child, or by any other person for whom payment was made by or on behalf of the petitioners. The report shall also include the dates of each payment, the names and addresses of each attorney, doctor, hospital, licensed adoption agency, or other person or organization who received any funds of the petitioners in connection with the adoption or the placement of the child with them, or participated in any way in the handling of such funds, either directly or indirectly.

The provisions of this section shall not apply to an adoption by a stepparent where one natural or adoptive parent retains his or her custody and control of the child.

The "reporting of expenses" requirement is a means of controlling unreasonable or illegal fees by subjecting them to court or state scrutiny. It is, however, the least restrictive of the three types of law discussed herein, because its only effect is to put the parties — particularly the adopting parents — on an "honor system." In a questionable or illegal independent placement situation, a couple desiring to adopt regardless of the cost might be tempted to avoid such a reporting requirement in order to expedite the adoption. Naturally, "black market" adoptions cannot succeed unless the parents cooperate with the intermediaries.

The second type of restrictive compensation law stipulates the kinds of fee that may be paid by the petitioners in connection with the adoption, prohibiting by inference any fees not specifically allowed. The laws of Florida, Idaho, Maryland, New Jersey and Utah allow for payment by the petitioners of medical expenses of the mother and child in connection with the birth. The Utah[111] law further allows the petitioners to pay any legal and court costs incurred by the placing agency and/or biological parents.

Florida's[112] adoption law allows the petitioners to pay to an intermediary up to $500, plus documented medical, hospital and court costs. As mentioned earlier, such expenditures must be reported by the petitioners, and any larger fee must be approved by the court.

Under proposed legislation in New Jersey,[113] that state's adoption and child welfare laws would be reformed in several respects, among which would be a provision effectuating the enforcement of the laws against unauthorized profit making by intermediaries in adoptive placement.

This second type of compensation provision is somewhat restrictive in the sense that it prohibits, by inference, the payment of unlimited fees to an intermediary or biological parent. Nevertheless, by allowing even a limited flow of money between adoptive parents and unlicensed private parties, these states may be leaving the door open for abuses of the independent placement system, with significant implications for "black market" adoptions.

The most restrictive compensation provisions are found in the laws of 10 states: Arizona, Colorado, Delaware, Illinois, Kentucky, Massachusetts, Minnesota, Nevada, North Carolina and Utah. These laws expressly prohibit the payment of any compensation except to the state or a licensed agency, or simply prohibit any fee from being paid or received for the placing of a child for adoption. This type of statute is found in states that do not allow independent third-party placements, as well as in some states that do not prohibit such placements but wish to discourage their "business" or "profit" aspects.

Regardless of the degree of severity of restrictions on compensation in adoptions, it seems that their effectiveness must depend largely on two factors: the honesty of the parties — biological parents, intermediaries and adoptive parents — in reporting adoption payments to the court involved in the proceeding, and the penalties provided by the state legislatures for violations of these laws.

PENALTIES

The vast majority of the states have enacted legislation that by one method or another sets parameters within which the adoptive placement process must operate. As has been indicated, attempts to curb misuse of (or illegal actions within) the adoption scheme vary greatly in terms of scope and approach. As noted, certain states bar independent placements outright. Some states have strictly limited and defined the circumstances that must first occur before a petition to adopt may even be filed. Other states have established stringent procedures for monitoring the adoption process. Furthermore, certain states have attempted to solve adoptive placement abuses by enacting protective legislation limiting the situations in which fees may be collected by third parties (such as doctors and lawyers who arrange placements), as well as limiting the compensation that may be given or received in facilitating adoptive placements.

Regardless of the form that the legislation takes in attempting to monitor placement practices, the real strength behind such legislation lies in 1) the ability to identify abuses, and 2) the statutory sanctions against those violating the placement laws. The effectiveness of this legislation can be guaranteed only by laws that call for meaningful penalties. A survey of the various state laws makes it clear that in this area there are different categories: states without statutory sanctions; states with statutory sanctions insufficient to support compliance; and states with adoptive placement limitations complemented by stringent penalties for violations.

At present only a few states (Alaska, Delaware, Kansas, Mississippi, South Dakota, West Virginia and Wyoming) have no penalty provisions for violations of their adoptive placement procedure. Among these states, the absence of penalties in Delaware[114] is particularly striking, since that state is one of the few that specifically prohibits all independent third-party placements.

All of the other states provide statutory penalties in some form for violations of adoptive placement procedures. As indicated previously, an explanation in part for the ineffectiveness of Georgia's independent placement prohibition is the inadequacy of the potential penalty:[115] an outlawed independent placement or advertising of placement practices without a license results merely in a $100 to $500 fine, and for unlicensed operation of a child-placing agency a fine of $50 to $200 may be imposed.

Other states also have weak penalty provisions. For example, Colorado's penalties[116] for receiving or offering unapproved or illegal placement fees are not rigorous: $100 to $500 fine and/or up to 90 days' incarceration. In Indiana[117] a fine of up to $100 and/or 30 days in jail may be imposed for selling or otherwise disposing of a child for any unlawful purpose. Iowa[118] provides for the same penalties as Indiana for giving or receiving a prohibited fee. In Oregon,[119] a fine of up to $500 may be imposed for advertising or soliciting child placement services without a license. Utah's[120] provision is made only for injunctive relief for operating a child-placing agency, advertising, or accepting certain fees without a license.

Some states do provide stringent penalties for violations of adoptive placement statutes. In Alabama,[121] a person may be fined up to $1000 and/or jailed for up to a year for facilitating and advertising independent placements without a license. In Arizona[122] it is a misdemeanor to facilitate an unauthorized third-party independent placement, to receive or give any compensation for placement by other than a state-licensed agency or the welfare department, or to commit any other procedural violation. Unauthorized independent placements and advertising placement facilities without a license are punishable as a misdemeanor in California.[123] In Florida[124] the following are punishable as third-degree felonies: independent placement outside the state unless with stepparents or relatives; paying or receiving an intermediary fee larger than $500 without court approval; failure of an intermediary to report any intended placement for adoption; and selling or surrendering a child for money or value. Idaho[125] has a strict baby-selling statute. In that state a person may be fined up to $5000 and/or imprisoned for up to 14 years for selling or bartering any child for adoption.

Penalty provisions in Illinois[126] are provided in cases of advertising child placement services without a license and paying or accepting compensation in connection with independent placements. First offenses are treated as Class A misdemeanors and subsequent offenses as third-degree felonies. It is noteworthy that the Illinois Supreme Court, in *State v. Schwartz,*[127] upheld that state's penalty provision against an attack of being unconstitutionally vague and overbroad, in violation of due process.

The Kentucky[128] penalty is $500 to $2000 fine and/or 6 months in jail for each day of violating the statute prohibiting certain independent placements, advertising, charging or accepting fees without a license for arranging a placement, or violating the confidentiality of adoption records.

Among the most stringent penalties imposed for placement violations are those recently enacted to augment the new independent placement prohibition in Massachusetts.[129] That state now imposes a fine of $100 to $1000 for offering or advertising an unlicensed independent placement. Accepting any payment for an unauthorized adoptive placement may result in a fine of $5000 to $30,000 and/or up to 5 years in prison.

In Nevada[130] a person may be fined up to $1000 and/or imprisoned for 1 to 6 years for receiving any compensation for child placement or being involved in child placement services or independent placements without a license.

Pennsylvania[131] imposes a fine of up to $10,000 and an imprisonment of up to 5 years for trading, bartering, selling or dealing in infant children.

In Washington,[132] penalties of up to $1000 and/or one year in prison may be imposed for placing children for adoption prior to receiving an order of relinquishment; or for inducing women to enter a hospital or maternity home for confinement care by offering, advertising or holding out that a placement or her child may be arranged.

As with adoptive placement practices in general, penalty provisions related to violations of placement practices vary greatly from state to state. The more stringent penalties place state officials in a better position to monitor and enforce adoptive placement statutes. Nevertheless, the solution to the problem of placement abuses requires more than the enactment of strict penalties. Such abuses can be perceived, ferreted out and properly dealt with only if proper monitoring of adoptive placements and concomitant enforcement are undertaken by duly authorized officials. The effectiveness of legislation regulating adoptions and the complementary penalty provisions, whether weak or strong, depends upon the ability and willingness of state officials to enforce the laws.

A state-by-state list dealing with compensation and penalties in adoption proceedings follows.

ALABAMA

Compensation: Court costs may be assessed to petitioner.
Penalties: For independent placement or advertisement without a license; for interstate placement without permission of Commissioner of Pensions & Security — $100 to $1000 and/or up to 1 year in jail.
Penalties — Ala. Code Tit. 49, § 84(16) (1973).

ALASKA

Compensation: Petitioner is required to report all itemized expenditures made in regard to the placement and adoption, including birth and hospital costs for child and mother, to the court.
Penalties: No provisions.
Compensation — Alaska Stat. § 20.15.090 (1974).

ARIZONA

Compensation: No person other than the state department or a licensed agency may receive any fee for placing a child. Petitioner is required to report to the court all disbursements made in connection with the adoption. Maximum agency fees: $100 for placement, $150 for social study.
Penalties: For independent third-party placement; for giving or accepting any compensation for placement by other than the state department of an agency; for procedural violations — Misdemeanor.
"Compensation" — Ariz. Rev. Stat. §§ 8-114, 8-126 (1974).
"Penalty" — Ariz. Rev. Stat. § 8-128 (1974).

ARKANSAS

Compensation: No fee may be collected from the petitioner where the state department has custody of the child and consents to the adoption.
Penalties: For failure to make an investigation of the adoption, disclos-

ing records or failing to file a copy of the decree — up to $100 and/or 3 months.
"Compensation" — Ark. Stat. Ann. § 56-120 (Cum. Supp. 1973).
"Penalty" — Ark. Stat. Ann. § 56-118 (Cum. Supp. 1973).

CALIFORNIA

Compensation: $500 maximum fee for public agency services; private agency fees must be approved by the state department.
Penalties: For independent placement without authorization (other than by natural parents); for advertising to place children without a license — Misdemeanor.
"Compensation" — Cal. Civ. Code § 224r (West Cum. Supp. 1976).
"Penalty" — Cal. Civ. Code § 224p (West Cum. Supp. 1976).

COLORADO

Compensation: No fees may be charged by other than the state department or licensed agency; all fees must be reported to the court.
Penalties: For illegal or unapproved fees and compensation (giving or receiving) — $100 to $500 and/or up to 90 days.
Colo. Rev. Stat. § 1904-115 (1973) (Compensation and penalties)

CONNECTICUT

Compensation: State department or agency may charge a reasonable fee for services.
Penalties: For unauthorized disclosure of confidential adoption records — up to $500 and/or 6 months.
"Compensation" — Conn. Gen. Stat. § 45-61(e) (1975).
"Penalty" — Conn. Gen. Stat. § 45-66 (1975).

DELAWARE

Compensation: Agency may charge a reasonable fee for its services. No natural parent may receive a fee for giving up a child. All fees must be reported and approved by the court.
Penalties: No provisions.
Compensation — Del. Code Tit. 13§ 916 (1975).

FLORIDA

Compensation: All fees must be reported to the court in the petition for adoption. An intermediary may charge up to $500, plus documented medical, hospital and court costs. Any larger fee must be approved by the court.
Penalties: For independent placement outside the state (except for

relatives or stepparent); for paying or receiving an intermediary fee larger than $500 without court approval; for selling or surrendering a child for money or value; for failure of an intermediary to report any intended placement for adoption — Third-degree felony.
"Compensation" — Fla. Stat. Ann. §§ 63.097, 63.132 (West Cum. Supp. 1976).
"Penalty" — Fla. Stat. Ann. § 63.212 (West Cum. Supp. 1976).

GEORGIA

Compensation: No provision.
Penalties: For independent placement or advertising without a license — $100 to $500 fine. For unlicensed operation of a child-placing agency — $50 to $200 fine for each offense.
Penalty — Ga. Code §§ 74-421, 99-214 (1975).

HAWAII

Compensation: No provisions.
Penalties: For operating a child-placing agency without state certificate of approval, $200 fine.
Penalty — Haw. Rev. Stat. § 346-17 (1968).

IDAHO

Compensation: Payment of any medical costs incurred by the mother or child by any person is allowed.
Penalties: For selling or bartering any child for adoption or any other purpose — Felony (up to $5000 and/or 14 years).
"Compensation" — Idaho Code § 18-1512 (Cum. Supp. 1974).
"Penalty" — Idaho Code § 18-1511 (Cum. Supp. 1974).

ILLINOIS

Compensation: No person or agency except a licensed child welfare agency may receive or pay any direct or indirect compensation for placing a child.
Penalties: For paying or accepting compensation in connection with an independent placement; for advertising child-placement services without a license — Class A misdemeanor (first offense), third-degree felony (subsequent offenses).
"Compensation" — Ill. Ann. Stat. ch. 4, § 12-1 (Smith-Hurd Cum. Supp. 1976).
"Penalty" — Ill. Ann. Stat. ch. 4 § 12-5 (Smith-Hurd Cum. Supp. 1976).

INDIANA

Compensation: County department may charge a placement fee not to exceed its central costs.
Penalties: For selling or otherwise disposing of a child for any unlawful purpose — up to $100 and/or 30 days.
"Compensation" — Ind. Code § 12-1-3-6 (1971).
"Penalty" — Ind. Code § 35-14-3-3 (1971)

IOWA

Compensation: Full accounting of all disbursements made in connection with the adoption.
Penalties: If the natural parent receives any prohibited thing of value, if a person gives a prohibited thing of value, or if a person charges a prohibited fee under this subsection each such person shall be, upon conviction, guilty of a misdemeanor, and shall be fined not more than $100 or imprisoned in the county jail for not more than 30 days.
Compensation and Penalties — Iowa Code Ann. § 600.9 (West Cum. Supp. 1976).

KANSAS

Compensation: No provisions.
Penalties: No provisions.

KENTUCKY

Compensation: No fee may be charged or accepted without a license.
Penalties: For independent placement, advertisement or charging or accepting fees without a license; for unauthorized disclosure of adoption records — $500 to $2000 fine and/or 6 months for each day of violation.
"Compensation" — Ky. Rev. Stat. Ann. § 199.590 (Baldwin 1974).
Penalties — same

LOUISIANA

Compensation: Reasonable court costs may be assessed to the petitioner.
Penalties: For unauthorized disclosure of adoption records — up to $500 and/or 90 days.
"Compensation" — La. Rev. Stat. § 9:441 (West Cum. Supp. 1976).
"Penalty" — La. Rev. Stat. § 9:437 (West Cum. Supp. 1976).

MAINE

Compensation: No provisions.
Penalties: For unlicensed placement or advertising for placement —
up to $500 and/or 11 months. For violations of procedural laws — up
to $500 and/or 6 months.
Penalty — Me. Rev. Stat. Tit. 22, § 3800 (1965).

MARYLAND

Compensation: No person or agency rendering any service in
connection with the placement of a child may charge or receive, from
natural parents or petitioner, any compensation other than reasonable fees for medical, hospital and legal services. The state department or licensed agency may charge for reasonable costs of adoptive
services.
Penalties: For unlicensed independent third-party placement —
Misdemeanor (up to $500 and/or 1 year). For charging unauthorized
fees in connection with placement or adoption — up to $100 and/or 3
months for each offense.
"Compensation" — Md. Ann. Code Art. 16, § 83 (Cum. Supp. 1974).
"Penalty" — Md. Ann. Code Art. 16, §§ 28, 31 (Cum. Supp. 1974).

MASSACHUSETTS

Compensation: No fee may be accepted for placing a child for
adoption.
Penalties: For offering or advertising independent placement without
a license — $100 to $1000 fine. For accepting any payment for
placing a child for adoption — $5000 to $30,000 fine and/or up to 5
years. For bringing a child into the state for adoptive placement
without permission from the state department — up to $100 and/or 6
months.
Mass. Gen. Laws Ann. ch. 210 § 11A (West Cum. Supp. 1976)
(Compensation and Penalties)

MICHIGAN

Compensation: All fees charged or paid in connection with placement
and adoption must be approved by the court.
Penalties: For placing a child in any home for adoption before an
order terminating the rights of its parents and making the child a
ward of the court has been entered; for giving or receiving any
compensation in connection with placement or consent to adoption
without court approval — Misdemeanor (first offense), felony

(subsequent offenses). For placement of a child in the control or care of a person by one other than the parent, guardian, or relative of the child, a licensed agency or governmental unit — up to $100/90 days. "Compensation" — Mich. Stat. Ann. § 27.3178 (555.54) (Cum. Supp. 1977).
"Penalties" — Mich. Stat. Ann. §§ 25.358(24-25), 27.3178 (555.69) (Cum. Supp. 1977).

MINNESOTA

Compensation: No fee may be solicited or paid for placing a child in an adoptive home.
Penalties: For independent third-party placement, advertising, charging fees or operating a child-placing agency without a license — Misdemeanor.
"Compensation" — Minn. Stat. § 257.03 (Cum. Supp. 1973).
"Penalties" — Minn. Stat. §§ 257.091, 257,123 (Cum. Supp. 1973).

MISSISSIPPI

Compensation: No provisions.
Penalties: No provisions.

MISSOURI

Compensation: No provisions.
Penalties: For independent third-party placement without court approval; for unauthorized disclosure of adoption records — Misdemeanor.
Penalties — Mo. Stat. Ann. § 453.110. (Vernon 1972).

MONTANA

Compensation: No provisions.
Penalties: For operating an unlicensed adoption agency — Misdemeanor (up to $1000).
Penalty — Mont. Rev. Code. Ann. § 10-706 (Cum. Supp. 1975).

NEBRASKA

Compensation: No provisions.
Penalties: For placing or assisting in placement of a child by other than the natural parents, state department or licensed agency; for advertising placement without a license — Misdemeanor ($50 to $200 and/or up to 30 days).
Penalty — Neb. Rev. Stat. §§ 43-701, 43-709 (1971).

NEVADA

Compensation: No fee may be paid to anyone involved in the adoption other than a licensed child-placing agency.

Penalties: For receiving any compensation for child placement or being involved in a child placement without a license — up to $1000 and/or 1 to 6 years. For advertising child placement services or for independent third-party placement without a license; for failure to deliver copies of all consents to adoption to state department within 48 hours of execution of consents — Misdemeanor.

"Compensation" — Nev. Rev. Stat. § 127.290 (1973).

"Penalty" — Nev. Rev. Stat. §§ 127.057, 127.280, 127.300, 127.310 (1973).

NEW HAMPSHIRE

Compensation: No provisions.

Penalties: For violating confidentiality of adoption proceedings and records — Misdemeanor.

Penalty — N.H. Rev. Stat. Ann. § 170-B:19 (Cum. Supp. 1975).

NEW JERSEY

Compensation: Petitioner must pay all court costs and agency fees. No one other than an agency shall receive or pay any money or thing of value except in connection with the birth and illness of the child.

Penalties: For independent placement other than by natural parents without proper authority — High misdemeanor.

"Compensation" — N.J. Stat. Ann. § 9:3-32 (West 1960).

"Penalty" — N.J. Stat. Ann. §§ 2A:96-6, 2A:96-7 (West 1969).

NEW MEXICO

Compensation: No provisions.

Penalties: For child placement without a license — Misdemeanor.

Penalty — N.M. Stat. Ann. § 22-2-42 (Cum. Supp. 1975).

NEW YORK

Compensation: All fees paid to an agent in an independent placement must be reported to court.

Penalties: For violations of confidentiality of adoption records — Contempt of court.

"Compensation" — N.Y. Dom. Rel. Law § 116 (McKinney Cum. Supp. 1976).

"Penalty" — N.Y. Dom. Rel. Law § 114 (McKinney Cum. Supp. 1976).

NORTH CAROLINA

Compensation: No fees whatsoever are allowed for placing or arranging the placement of a child.

Penalties: For advertising without a license; for accepting any compensation for placement; for violation of confidentiality of adoption records — Misdemeanor. For procuring the custody of a relinquished child (by forfeiting parents) — Abduction.

"Compensation" — N.C. Gen. Stat. § 48-37 (1975).

"Penalty" — N.C. Gen STat. §§ 48-25, 48-33, 48-37, 48-38 (1975).

NORTH DAKOTA

Compensation: Petitioner may pay reasonable costs of birth of child, hospital and medical care of the mother and placement services. All expenditures must be reported to court.

Penalties: For independent placement by other than natural parents — up to $5000 and/or 5 years.

"Compensation" — N.D. Cent. Code § 14-5-10 (Cum. Supp. 1975).

"Penalty" — N.D. Cent. Code § 50-12-17 (Cum. Supp. 1975).

OHIO

Compensation: No provisions.

Penalties: For independent placement except with relatives or stepparent; for advertising for placement without a license — up to 6 months and/or $500 to $1000 fine.

Penalty — Ohio Rev. Code Ann. § 5103.99 (Baldwin Cum. Supp. 1974).

OKLAHOMA

Compensation: No compensation other than court-approved medical and legal fees may be accepted from petitioner in connection with placement or adoption.

Penalties: For "trafficking" in children; for accepting any unauthorized compensation in connection with placement or adoption; for offering or advertising to place a child as an inducement to any woman to enter an institution or home for delivery of a child and maternity care; for bringing or causing to be brought into the state any child (or sending the child out of the state) for placement by parents or placement with relatives — Misdemeanor (up to 1 year) for first offense, felony (up to 2 years) for subsequent offenses. *No suspension of sentence is permitted.*

Penalty — Okla. Stat. Ann. Tit. 21, §§ 866, 867 (West Cum. Supp. 1976).

OREGON

Compensation: No provisions.
Penalties: For advertising or soliciting child placement services — up to $500 fine.
Penalty — Ore. Rev. Stat. § 167.645 (Cum. Supp. 1975).

PENNSYLVANIA

Compensation: Petitioners may be required to pay court and agency costs. All fees paid in connection with placement and adoption must be reported by petitioner to court.
Penalties: For trading, bartering, buying, selling or dealing in infant children — Misdemeanor (up to $10,000 and/or 5 years).
"Compensation" — Pa. Stat. Ann. Tit. 1, §§ 333,424 (Purdon Cum. Supp. 1977).
"Penalty" — Pa. Stat. Ann. Tit. 18, § 4305 (Purdon Cum. Supp. 1973).

RHODE ISLAND

Compensation: No provisions.
Penalties: For independent placement without contemplation of adoption through a licensed agency; for any procedural violation — up to $500 and/or 1 year.
Penalty — R.I. Gen. Laws § 15-7-22 (Cum. Supp. 1974).

SOUTH CAROLINA

Compensation: No provisions.
Penalties: For removing a child from its natural mother within 6 months after its birth without reporting to the Children's Bureau the names and addresses of the persons with whom the child is placed; for bringing a child into the state for placement without permission from the Children's Bureau — Misdemeanor.
Penalty — S.C. Code §§ 71-206, 71-207, 71-211 (Cum. Supp. 1974).

SOUTH DAKOTA

Compensation: No provisions.
Penalties: No provisions.

TENNESSEE

Compensation: No provisions.
Penalties: For independent placement; for disclosure of confidential records; for procedural violations — Misdemeanor — $250 to $1000

and/or up to 1 year. For illegally obtaining repossession of the child (by natural parents) — Abduction.
Penalty — Tenn. Code Ann. §§ 36-130, 36-133, 36-134 (Cum. Supp. 1976).

TEXAS

Compensation: No fee may be given or accepted for child placement.
Penalties: For advertising or accepting any compensation in connection with an adoption without a license — Felony third degree. For operating a child placement agency without a license, $50 to $1000 for each day of violation.
"Compensation" — Tex. Fam. Code Ann. Tit. 20 § 8A (Vernon 1975).
"Penalty" — Tex. Fam. Code Ann. Tit. 20 § 23, Tit. 22 § 524 (Vernon 1975).

UTAH

Compensation: No fee may be charged for independent placement, but fees may be paid to an independent placement agent or directly to the natural parents for birth, hospital, medical and legal costs.
Penalties: For operating a child-placing agency, advertising or accepting fees (except as provided above) without a license — Injunctive relief may be obtained.
Compensation and Penalty — Utah Code Ann. § 55-8a-1 (1971).

VERMONT

Compensation: No provisions.
Penalties: For failure to file adoption papers with Secretary of State — $25 fine (pending legislation would make independent third-party placements illegal).
Penalty — Vt. Stat. Ann. Tit. 15 § 451 (1974).

VIRGINIA

Compensation: No provisions.
Penalties: For operating a child-placing agency without a license; for misleading or deceptive advertisements (by a licensed agency or other) — up to $100 and/or 1 year.
Penalty — Va. Code §§ 63.1-196, 63.1-215 (Cum. Supp. 1975).

WASHINGTON

Compensation: Petitioner may be assessed fees for preparation of investigation and report by agency.
Penalties: For directly or indirectly disposing of infants by placing

them for adoption before an order of relinquishment has been entered (except for stepparent adoptions); for offering, advertising or holding out to be able to dispose of any child as an inducement to a woman to go to a hospital or maternity home for confinement care — Gross misdemeanor (up to $1000 and/or 1 year).
"Compensation" — Wash. Rev. Code Ann. § 26.32.230 (Cum. Supp. 1974).
"Penalty" — Wash. Rev. Code Ann. § 26.32.040-060 (Cum. Supp. 1974).

WEST VIRGINIA

Compensation: No provisions.
Penalties: No provisions.

WISCONSIN

Compensation: No provisions.
Penalties: For independent third-party placement — up to $500 and/or 1 year; injunction.
Wis. Stat. Ann. §§ 48.76, 48.77 (Cum. Supp. 1976).

WYOMING

Compensation: No provisions.
Penalties: No provisions.

FINALITY PROVISIONS

Every state adoption law includes a section dealing with the legal effects of an adoption decree. Such sections invariably provide, among other things, that the final decree of adoption terminates any and all rights of the biological parents in the child, and gives the adoptive parents all the legal rights in the child, exactly as if the child had been born to them.

Standing alone, the "legal effects of adoption" provisions appear emphatic and absolute and seems to leave no room for doubt as to the status of the new parent-child relationship created by an adoption decree. However, upon the issuance of the decree, two legal concepts come into play that leave the adoption in a tentative state for at least 1 month and, in some cases, as long as 5 years or more.

The first of these concepts is the appeal from the adoption order. This fundamental legal remedy is found in every state, and whether it is specified in the adoption statute itself or not, no adoption decree is immune from a civil appeal as of the date that the decree is entered. The ordinary appeal is the means by which a *party* to the adoption proceeding — the biological parents, adoptive parents, state welfare department, child placing agency or even the child (by his appointed guardian *ad litem*) — can challenge the final decision of the judge in the first instance to allow or deny the adoption.

The second legal concept that can cause the status of an adoption to remain in doubt for a period of time is the collateral attack. A collateral attack is the means by which any person — whether or not he was directly involved in the original proceeding — may bring an action to challenge the validity of the adoption decree after it has been entered. Such an action, separate from the original adoption action and thereby termed "collateral," seeks to set aside or modify the adoption decree on either jurisdictional, procedural or substantive grounds. A collateral attack based on jurisdiction might allege that the court issuing the decree had no jurisdiction and was approached solely for the purpose of taking advantage of a more liberal adoption law or policy. A procedural collateral attack could charge that an adoption was invalid because a formal requirement of the law — such as minimum length of the adoptive placement or signatures of necessary affidavits — was not met prior to allowance of the adoption. Finally, a substantive ground for collateral attack could be that the adoptive parents are not fit to care for the child, or that the consent to the adoption given by an unwed mother was obtained through fraud, duress, undue influence or lack of capacity to consent.

Although every state must provide a mechanism for appealing an adoption decree, not every state has a finality statute that provides for collateral attack. The reason for this is unclear, but one possible factor is that a collateral attack statute may be a two-edged sword.

On one hand, it seems reasonable that a person discovering some problem or fact that could affect the judge's decision on the adoption petition should not be foreclosed from bringing it to the attention of the court within a certain time. Although most states have an "interlocutory decree" prior to the final decree for just this purpose, in many cases a defect in the adoption may not be discovered until after the adoption has become final.

On the other hand, the state, as well as the parties involved, has a legitimate interest in protecting the stability of the adoptive home by drawing a line at some specified time, after which the adoption may not be attacked for any reason whatsoever. This policy also seems reasonable, although it may in some cases mean the legitimation of an adoption that should not have been allowed in the first place.

In the context of independent adoptive placements, finality statutes providing for collateral attack can have great significance. Again, such a law can have contradictory effects: although it can be used to terminate an unsupervised private placement that is not in the best interests of the child, it can also allow a biological parent who is confused or who has had a change of mind to stay involved in the relinquished child's life for an unreasonable time.

Presumably, consideration of these and other factors has resulted in the various finality provisions found in state adoption laws. The varying emphases that the state legislatures have placed on these factors account for the wide differences between finality statutes from state to state.

Of the 50 states, 13 (Georgia, Idaho, Iowa, Louisiana, Michigan, Minnesota, Montana, Nevada, North Carolina, Oregon, South Carolina, Tennessee and Wisconsin) have finality statutes that allow an adoption decree to be attacked only by normal civil appeal. In these states, therefore, only the parties to the adoption proceeding are given standing to contest the decision of the judge in the first instance, and such action must be taken promptly. The standard time limit on civil appeals ranges from 10 to 90 days after the entry of the judgment or order in question.

The Georgia[133] statute is somewhat different from other "appeal only" finality laws in that the objection to the adoption must be filed at least 10 days before the date assigned for hearing on the final decree. In other words, any formal objection to the adoption must be heard concurrently with the arguments in favor of allowing the adoption, rather than subsequent to issuance of a final decree. The Georgia courts have further clarified this state policy by declaring that a final order of adoption cannot be collaterally attacked.[134]

The Louisiana[135] statute gives the right of appeal to "any party to the proceedings or any other party in interest." This law is unique in that it allows a person not directly involved in the adoption proceeding to intervene by appeal. The statute allows a collateral attack on the adoption for a limited period (30 days).

Oregon's[136] finality statute makes the adoption decree binding on all parties, except by appeal, as of the date of the decree. All other persons, however, have 1 year in which to bring a collateral attack before they become bound by the decree. This statute, then, distinguishes between parties and nonparties, and the distinction is important. It represents an acknowledgment by the Oregon legislature that persons not directly involved in the adoption proceedings may not become aware of defects in the adoption until a decree has already been issued, and therefore that such persons should have additional time in which to object to the adoption. On the other hand, parties to the adoption should be able to make all arguments pro and con prior to the judge's decision and are therefore estopped from objecting as of the date of the final decree.

The Tennessee[137] statute makes the appeal period the time between the entry of the interlocutory decree and the final decree, which must be at least 1 year. This is a curious provision; it makes an adoption subject to attack for an entire year while apparently precluding persons other than parties to the original proceeding from making use of the law.

It is interesting to note that those state laws that allow for collateral attack of an adoption decree place the same time limit on regular appeals of the decree as on collateral attacks. Thus, in the states described in the following sections, the time limits imposed on collateral attacks apply to party appeals as well — with the exception of the Oregon law already described.[138]

Those state laws that do provide for collateral attack of an adoption decree vary in the time they allow for such an attack to be made. Three states (Mississippi, Virginia and Washington) limit the period of attack to 6 months from the date of the final decree. The most popular time limitation on collateral attacks of adoption decrees is 1 year. Eleven states (Alaska, Arizona, Florida, Hawaii, Maryland, Missouri, New Hampshire, New Mexico, North Dakota, Oklahoma and Oregon) provide for a 1-year period.

The Alaska[139] and North Dakota[140] statutes both contain an exception to this limitation. The period of attack is not limited to 1 year in cases where the petitioners (adoptive parents) have not taken custody of the child at the time of the final decree. Presumably, this means that the 1-year period does not begin to run until such time as the custody of the child is given to the petitioners.

Five states (Arkansas, Colorado, Delaware, Kentucky and Nebraska) provide for a 2-year period for direct or collateral attack. The Arkansas[141] law conditions this limitation on the adopted child's having lived with the adopting parents for that length of time, and provides for several additional exceptions to the 2-year limitation.

California[142] law distinguishes between grounds for collateral attack: an attack based on procedural grounds must be brought within 3 years of the entry of the decree; for any other ground, the attack period is extended to 5 years.

Alabama's[143] adoption law contains a 5-year limitation on direct or collateral attacks of adoption decrees. Of those states that specify a time limitation, the Alabama and California laws leave the adoption open to attack for the longest period.

In addition to finality statutes that impose time limitations on direct and collateral attacks on adoption decrees, six states (Arkansas, Indiana, Maine, Massachusetts, Vermont and West Virginia) provide for attacks not subject to time limits where certain grounds are involved. These states apparently hold that when certain conditions can be proved, the adoption should not be allowed to continue regardless of the time that has expired since issuance of the final decree.

The Arkansas law limiting the period of attack to 2 years contains several exceptions.[144] A petition to annul a final adoption decree may be brought on any of the following grounds: a) the adopting parents have failed to perform their obligations to the child; b) the adopting parents have become separated or divorced within 2 years after the entry of the decree; c) the adopted child, within 5 years after the adoption decree, has developed a mental, venereal or incurable disease as a result of a condition that existed prior to the adoption and was unknown to the adopting parents. Upon proof of any of these grounds, the court in its discretion may set aside the adoption.

Indiana's[145] code of civil procedure allows a person who is under a "legal disability" when a cause of action accrues to bring his action within 2 years after the removal of the disability. In *Aramovich v. Doles*,[146] the Indiana Supreme Court implied that this statute may allow a collateral attack on an adoption decree to be made by a person whose consent was required but who was not notified of the adoption proceeding.

The Maine[147] finality statute is extremely liberal, allowing the probate judge virtually unfettered discretion to annul an adoption at any time. The law provides:

> Any judge of probate may, on petition of two or more persons, after notice and hearing and for good cause shown, reverse and annul any decree of the probate court in his county, whereby any child has been adopted under this chapter.

Case law indicates that the traditional equitable grounds of duress, fraud or incapacity in the taking of consent to adoption are valid grounds to annul an adoption under this provision.[148]

Massachusetts[149] law provides:

> The supreme judicial court may allow a parent, who, upon a petition for adoption, had no personal knowledge of the proceedings before the decree and had neither waived notice . . . nor been the subject of

> a decree dispensing with need for notice. . . , to appeal therefrom
> within 2 years after actual notice thereof.

This law contemplates, among other situations, one where an unwed father or parent who has been absent from home during the adoption proceedings may not want his child to be adopted, but was not informed of the proceedings before the decree was entered. Conceivably, "actual notice" of the adoption could occur at any time, which raises the question whether an open-ended period of attack in this context is fair to the adoptive child and parents.

The Vermont[150] statute provides for a proceeding to challenge the validity of an adoption, but does not specify any time limitation on the bringing of such an action. This law provides further that the state welfare department and any licensed agency involved in the adoption shall be made parties to any such proceeding. Another section of the Vermont adoption law[151] provides that if a person is adopted while a minor, he may file a "dissent" from the adoption within 1 year after becoming of age, and the court shall thereupon vacate the adoption. Under this extraordinary law, an adoption could conceivably be subject to annulment as many as 19 years after the decree is issued.

West Virginia's[152] adoption law contains a provision identical to the Vermont law, which allows an adopted person to petition to vacate the adoption upon becoming of age. Additionally, the law provides that a person whose consent to the adoption was required but who did not give such consent may, at any time within 1 year after learning of the adoption, petition the court to vacate the decree. This provision, like that of Massachusetts, seems designed to protect unnotified parents who are helpless to object to the adoption before the decree is issued.

Finally, 12 states (Connecticut, Illinois, Kansas, New Jersey, New York, Ohio, Pennsylvania, Rhode Island, South Dakota, Texas, Utah and Wyoming) have no finality provisions in their adoption statutes. This seems to indicate that the only available means of challenging an adoption decree in any of these states is by normal civil appeal. The case law analysis that follows clarifies the status of the collateral attack in several of these states.

The Illinois courts have consistently held that an adoption order is not subject to collateral attack when "substantial compliance" with the provisions of the Illinois Adoption Act is shown, except on the issue of jurisdiction of the court entering the order.[153] The Kansas Supreme Court, in *Jones v. Jones*,[154] has also held that adoption decrees may not be attacked collaterally.

Analysis of State Adoption Laws and Regulations:
Finality Provisions

Key
1. Adoption may be attacked by appeal only
2. Collateral attack allowed up to 6 months after final decree
3. Collateral attack allowed up to 1 year after final decree
4. Collateral attack allowed up to 2 years after final decree
5. Collateral attack allowed up to 5 years after final degree
6. Collateral attack may be brought at any time on certain grounds
7. No relevant statute

State	1	2	3	4	5	6	7
Alabama					x		
Alaska			x				
Arizona			x				
Arkansas				x		x	
California					x[1]		
Colorado				x			
Connecticut							x
Delaware				x			
Florida			x				
Georgia	x						
Hawaii			x				
Idaho	x						
Illinois							x
Indiana						x	
Iowa	x						
Kansas							x
Kentucky				x			
Louisiana	x						
Maine						x	
Maryland			x				
Massachusetts						x	
Michigan	x						
Minnesota	x						
Mississippi		x					
Missouri			x				
Montana	x						
Nebraska				x			

Nevada	X				
New Hampshire			X		
New Jersey					X
New Mexico			X		
New York					X
North Carolina	X				
North Dakota			X		
Ohio					X
Oklahoma			X		
Oregon	X^2		X^3		
Pennsylvania					X
Rhode Island					X
South Carolina	X				
South Dakota					X
Tennessee	X				
Texas					X
Utah					X
Vermont				X	
Virginia		X			
Washington		X			
West Virginia				X	
Wisconsin	X				
Wyoming					X

[1] An attack based on procedural grounds must be brought within 3 years of the decree.

[2] Parties to the adoption proceeding may not attack the decree except by appeal.

[3] Persons other than parties to the adoption are bound by the decree after 1 year.

In spite of the absence of collateral attack provisions in their adoption laws, the courts of three states have indicated that such attacks may be made in certain circumstances. In *In re Anonymous*,[155] as well as in other cases, the New York courts have held that decrees of adoption are subject to being reopened, set aside or vacated on the ground of newly discovered evidence. Such evidence would, presumably, have to affect significantly the factors involved in the judge's decision on the adoption petition.

The same test appears to have been applied by the Rhode Island Supreme Court in the case of *In re Adoption of Minor Child*.[156] The court held there that a final decree of adoption may be set aside by collateral attack, but only after a showing of clear and convincing evidence on the issues pleaded.

The Utah Supreme Court, in *Taylor v. Waddoups*,[157] held that a natural mother's "diligent attack" on a voidable adoption decree entitled her to regain the custody of her children. In that case, the court held that a decree procured through fraudulent conduct by the adopting parents was voidable. It appears, then, that in Utah the court has the discretion to decide what constitutes a reasonable time for collateral attack before the adoption becomes binding on all persons.

The Ohio legislature is currently considering House Bill 156, which contains several proposals for change in that state's adoption law. Among the proposed additions to the law is a finality statute that would make adoption decrees immune from attack after 1 year from the date of the decree,

> . . . unless, in the case of the adoption of a minor the petitioner has not taken custody of the minor, or in the case of the adoption of a minor by a stepparent, the adoption would not have been granted but for fraud perpetrated by the petitioner or the petitioner's spouse.

Because of the variety of finality provisions among the 50 states, it is difficult to discern any trend in favor of or against allowing adoption decrees to be attacked beyond the time limit for normal appeals. In light of the implications that these laws can have for parties to an adoption, however, it seems important that those states without such statutes make their policies clear by enacting explicit finality provisions as part of their comprehensive adoption laws. In this way, all persons involved in the adoption process will have a better idea as to where the adoption stands, and what their rights are, at any given time.

REFERENCES

1. 405 U.S. 645 (1972).
2. Georgia Department of Human Resources, Division of Family and Children Services, County Letter No. 422.
3. Wyoming County Director Manual, Volume 3 § 872.3.
4. 360 A. 2d 603 (Pa. 1976).
5. 71 Misc. 2d 666, 337 N.Y.S. 2d 102 (Sup. Ct. 1972).
6. Id. at 671, 337 N.Y.S. 2d at 107.
7. 36 N.Y. 2d 568, 331 N.E. 2d 486, 370 N.Y.S. 2d 511 (1975).
8. N.Y. Sur. Ct. Kings County, Aug. 9, 1976, 2 Fam. L. Rep. 2727 (Sept. 7, 1976).

9. Tex. Sup. Ct., 2 Fam. L. Rep. (B.N.A.) 2456 (May 11, 1976).

10. Idaho Code §16-1504 (Cum. Supp. 1975).

11. 2 Fam. L. Rep. (B.N.A.) 2357 (Mar. 30, 1976).

12. *See,* Mass. Gen. Laws Ann. ch. 210 §4A (West Cum. Supp. 1977)
     (Amending Mass. Gen. Laws ch. 210 §4); S. 1631, 197th N.J. Leg., 1st
     Sess., 2 Fam. L. Rep. (B.N.A.) 2773 (Sept. 28, 1976); HB 1426, 35th Okla.
     Leg., 2d Sess., 2 Fam. L. Rep. (B.N.A.) 2221 (Feb. 10, 1976); Bill 108,
     1976 W. Va. Leg., Regular Sess., 2 Fam. L. Rep. (B.N.A.) 2283 (Mar. 2,
     1976).

13. Ky. Rev. Stat. §199.500(2) (Cum. Supp. 1976); Wash. Rev. Code
     §26.32.070 (1974); Wisc. Stat. Ann. §48.84(2) (a) (West 1957).

14. Ind. Code §31-3-1-6(a) (1973).

15. N.H. Rev. Stat. Ann. §170-B:5 (Supp. 1975).

16. Vt. Stat. Ann. Tit. 15 §435 (Cum. Supp. 1976).

17. Mich. Stat. Ann. §27.3178 (55.28) (2) (1975).

18. Minn. Stat. Ann. §259.24 (West Cum. Supp. 1976).

19. Okla. Stat. Ann. Tit. 10, §60.5 (West 1966).

20. Pa. Stat. Ann. Tit. 1 §411 (Purdon Cum. Supp. 1977).

21. R.I. Gen. Laws §15-7-10 (Cum. Supp. 1976).

22. Ga. Code §74-403(5) (1975).

23. Georgia Service Manual Transmittal No. 28, p. 8, (1975).

24. Conn. Gen. Stat. §45-61(e) (1975).

25. Iowa Code Ann. §§600.1-600.23 (West Cum. Supp. 1976).

26. *State ex rel. Simpson v. Salter,* 211 La. 918, 31 So. 2d 163 (1971).

27. Alaska Stat. §20.15.60(a) (1975).

28. Fla. Stat. Ann. §63.0626 (West Cum. Supp. 1976).

29. Ind. Code §31-3-1-6(B) (1973).

30. Nev. Rev. Stat. §127.070 (1973).

31. N.M. Stat. Ann. §22-2-27 (Supp. 1975).

32. N.D. Cent. Code §14-15-07 (1971).

33. Ariz. Rev. Stat. §8-107 (1974).

34. Ill. Rev. Stat. ch. 4 §9.1-9 (1973).

35. Miss. Code Ann. ch. 17 §93-17-7 (1972).

36. N.H. Rev. Stat. Ann. §170-B:7 (Supp. 1975).

37. Mass. Gen. Laws Ann. ch. 210 §2 (West Cum. Supp. 1977).

38. Va. Code §63.1-225 (Cum. Supp. 1975).

39. Children Act, 1975 §§12(4), 14(4).

40. *See Infra,* p. 18, discussion of *In re Stone's Adoption,* 398 Pa. 190, A. 2d
     808 (1959).

41. Kan. Stat. §59-2102 (Supp. 1975).

42. Mass. Gen. Laws Ann. ch. 210, §2 (West Cum. Supp. 1977).

43. 271 N.E. 2d 621 (Mass. 1971).

44. 295 N.E. 2d 693 (Mass. App. Ct. 1973).

45. Mich. Stat. Ann. §27.3178 (555.29.8) (Cum. Supp. 1977).

46. Nev. Rev. Stat. §127.080 (1973).
47. N.Y. Dom. Rel. Law §§115, 116 (McKinney Cum. Supp. 1976).
48. 81 Misc. 2d 563, 364 N.Y.S. 2d 709 (Fam. Ct. 1975).
49. Alaska Stat. §20.15.070 (1974).
50. Ga. Code §74-403 (1975).
51. Ga. Dept. of Human Resources, Service Manual Transmittal No. 28 (1975).
52. 234 Ga. 204, 214 S.E. 2d 890 (1975).
53. La. Rev. Stat. §9:429 (West 1965).
54. Md. Ann. Code Art. 16 §74 (1973).
55. N.C. Gen. Stat. §48-11 (1976).
56. Pa. Stat. Ann. Tit. 1, §411 (Purdon Supp. 1977).
57. Tenn. Code Ann. §26-117 (1955).
58. Tex. Fam. Code Ann. Tit. 2, §§15.03, 16.06 (Vernon 1975).
59. 289 S. 2d 304 (La. App. Ct. 1973).
60. 398 Pa. 190, 156A 2d 808 (1959).
61. Miss. Code Ann. §93-17-7 (1972).
62. Va. Code §63.1-227 (Cum. Supp. 1975).
63. Minn. Stat. §259.24(6) (West Cum. Supp. 1976).
64. 224 Ark. 993, 277 S.W. 2d 842 (1955).
65. 252 Ark. 541, 480 S.W. 2d 336 (1972).
66. Okla. Stat. Ann. Tit. 10, §60.10 (West Cum. Supp. 1976).
67. 481 P. 2d 136 (Okla. 1971).
68. Wis. Stat. §48.86 (1973).
69. 260 Wis. 50, 49 N.W. 2d 759 (1951).
70. Ohio Rev. Code Ann. §3107.09(B) (Baldwin Cum. Supp. 1976).
71. 256 A. 2d 583 (Me. 1969).
72. 149 Colo. 404, 369 P. 2d 434 (1962).
73. 109 R.I. 443, 287 A. 2d 115 (1972).
74. 26 Utah 2d 255, 488 P. 2d 130 (1971).
75. Iowa Code Ann. §§600.1-600.23 (West Cum. Supp. 1976).
76. Iowa Code Ann. §600 A. 4 (1) (West Cum. Supp. 1976).
77. Iowa Code Ann. §600.9 (1) (West Cum. Supp. 1976).
78. Ind. Code §31-3-1-3 (1973).
79. Ariz. Rev. Stat. §8-105 (Cum. Supp. 1976).
80. Ky. Rev. Stat. §199.473 (1) (1970).
81. Id.
82. Fla. Stat. Ann. §63 (West Cum. Supp. 1976).
83. Fla. Stat. Ann. §63.022, (2) (F) (West Cum. Supp. 1976).
84. Fla. Stat. Ann. §63.092 (West Cum. Supp. 1976).
85. Id.
86. N.Y. Dom. Rel. Law §115 (McKinney Cum. Supp. 1975).
87. N.Y. Dom. Rel. Law §115-A (McKinney Cum. Supp. 1975).
88. Pa. Stat. Ann. Tit. 1 (Purdon Cum. Supp. 1977).
89. Pa. Stat. Ann. Tit. 1, §102(5) (Purdon Cum. Supp. 1977).

90. Pa. Stat. Ann. Tit. 1, §302 (Purdon Cum. Supp. 1977).
91. Pa. Stat. Ann. Tit. 1, §333 (Purdon Cum. Supp. 1977).
92. Pa. Stat. Ann. Tit. 1, §424 (Purdon Cum. Supp. 1977).
93. N.M. Stat. Ann. §22-2-37 (Cum. Supp. 1975).
94. Colo. Rev. Stat. §19-4-108 (Cum. Supp. 1975).
95. Colo. Rev. Stat. §19-4-103(1) (d) (Cum. Supp. 1975).
96. Ariz. Rev. Stat. §8-105 (Cum. Supp. 1976).
97. Md. Ann. Code Art. 88A §20 (Cum. Supp. 1976).
98. Pa. Stat. Ann. Tit. 1 §331 (Purdon Cum. Supp. 1977).
99. Wisc. Stat. Ann. §48.63(2) (West Cum. Supp. 1976).
100. Nev. Rev. Stat. §127.280 (1973).
101. Fla. Stat. Ann. §63.092 (West Cum. Supp. 1976).
102. Cal. Civ. Code §2266 (West 1973).
103. *See* Cal. Dept. of Health Regs. Tit. 22, ch. 3 (1972).
104. N.Y. Dom. Rel. Law §116 (McKinney Cum. Supp. 1975).
105. Ohio Rev. Code Ann. §3107.05 (Baldwin Cum. Supp. 1976).
106. Pa. Stat. Ann. Tit. 1, §§335, 424 (Purdon Cum. Supp. 1977).
107. Pa. Stat. Ann. Tit. 1, §§331-334 (Purdon Cum. Supp. 1977).
108. These states are: Georgia, Hawaii, Kansas, Maine, Mississippi, Missouri Montana, Nebraska, New Hampshire, New Mexico, Ohio, Oregon, Rhode Island, South Carolina, South Dakota, Tennessee, Vermont, Virginia, West Virginia, Wisconsin and Wyoming.
109. Conn. Gen. Stat. §45-63 (1975).
110. Cal. Civ. Code §224r (West Cum. Supp. 1976).
111. Utah Code Ann. §55-8a-1 (Cum. Supp. 1975).
112. Fla. Stat. Ann. §63.097 (West Cum. Supp. 1976).
113. S. 1631, 197th N.J. Leg., 1st Sess. (1976); *See also* 2 Fam. L. Rep. 2773 (Sept. 28, 1976).
114. Del. Code Tit. 13, §904 (1975).
115. Ga. Code §§74-421, 99-214 (1975).
116. Colo. Rev. Stat. §19-4-115 (1973).
117. Ind. Code §35-14-3-3 (1973).
118. Iowa Code Ann. §600.9 (West Cum. Supp. 1977).
119. Or. Rev. Stat. §167.645 (Cum. Supp. 1975).
120. Utah Code Ann. §55-8a-1 (Cum. Supp. 1975).
121. Ala. Code Tit. 49, §84(16) (1973).
122. Ariz. Rev. Stat. §8-128 (1974).
123. Cal. Civ. Code §224p (West Cum. Supp. 1976).
124. Fla. Stat. Ann. §63.212 (West Cum. Supp. 1976).
125. Idaho Code §18-1511 (Cum. Supp. 1974).
126. Ill. Ann. Stat. ch. 4 §12-5 (Smith-Hurd Cum. Supp. 1976).
127. Decided Oct. 1, 1976. *See,* 2 Fam. L. Rep. 2804 (Oct. 12, 1976).
128. Ky. Stat. §199.590 (Supp. 1975).
129. Mass. Gen. Laws Ann. ch. 210 §11 A (West Cum. Supp. 1976).

130.   Nev. Rev. Stat. §§127.280, 127.300, 127.310 (1973).

131.   Pa. Stat. Ann. Tit. 18, §4303 (Purdon Cum. Supp. 1975).

132.   Wash. Rev. Code §26.32.040-060 (1974).

133.   Ga. Code §74-414 (Cum. Supp. 1975).

134.   *Jossey v. Brown*, 47 S.E. 350 (Ga. 1904).

135.   La. Rev. Stat. §9:438 (West 1975).

136.   Ore. Rev. Stat. §109.381 (1974).

137.   Tenn. Code Ann. §§36-124, 36-127 (1956).

138.   *See* note 136 *supra* and accompanying text.

139.   Alaska Stat. §20.15.140 (Cum. Supp. 1975).

140.   N.D. Cent. Code §14-15-15 (1971).

141.   Ark. Stat. Ann. §56-112 (Cum. Supp. 1973).

142.   Cal. Civ. Code §227(d) (West 1954).

143.   Ala. Code Tit. 27, §5 (Cum. Supp. 1973).

144.   Ark. Stat. Ann. §56-110 (Cum. Supp. 1973).

145.   Ind. Code §34-1-2-5 (1973).

146.   244 Ind. 658, 195 N.E. 2d 481 (1964).

147.   Me. Rev. Stat. Tit. 12, §538 (1964).

148.   *See In re Cote's Estate*, 144 Me. 297, 68 A.2d 18 (1949).

149.   Mass. Gen. Laws Ann. ch. 210, §11 (West Cum. Supp. 1976).

150.   Vt. Stat. Ann. Tit. 15, §45 (1974).

151.   Vt. Stat. Tit. 15 §454 (1970).

152.   W. Va. Code §48-4-6 (West Cum. Supp. 1976).

153.   *See Keal v. Rhydderck*, 148 N.E. 53 (1925); *In re Wolfner's Estate*, 120 N.E. 2d 62 (Ill. App. 1963).

154.   215 Kan. 192, 523 P.2d 743 (1974).

155.   76 Misc. 2d 1077, 352 N.Y.S. 2d 743 (1968).

156.   109 R.I. 443, 287 A.2d 115 (1972).

157.   121 Utah 279, 241 P.2d 157 (1952).

9

The Attorneys General/ District Attorneys

THE SCHEDULE

A seven-page questionnaire was developed to obtain information on the monitoring of independent adoption practices by state and local law enforcement offices and on the extent to which violations of state law are prosecuted.

Data were sought on reports from 1971 to 1976 of violations of state laws in five specific areas:

1. placing children for adoption without a license;
2. acting as an intermediary in the adoptive placement process;
3. advertisement of placement services requesting/offering children for adoption;
4. fees and compensation offered/received/requested for adoptive placement or failure to report such fees;
5. failure to follow required procedures in independent adoptions, such as notifying the designated agency of placement, obtaining the required consents, meeting the requirement for a home study, etc.

In each of the five categories, if a relevant provision in the law existed, the respondents were asked to indicate whether there had been reports of violations since 1971, and if so, how many reports had been received and in what manner had their office been made aware of the irregularities.

If violations had been brought to their attention, respondents were then asked to cite the specific law violated and to indicate whether there had been prosecutions under this law since 1971. Subsequent questions concerning prosecutions sought more information on the number of cases, their nature, their disposition and the imposition of penalties, when indicated. If there were reports of violations but no prosecutions, a brief explanation was requested.

The latter part of the questionnaire consisted of open-ended questions concerning the extent of the role of the respondent's office in monitoring adoptive placement practice and in enforcing the law pertaining to such practice. Perceptions of problems in the law and their enforcement were also sought, as well as any suggestion for reform of existing statutes.

THE RESPONSE

Major difficulties were encountered in obtaining a sufficient response to the questionnaire. The effort was unsuccessful on two counts: 1) more than one-third of the completed schedules were forwarded to, and completed by, state or local public social service agencies rather than law enforcement officials, and 2) the total number of completed questionnaires (42) was too small to allow reliable analysis of the data. Table 9-2 indicates the response rate for attorneys general and district attorneys separately and in total.

Table 9-1
Response Rate for Attorneys General/
District Attorneys Questionnaire

		Number Completed		
	Number Sent	Appropriate Office	Other Office	Total
Attorneys general	50	11	14	25
District attorneys	50	14	3	17
Total	100	25	17	42

In addition to the 42 questionnaires received, letters indicating inability to complete the schedules were sent by 12 attorneys general and three district attorneys or members of their staff. The reasons most often cited for not filling out the questionnaire were lack of available statistics and the absence of reports of violations in the period covered by the inquiry. In spite of a followup letter by the Research Center, no response at all was received from 13 attorneys general and 30 district attorneys in the projected sample.

THE DATA

With only 42 completed questionnaires, 17 of which were filled out by personnel outside the field of law enforcement, attempts at analysis, comparison of the attorneys general sample with that of the district attorneys, or in-depth interpretation of the data appeared futile. Furthermore, initial reading of the completed schedules indicated that there was a scarcity of information in almost all areas. Tabulation of responses to key questions confirmed this impression.

In the five specific areas where information regarding reported violations of the law was requested, the following results were obtained:

Question 1 — Since 1971, were there any reports of violations of your state's law regulating placement of children for adoption without a license?

	No.
Not applicable — no provision in the law	6
No reports of violations	17
Yes, reports of violations	17*
No response	2
Total	42

*Of the 17 respondents indicating reports of violations, seven were not connected with an attorney general or district attorney office.

Question 2 — Since 1971, were there any reports of violations of your state's law regulating acting as an intermediary in the adoptive placement process?

	No.
Not applicable — no provision in the law	9
No reports of violations	20
Yes, reports of violations	12*
No response	1
Total	42

*Six of these 12 respondents were not connected with an attorney general or district attorney office.

Question 3 — Since 1971, were there any reports of violations of your state's law regulating advertisement of placement services requesting/offering children for adoption?

	No.
Not applicable — no provision in the law	17
No reports of violations	17
Yes, reports of violations	8*
No response	—
Total	42

*Six of these eight respondents were not connected with an attorney general or district attorney office.

Question 4 — Since 1971, were there any reports of violations of your state's law regulating fees and compensation

offered/received/requested for adoptive placement or
failure to report such fees?

	No.
Not applicable — no provision in the law	15
No reports of violations	20
Yes, reports of violations	6*
No response	1
Total	42

*Three of these six respondents were not connected with an attorney general or district
attorney office.

Question 5 — Since 1971, were there any reports of violations of
your state's law regulating failure to follow required
procedures in independent adoption?

	No.
Not applicable — no provision in the law	8
No reports of violations	22
Yes, reports of violations	11*
No response	1
Total	42

*Seven of these 11 respondents were not connected with an attorney general or
district attorney office.

It is noteworthy that in all but the first area of law, reports of more
than half the violations were obtained from persons other than law
enforcement officials. Since the largest single number of responses
originating from a law enforcement office acknowledging reports of
violations within a specific area of the law was 10, answers to questions
relating to prosecution of reported violations could not be undertaken. In
addition, the only safe conclusion to be drawn from the data is that in the

five areas of concern, the 25 attorneys general and district attorneys in the sample were aware of few violations in the law.

Considering the responses, it would have been surprising to find many attorney general and district attorney offices actively engaged in monitoring adoptive placement practices and enforcing the adoptive placement laws. The answers to the question, "How active a role does your office take in monitoring?" were consistent with this supposition. Of the 42 respondents, only 32 answered the question at all. Of those that did answer, almost half (14) were from offices other than those dealing with law enforcement. Table 9-2 summarizes the responses:

Table 9-2
Activity in Monitoring Adoptive Placement Practices
and Enforcing Adoptive Placement Laws
(N = 32)

	Office Other Than AG/DA No.	AG/DA Office No.	Total Respondents No.
None/not active at all	1	9	10
Enforcement only — when violations referred/ complaints made	1	7	8
Monitoring only	6	1	7
Monitoring and enforcement	3	—	3
Very active — nonspecific	2	—	2
Answer unclear/irrelevant	1	1	2
Total	14	18	32

Nine of the 18 law enforcement offices responding to this question indicated that they were in no way active in the monitoring and enforcement of adoptive placement laws, while seven additional offices were involved only with enforcement.

The inquiry into respondents' perceptions of major problems in their state's adoptive placement laws that cause continued illegal or legally questionable activity produced the results shown in Table 9-3.

Half of the attorneys general and district attorneys who answered the question saw no major problems in their state's adoption laws, while two of 18 law enforcement respondents indicated that they were not familiar enough with the laws to render an opinion. An overwhelming majority (14 out of 16) of the personnel in the social service offices responding to the

Table 9-3
Respondents' Perceptions of Major Problems in Their
State's Adoptive Placement Laws
(N = 34)*

	AG/DA Office No.	Other Office No.	Total Respondents No.
No major problems/law effective	8	2	10
One or more major problems	8	14	22
Don't know	2	–	2
Total	18	16	34

*Seven law enforcement offices and one other respondent did not reply to the question.

inquiry did feel that there were major problems in their current adoption laws.

A state-by-state breakdown might 'have indicated that those respondents who saw no major problems came from states with more stringent legislation. However, since the total sample was too small to justify further analysis, any conclusions about the responses to this question would be mere conjecture.

Forty of the 42 respondents in the sample did reply to the inquiry into whether they saw a need for reform of their state's adoptive placement laws. Twenty-three persons thought that reform was necessary and 21 gave specific suggestions for changing the laws in their states. However (as shown in Table 9-4), more than half of the 23 respondents wishing to see the laws changed were not law enforcement personnel.

Table 9-4
Respondents' Perceptions of Need for Reform
in Their State's Adoptive Placement Laws
(N = 40)*

	AG/DA Office No.	Other Office No.	Total Respondents No.
No need for reform	13	4	17
Yes, need for reform	10	13	23
Total	23	17	40

*Two law enforcement offices did not answer the question.

CONCLUSIONS

Much of what can be gleaned from the results of this inquiry into the monitoring and enforcement of adoptive placement laws comes not from the data themselves, but from the lack of them. In spite of the attention paid by the media to occasional investigations of the "black market" area of independent adoptions, this type of crime and other abuses of the adoption law are apparently not given a high priority within the offices having the authority to prosecute violators. It may well be that only the most flagrant abuses come to the attention of law enforcement agencies. Both the failure to respond to an inquiry into the area of independent adoptions and the tendency to divert the questionnaire to more "appropriate" personnel (i.e., social welfare officials) indicates a probable lack of interest or knowledge in this area and certainly a scarcity of information on the part of the agents of law enforcement across the country.

The data themselves reveal minimum reports of violations, and basic inactivity in the monitoring of adoptive placement practices and, to a somewhat lesser degree, the enforcement of the laws. Law enforcement officials see fewer problems in their local laws and less need for reform than do personnel in the social service departments. These personnel appear to be more active, more concerned and more knowledgeable, but are not in a position to prosecute violations of law.

10

Summary, Synthesis
and Policy Recommendations

The purposes of the study of independent adoptions were: 1) to determine the experience of the parties involved in independent adoptions; 2) to identify agency policies, procedures and resources that deter agency adoptions and thus encourage independent adoptions; and 3) to identify weaknesses in state laws and regulations, and their enforcement, that allow abuses of the independent adoption process to continue.

The study was conducted between July 1975 and August 1977 and was divided into three major phases. The first was a survey conducted through a detailed, mailed questionnaire to one public and one voluntary agency in each state, selected for their knowledge of independent adoptions. Data were collected concerning their observations and opinions about independent adoptions, as well as their policies and practices in providing services to adoptive families and unmarried parents.

The second component was a detailed investigation of independent adoptions through personal interviews with participants in five cities: Des Moines, Los Angeles, Miami, New York and Philadelphia. These areas were chosen because of the high incidence of independent adoptions and the concern of people in these communities about the attendant problems. A total of 321 interviews were conducted: 131 interviews with adoptive parents who received their children through independent placement, 115 interviews with biological mothers who relinquished their children independently, and 75 interviews with facilitators who helped to arrange independent adoptions.

The final component of the study was an analysis of the state laws and regulations in all 50 states and a mailed inquiry to attorneys general and district attorneys throughout the country about their enforcement.

This experiential, descriptive study had two major goals: 1) documentation of the possible risks involved in independent adoptions, including illegal activity in the field; and 2) identification of deterrents in agency practices and services that encourage biological and adoptive parents to turn to independent adoptions for help in relinquishing or adopting a child.

THE RISKS OF INDEPENDENT ADOPTION

The introductory chapter lists nine conditions that should be met if the best interests of all parties in an adoption are to be protected. The data reported by the various respondents in the study are examined in relation to these conditions.

The Biological Mother Who Surrenders Her Baby Should Have an Opportunity to Consider Alternatives and to Be Given Help in Selecting Among Them.

The Child Has a Right to Protection From Unnecessary Separation From His or Her Biological Parents.

As noted in the introduction, these two conditions are related.

The data show that for some women, the conflict over the surrender of their child continues well after contact with the intermediary has taken place. Sixty-seven of the 115 women had doubts during their pregnancy that adoption was the best plan for their child. Over half of the women were troubled by some aspect of signing the consent, including some who expressed concern about the irrevocability of the action. Over one-third of the women would advise their friends to act differently than they had acted, including some who would advise them to keep the child. Almost one-fifth of the mothers felt that the adoption process did not go as well as they had expected.

A substantial number of mothers (18%) felt that pressure was placed on them to relinquish their child. In addition, almost one-third felt that the intermediaries' primary interest was in arranging the adoption — not in the mother's well-being.

Yet, despite the doubts expressed by many of the mothers and the pressure placed on some, it is clear that the majority did not receive counseling about the decision to relinquish their child. Only 40% of the mothers reported discussing alternatives with the intermediary. Of the women who wanted to talk about the decision to surrender their child (85% of the sample), only one-quarter talked with someone qualified to provide counseling.

Fewer than half of the intermediaries ever suggest that the biological mother go to an agency, and only seven do this as a matter of routine. Fully half of the agencies and one-third of the intermediaries cited at least one case in the last year in which they had direct knowledge of a biological mother in need of counseling but not receiving it.

It is clear, also, that agencies have not been mandated to provide this service to the biological mother relinquishing her child independently. Over one-third of the agencies reported that they do not see the biological mother as part of their mandated investigation into an independent adoption. Only 12% of the agencies see her more than once as part of this process.

The Biological Mother's Decision to Surrender Should Not Be Linked to the Provision of Services.

It is evident from the data that the manner in which concrete services (medical, housing, financial and other material assistance) were provided in these independent adoptions was more acceptable to many of the biological mothers than the way such services are provided through agencies. Most of the agencies recognize this situation, with almost two-thirds stating that there are problems in the provision of services; less than half of the agencies can provide direct financial aid (and this, usually, through public assistance); even fewer can provide for private medical care or housing that allows the biological mother to live independently. Those mothers who were aware of how the agency would provide for concrete services tended to be more negative in their attitudes toward agencies than other mothers. One-third of the mothers who actually approached agencies cited the way such services were provided as a reason for their not relinquishing through the agency.

Almost all the mothers in the study received their medical help through private physicians. The majority of them received financial help in this area from the adoptive couple. In addition, some of the women received financial help for housing and living expenses both before and after the relinquishment. (The provision of assistance in these areas was confirmed by the adoptive couples and the intermediaries.)

The data show that for almost one-third of the women the provision of such services was influential in their decision to relinquish their child independently. One-third of the intermediaries believed this to be true and 29% of the biological mothers reported that this was the case. When asked about the positives of independent adoption, one-third of the intermediaries stated that the financial and other assistance provided to the biological mother was a major reason they chose to relinquish their child independently.

Yet, for at least 15 of the biological mothers, the provision of such services was contingent on their relinquishment of the child. Twenty percent of the women who discussed what would happen if they decided not to relinquish their child were told directly by the intermediary that all compensation would have to be paid back.

The Biological Father's Interest Should Be Considered in the Relinquishment of His Child.

A fairly large number of the interviews showed that the biological father's rights were either ignored or consciously denied. The biological mothers reported that although 85% of the fathers knew about their pregnancy, only 40% were involved in the relinquishment of the child.

More than 20% of the intermediaries stated that they were not required to obtain the father's consent for the adoption or a termination of his rights. In only one site did all the intermediaries recognize the need to obtain such consent or termination. In addition, 10% of the intermediaries consciously attempted to avoid involving the biological father in the relinquishment.

Thirty-eight percent of the adoptive parents did not have information about whether the biological father had consented to the adoption. Many of these adoptive couples were unaware of any necessity for this.

There are strong, consistent, geographic differences in the data about the biological fathers' rights — in states with strong consent statutes the rights of the biological father are better protected. In these jurisdictions there was also greater knowledge of his involvement by the sample's adoptive parents and a greater recognition on the part of the intermediaries of the need for such involvement.

The Child Has a Right to a Secure, Permanent Home.

Our data indicate that permanency may never be achieved in some independent adoptions. Twenty-nine percent of the agencies and 15% of the facilitators were aware of cases occurring within the last year where an independent adoption, eligible for finalization, had not been brought before the court.

There also appear to be a number of situations arising in independent adoptions in which placement plans are not realized, thus jeopardizing the child's right to a secure, permanent home. This occurs when the child is born with a physical or developmental handicap or when, for some other reason, the prospective adoptive couple choose not to go through with the placement. Almost 40% of the biological mothers either were told directly or believed that if the child were born with a physical or developmental problem, the adoptive couples would not accept the child and they would have to plan for it. Thirty percent either were told or believed that, if for some other reason the adoptive couple could not accept the child, they would be responsible for planning.

Almost one-quarter of the agencies were aware of the return in the last year of a child to the biological mother due to a physical/ developmental problem. Over half of the intermediaries had direct knowledge of a prospective adoptive child's being born with some condition contrary to expectation; some of these children were returned to the biological mothers.

The Child Has a Right to the Best Suitable Home Available.

The study did not attempt to compare the quality of homes in which children were placed independently with the quality of homes in which children were placed by agencies. Rather, the concern was with problems that may arise in the placement process. Because of this focus, the placement process in independent adoptions was examined to see if there were potential problems regarding the selection of homes. This is not to say that the homes were found unsuitable, or that the adoptive parents were not providing satisfactory care for the children.

From the analysis of state laws and regulations, it is clear that the possibility for the placement of a child in a home that cannot meet his/her needs is greater in independent adoptions than in agency adoptions. Only six states require an investigation of the home prior to the placement of a child. This means that in the vast majority of independent placements in this country, there is no assessment of the home by an authorized agent of the state prior to the placement. Although most states require a home study prior to the completion of an independent adoption, a few allow the investigation to be conducted by a "disinterested person," not necessarily someone trained to examine the adoptive couples' ability to provide for the child or the quality of care the child is receiving. Seventeen states allow waiver of the home study at the discretion of the court. Thus, under certain circumstances, there may be no scrutiny of the home.

Few doctors or lawyers are trained to assess the ability of adoptive parents to provide for the emotional needs of the child. In addition, many of the intermediaries do not see this as their function. Fewer than half the sample's intermediaries collect information about the adoptive couple's health, reason for wanting to adopt the child, marital history, attitudes toward rearing a child not their own, etc. One-quarter of the intermediaries stated that they make no attempt whatsoever to screen the adoptive couple. Over one-quarter of the intermediaries reported that they have only one or two contacts with an adoptive couple. This does not seem sufficient for the facilitators to assess the couple's ability to care for the child.

This lack of scrutiny by the facilitators was confirmed by the adoptive couples. One-third had fewer than three contacts with the intermediary. Only one-quarter of the adoptive parents discussed their own background or current feelings and attitudes about adoption with the intermediary. Few were seen by the intermediary in their homes.

It is clear that the agency investigation (usually postplacement) into the circumstances of an independent adoption may also be cursory. Over one-fifth of the agencies reported that the adoptive couple may not be seen as part of this effort. (Six couples in this study, whose adoptions were finalized, had never seen an agent of the court prior to the finalization of the adoption.) Over four-fifths of the agencies reported that their investigation into independent adoptions takes less time and may be less thorough than is the case in agency adoptions. Over half of the agencies reported that different criteria are used in judging a home for an independent placement. The standard applied is not the best suitable home for the child, but whether the home meets minimum requirements. Almost one-third of the agencies knew of cases in which a child was placed with an adoptive couple who had applied to a social agency and were not approved.

For the Child to Develop a Sense of Identity and Emotional Well-Being, His/Her Adoptive Parents Have the Right to Accurate and Appropriate Information About the Biological Parents, Including Full Knowledge of Physical and Developmental Factors That Might Affect the Child's Growth.

There is evidence in the data that the adoptive parents may not have received critical information about the child, that the biological mother may not have been asked or may not have shared this information, and that the facilitator may not have gathered such information. About 20% of the adoptive couples had no information about the biological mothers in each of the areas (health, education, occupation, etc.) covered in the interview. Between 40% and 55% had no information about the biological fathers in these areas. There was strong indication that many couples were dissatisfied with the amount of information they had received about their children.

About 15% of the biological mothers reported that they did not share information about these aspects of their own background with the intermediary. More than one-quarter did not furnish information about the biological father.

The facilitators confirmed the reports of the adoptive couples and the biological mother. Fifteen percent do not routinely elicit a medical history from the biological mother and one-third do not receive this type of information regarding the biological father. Over one-quarter do not elicit information about the biological parents' occupations, reasons for surrender, or feelings about each other.

Only about half of the facilitators reported that they share information about the biological parents' medical history or family background with the adoptive parents. Less than one-quarter said they share information about the reasons the child was surrendered. Nineteen of the intermediaries stated that they disclose only limited or positive information to the adoptive couples.

In addition, 31% of the agencies and 21% of the facilitators knew of cases in the last year in which a critical factor in the child's background was not revealed to the adoptive couple at the time of placement, precipitating difficulties in the adoption.

The Adoptive Parents Have the Right to Assurance That the Biological Parent(s) Will Not Intervene in the Child's Life After Placement.

The data reveal that the potential for intervention in the child's life by the biological mother was present in many adoptions because the biological and adoptive parents were known to each other. Almost one-third of the biological mothers in the study knew the identity of the adoptive family. Over 50% reported that the adoptive couple's names were on the consent they signed. Half of the adoptive couples knew the identity of the biological mother. Almost one-fifth were concerned that the biological mother would interfere in the child's life. Nearly half of the facilitators had been involved in cases where the identities of the adoptive and biological parents were known to each other.

Not only is the potential for intervention in the child's life by the biological mother present in independent adoptions, but there was evidence that such interventions occur. Over 40% of the agencies and about one-fifth of the facilitators knew of a case within the last year in which difficulties arose because the biological mother attempted to intervene in the life of the child. In some instances reported, the adoptive couple moved away to avoid such harassment.

An even more serious situation arises when the biological mother attempts to withdraw her consent to the adoption. Withdrawal of consent was a concern to the adoptive parents — 45% reported that they were worried about this possibility. Almost one-quarter of the agencies and 44% of the intermediaries had direct knowledge of such situations occurring in the last year.

The Adoptive Parents Should Have Available Help in Understanding the Special Needs of an Adopted Child and the Difficulties Inherent in Adoptive Parenthood.

It is apparent that many of the sample's adoptive couples did not receive help in understanding the needs of their adopted children. Most of the facilitators (85%) did not talk with the couple about the problems in rearing an adopted child. Over half never explored with the couple their reason for wanting to adopt and almost two-thirds never explored the adoptive parents' attitudes toward rearing a child not biologically theirs.

This lack of available help in recognizing the special situation of the adopted child is reflected in the responses of the adoptive couples. Almost one-fifth of the couples stated that they did not want to know about the child's background and appeared to be denying the importance of such information to the child. Half of the adoptive parents interviewed saw no difference between rearing an adopted child and rearing a biological child. Thirty-five percent did not feel that adopted children faced problems in growing up that other children did not face. Sixteen of the adoptive couples said they did not know how they would handle questions that the child might raise about adoptive status or said they would lie to the child or discourage such questions. Two couples did not plan to tell the child that he/she was adopted.

It appears clear that in independent adoptions there is much greater risk than in agency adoptions of failure to meet the conditions generally agreed necessary to protect the interests of child, biological parents and adoptive parents.

LEGALLY QUESTIONABLE ACTIVITIES

The review of state laws and regulations revealed disturbing facts regarding adoptions for profit and other legally questionable activities in the area of independent adoptions. Over half of the states have either no provision regarding fees and compensation for adoptions, or provisions that apply only to agencies. Only 10 states prohibit payment of compensation for placing a child for adoption. In addition, seven states were found to have no penalty provision for violation of their adoption statutes, and many other states impose such small fines or other penalties as to make these provisions almost meaningless. It is clear that adoptions for profit, although receiving much attention in the press, are not perceived as a major area of concern by many state lawmakers.

The sparse reponse to the questionnaire sent to the attorneys general and district attorneys, and the fact that many who did respond stated that their office was not at all active in the enforcement of adoptive placement laws, seemed to confirm that adoptions are not a high priority for law enforcement officials.

This problem appears to be of little concern to legislators or law enforcement officials. Whatever the reason for this, it cannot be for lack of evidence that adoptions for profit occur. Almost half (45%) of the intermediaries had direct knowledge of couples paying or being asked to pay high fees in the last year. Ten percent believed that nearly all independent adoption activity in their area could be classified as "for profit." Over half thought that organized rings specializing in these activities were in operation.

Almost one-quarter of the agencies in the study had direct knowledge of "for-profit" activities within the last year. Nineteen percent thought that most or nearly all of the independent adoption activity in their area was of this type. An additional 26% thought that half or a substantial minority of the independent adoption activity could be classified as "for profit."

There were also indications of adoptions for profit and other legally questionable activities in the data gathered from the adoptive couples. It should be noted that the reliability of these data is questionable. By admitting the payment of high fees, many of the couples would also be admitting to breaking the law and/or perjury. It is therefore likely that the results reported in this area were understated.

Even with the possibility of underreporting, 15% of the adoptive couples stated that they were worried about the legality of their adoption. Twelve percent admitted that part of all of the payment to the intermediary was made in cash. One-fifth of the sample felt that at least some of the costs in the adoption were inflated. Fifteen percent reported that during their wait for a child the intermediary attempted to raise the costs of the adoption. A conservative estimate by the research team was that 13% of the adoptions were legally questionable. Interstate adoptions were more often judged legally questionable than adoptions completed intrastate.

It seems, therefore, that current state laws and regulations are not effective in preventing illegal operations.

FACTORS IN AGENCY PRACTICE THAT ENCOURAGE INDEPENDENT ADOPTIONS

Clearly, the primary factor encouraging prospective adoptive couples to seek children independently is the shortage of white, healthy infants available through agencies. Seventy percent of the adoptive couples interviewed approached agencies regarding their decision to adopt. Many were discouraged about this prospect primarily because of the long waiting lists and the unavailability of infants. Although many were not given an estimate of the waiting period for a child, fewer than 20% were told that the wait for a healthy, white infant would be less than 3 years. Almost half of the couples who approached agencies cited the shortage of infants as the primary factor in their decision to adopt independently.

This is not surprising in light of the data collected from the agencies. Almost two-thirds cited the shortage of white, healthy infants as a deterrent to adoptive couples. Almost all of the agencies (97%) reported a decrease in the number of completed adoptions of healthy, white infants between 1970 and 1974. Over half of the agencies reported that their waiting list for adoptive couples was currently closed.

Over half of the intermediaries stated that the availability of white infants was a major advantage of independent adoptions. In addition, almost half stated that independent placements take less time to complete. Thus, the facilitators also perceive the shortage of healthy, white infants available through agencies as a primary deterrent to their use.

There are major differences between agency and independent adoptions in the amount of time between the inquiry about adoption and the placement of a normal white infant. Almost half the agencies reported that it takes at least 1 year between inquiry to the agency and approval of the home. Almost two-thirds of the agencies stated that it is at least 1 year between approval and the placement of a child. When these figures are compared with the reports of the adoptive couples (half had a child placed within 6 months of contact with an intermediary) and the intermediaries (half reported that placement occurs within 1 year of inquiry), it becomes evident that independent placements take significantly less time to accomplish. Couples who are anxious for children will seek the fastest alternative. For many, independent adoptions may seem the only viable alternative. Another factor that appears to discourage some prospective adoptive couples from using agencies is the presence of policy-determined eligibility requirements. The presence of such requirements was confirmed by the agency questionnaire; almost one-quarter of the agencies felt that such requirements did stop prospective couples from adopting through an agency.

The data seem to confirm that, at least for a minority of the couples, agency requirements were a deterrent to agency use. Fifteen percent of the adoptive couples who felt discouraged by agencies cited agency requirements as the reason. Those who were told explicitly or by inference that they were not eligible to adopt through an agency (N = 20) most often said that they were above the age limit set by the agency, that there were children present in their home and the agency would not place an additional child, or that they had not been married long enough.

From the preceding discussion we might generalize that the primary deterrent to the use of agencies is the shortage of healthy infants; most couples would be willing to adopt through agencies if such children were available. Only a small minority would avoid agencies because of ineligibility.

Although the deterrents to the use of agencies by adoptive couples seemed fairly clear cut, this was not so in the case of the biological parents. Several simultaneous forces seemed to be operating that deterred the use of agency services by this group.

For at least a minority of the women, a major deterrent to the use of agencies appeared to be the way concrete services, especially medical care, were provided. About 30% of the mothers reported that the way services were provided in independent adoptions influenced their decision to relinquish their child independently. Agencies, for the most part, are unable to provide such services in a way acceptable to unmarried women.

Another deterrent to the use of agency services by the biological mother was her understanding that the child would spend a period of time, for evaluation, in foster care. This does appear to be general agency practice, with 53% of the agencies reporting that no child goes directly into an adoptive placement, and only 7% reporting that all of their children go directly into their adoptive homes. Two-thirds of the biological mothers said if the agency had to place their child in foster care, they would be deterred from using agency services; one-quarter felt that this requirement did, in fact, influence their decision to arrange the adoption without the help of a social agency. Thirteen percent of the agencies felt placement of the child in foster care was a deterrent to the biological mother. The same percentage of the facilitators considered this a reason biological mothers chose independent adoption.

A further deterrent, not generally recognized by the agencies, is the biological mothers' lack of knowledge about agency services. Only 9% of the agencies perceived this as a problem. Yet, almost half of the women were not aware of a specific agency in their community that could help them in planning for their child, and 18 of the women did not know that any agencies existed for this purpose.

There is also some indication from the data that the involvement of other persons or a state agency in the adoption process may have dissuaded some biological mothers from approaching social agencies for help. Over one-fifth of the agencies stated that out-of-wedlock pregnancies must be reported to a government agency. About the same number said that parents had to be notified in the event of out-of-wedlock pregnancy if the woman were a minor, or if social services were to be rendered to a minor. Most of the agencies reported that the biological father had to be involved in the relinquishment of the child. The legal analysis revealed that 12 states require consent from someone other than the biological mother if she is a minor, and most have provisions for the involvement of the biological father.

In response to hypothetical questions, more than one-quarter of the mothers felt that the involvement of various other parties might deter them from using the services of an agency. The responses showed that six were deterred from using agency services because of the notification requirement to state agencies, and seven were deterred because of the mandated involvement of the biological father. About one-quarter of the agencies believed that involvement of the biological father was a block to the use of their services by biological mothers.

The data also indicate that, for a small number of biological mothers, the belief that they would not receive adequate information about the adoptive couple was a deterrent to their use of agencies. Few of the biological and adoptive parents were known personally to each other, and only 10% of the adoptions were arranged directly between the adoptive couple and the biological parent. However, some women stated that they did not approach social agencies because they would not be allowed to "choose" the adoptive parents. Three of the mothers who did approach agencies did not feel that they received satisfactory information about the adoptive couple. Over one-quarter of the facilitators believed that biological mothers chose the independent route because of the opportunity to select the adoptive couple with whom their child would be placed.

Although the majority of both the adoptive couples and the biological mothers reported that their experience with the social agencies was positive, the data indicate that there were some aspects of the relationship with the agency that might deter both of these groups from using their services. On the one hand, 30% of the adoptive couples felt that they were treated impersonally by the worker, and 11% of the biological mothers who did not approach agencies thought that agencies were impersonal or uncaring. One-quarter of the intermediaries believed that the reason adoptive parents approached them was because their services were more individualized and personal. On the other hand, half of the adoptive couples felt that the worker asked too many personal questions and 37% of the biological mothers had the impression that agencies were too nosy. Thus, there appears to be criticism on both ends of a continuum — some of the parties believed that agencies were impersonal and bureaucratic, while others thought that their privacy was or would be invaded because of the nature of the contacts with the worker.

It should be noted that one commonly held belief about the group of biological mothers relinquishing their children independently was not upheld by the data. The women interviewed were not, for the most part, mature, sophisticated, educated, middle class women. They were young. The majority were living at home at the time of the pregnancy and continued to do so through delivery. Many were under the strong and sometimes overwhelming influence of their parents. A few did not have control over the decision to surrender the child or the way the surrender was accomplished. Rather, their parents, embarrassed by the situation, usurped their right to plan for themselves and their child.

It thus appears that although the shortage of healthy white infants is a stronger deterrent to adoptive parents than are agency policies and procedures, the latter do play a role in diverting couples to the independent route. Agency factors are a more serious deterrent to use of agencies by biological mothers than by adoptive parents, and this very fact aggravates the shortage of adoptable infants available through agencies.

POLICY RECOMMENDATIONS

This study of independent adoptions indicates that many of the suspected risks of independent adoptions do become a reality or are potential in a substantial minority of the cases explored. There are several policy options that could lead to reduction of these risks.

The first is to allow the placement of children for adoption only through licensed social agencies. Five states have done this and effectively outlawed independent placements. However, such a recommendation appears premature, on the basis of the results of this study. Although it is believed that agency placements would reduce the risks explored, there are no hard data to support this assumption. In addition, this study did not attempt to compare the outcomes of independent and agency adoptions. Therefore, it is not known what the effects of the risks of independent adoptions are on the children involved in these placements. Finally, it should be remembered that all but one of the adoptive couples in this study who completed an agency home study were approved; the majority of the homes in which children were placed independently were rated by the agencies as being as good or better than agency homes in their physical and emotional care of the child; some of the adoptive couples in this study had adopted through agencies prior to this adoption; and almost all the homes were rated positively by the trained personnel who interviewed the adoptive couples.

In considering legislation to outlaw independent adoptions, several factors should be taken into account.

If independent adoptions were outlawed, the demand for agency services would increase precipitously. Given the current limitations of agency resources and funding, agencies might find themselves unable to meet effectively the demands for this service.

Further, if adoptive placements were restricted to licensed social agencies, a monopoly would be created. As with any monopoly, there would be the possibility of abuse. Thus, built into any statute of this type should be an appeal process for those adoptive couples rejected by an agency. Any prospective adoptive parent denied approval by an agency should have the right to have this decision reviewed.

In addition, licensing statutes governing adoption agencies would have to be reviewed and strengthened to ensure the presence of mandated resources, services, and administrative structures (boards of directors, etc.). If this were not done, intermediaries would simply have to apply for a license as an adoption agency in order to continue their placement of children.

Finally, it should be remembered that there is a great demand for healthy infants freed for adoption. It has been suggested that outlawing independent adoptions would simply create a larger "black market." There is strong evidence that desperate couples will use illegal means and pay high fees for children. Devices such as finalization of the adoption of an American child in a foreign country, and the biological mother admitting herself to the hospital for delivery in the adoptive mother's name (thus avoiding the need for the issuance of a new birth certificate and any legal scrutiny) that have been reported in the press were confirmed in this study. If independent adoptions were outlawed, such practices might increase.

There are alternatives to the outlawing of independent adoptions. There is evidence in the study data that some of the risks of independent adoptions are significantly diminished in the geographic areas where state laws and regulations are strong and specific, and where agency involvement in independent adoptions is mandated by law — Los Angeles and Iowa. In these areas, biological fathers are more likely to be involved; adoptive couples are more likely to have knowledge about the father's involvement; biological mothers are likely to perceive their relationships with the facilitators in a positive light; and adoptions are less likely to be judged legally questionable. It appears, then, that legislative and judicial reform, and the strengthening of the involvement of social agencies in the independent adoption process, can affect the nature of this process. In light of this, the following recommendations are suggested:

1. A requirement of preplacement investigations of prospective adoptive homes (already in effect in seven states), with agencies given ample time to do a thorough job in evaluating a given home, based on the same standards currently applied in agency adoptions. This would help to guarantee a suitable home to a child, and negate the tendency of judges to allow children to remain in homes that may not meet their needs, since no bonds would be formed between adoptive parents and child prior to approval of the home.

2. Mandatory involvement during the preplacement investigation of all parties to the adoption, so that they are aware of their rights and the alternatives open to them. Such involvement

would allow qualified personnel to offer counseling to the biological mothers who want it, and prepare the adoptive couple for the task of rearing a child not biologically theirs. It would also guarantee the rights of the biological father and ensure proper termination of these rights. Such mandated involvement would also assure an agency presence in the event that the child is born with a physical or developmental disability, or is unacceptable to an adoptive couple for some other reason. Alternate plans for the child could then be made quickly. In addition, agency workers supervising independent placements could collect and disseminate background information crucial to the development of the child and his/her sense of identity.

3. Prior to or immediately after placement (and following voluntary relinquishment), a judicial proceeding terminating parental rights, so that the right of the adoptive parents to security in their relationship with the child is guaranteed. To implement such a requirement effectively, it would be necessary also to establish standard procedures for the termination or relinquishment of the biological father's rights that are least intrusive to the life of the biological mother, and can be accomplished within a reasonable time. Both relinquishment and termination of rights, if accomplished properly, should be irrevocable.

4. The legal requirement that an adoption petition be filed no later than 1 year after the placement of the child. This would guarantee that a determination on the status of the child would be made expeditiously, and that the child would not remain in legal limbo.

5. The protection of the anonymity of the adoptive couples and biological parents until the child has reached his/her majority, to eliminate the possibility of blackmail and harassment of one party by the other. Such protection might be waived if both parties were agreeable. In addition, any statutes requiring the revealing of the identity of the biological and adoptive parents to each other, or requiring a meeting between these parties should be eliminated.

6. The establishment, by law and/or by the professional associations of the various intermediaries, of reasonable fee scales for intermediaries in the adoption process. Such established scales would, it is hoped, reduce the willingness of the various parties to charge or pay fees above those that are "reasonable and customary."

7. The requirement of an itemized declaration of all costs in the adoption at the time of filing an adoption petition, so that the laws regarding the buying and selling of children could be more strictly monitored. In addition, a list of legally reimbursable expenses should be established so that biological mothers would not be induced to relinquish their children for monetary or other gains.

8. The establishment or strengthening of statutes concerning the sale of children, with mandatory prosecution of suspected abusers, in order to diminish the trafficking in "black market" babies. Linked with this should be the establishment or strengthening of penalty provisions in the law so that abusers face heavy, rather than nominal, penalties. In addition, all parties to the adoption should be held liable for action in the adoption. Not only should the facilitator be prosecuted for arranging adoptions for high fees, but adoptive couples willing to pay fees above those established, as well as biological parents accepting payments above medical and living expenses for the relinquishment of their child, should also be held accountable for their actions.

9. Passage of state laws prohibiting the importation of children from or exportation to another state for the purpose of placement or adoption in an unrelated home except by a licensed social agency. Much of the legally questionable activity appears to occur in the interstate transport of children.

At the same time as these legal recommendations are implemented, there are steps that can be taken in agency policy and practice, and in the funding of social services, that would remove some of the deterrents to the use of social agencies by biological and adoptive parents. These include:

1. Earmarking of funds to social agencies for the provision of "hard" services, so that medical care and living expenses could be provided without the stigma associated with public assistance and in a manner more acceptable to the biological parents. Medical care by private physicians could then become an option that agencies could offer.

2. A reduction of the nonessential eligibility requirements currently present in social agencies and greater flexibility in the application of the requirements retained. Rigid requirements tend to screen out rather than screen in prospective adoptive parents, and may not be essential to the well-being of the child.

Such reduction is already a trend and should be continued. The appropriateness and application of such requirements should be a consideration of state authorities in the licensing of adoption agencies.

3. A reassessment of patterns within social agencies in which children spend time in foster care prior to adoptive placement. For many children, this appears to be an unnecessary precaution that inhibits the biological mothers from using agency services. As many children as possible should be placed directly in adoptive homes. Efforts should be made to move those children placed in foster care for evaluation or clearance of legal complications into adoptive placement as soon as possible.

4. A concerted public relations effort by the social agencies offering services to biological parents, so that women in the community not only know of the availability of services, but of a specific agency that can assist them.

5. A reassessment within agencies of casework practice with the parties in the adoption. Some social agencies routinely involve both the adoptive couple and the biological mother in analytically oriented casework. Although some might benefit from such services, it is apparent that this is not true for many in this study. For some, such involvement may be a deterrent to the use of agencies. It is important that the counseling focus on the adoptive couples' ability to parent and the biological mother's planning for her child. It need not be equated with painful exploration of feelings about infertility or the psychodynamics of illegitimate pregnancy.

6. The establishment of procedures that allow responsible unmarried mothers to become involved in agency services without the mandatory involvement of other government agencies or their parents. This would require a broadening of the use of the concept of the "emancipated minor," and its application in the adoption field.

7. Establishment or expansion within agencies of procedures that allow the biological mother a say in the selection of the adoptive family. This is not to say that confidentiality should be breached, but rather that nonidentifying information about the families available for the child should be discussed with the biological mother. Together, she and the agency worker could decide which family would be best for her child.

8. A redoubling of efforts by social agencies to work with families who approach them with a willingness to adopt other than a healthy infant. Some of these families might be able to provide care for children currently under agency supervision and awaiting adoptive homes.

It is anticipated that the legislative and policy recommendations outlined here would have several effects, including:

1. A guaranteed, early presence of a licensed adoption agency in every independent adoption. Such a presence would reduce many of the risks in independent adoption. However, if such a presence were mandated, the agency might find itself in the position of dealing with independent placements that were planned but not completed. This would increase the number of "difficult to place" children under agency care. To provide for such children, and do a proper home study in all independent adoptions, resources of the agency would have to be reallocated or new resources would have to be found to meet the increased demand for adoption services.

2. Greater control on the fees and compensation in independent adoption, with all parties held accountable for the financial transactions that take place. This would reduce the possibility of legally questionable activities in the field. For this to be effective, law enforcement officials would have to take a more active role in the monitoring of adoption practice and in the enforcement of adoption laws.

3. Reduction of the deterrents to the use of agency service, to encourage prospective adoptive and biological parents to use agency services. This, also, would increase the demand placed on the resources of the agency.

4. An increased involvement of the judiciary in the adoption process. This would cause delays in the placement of children in permanent homes unless court procedures for the termination of parental rights were streamlined and made more responsive to the needs of the children, allowing termination to be carried out quickly.

William Meezan received his BA from the University of Vermont, his MSW from the Florida State University School of Social Welfare and his DSW from the Columbia University School of Social Work. He is Adjunct Assistant Professor in Research at the Graduate School of Social Work at New York University. He is coauthor of *Foster Care Needs and Alternatives to Placement* (New York State Board of Social Welfare) and *The Impact of Welfare on Family Stability* (New School for Social Research).

Sanford Katz is Professor of Law at the Boston College Law School. He received his AB from Boston University and his JD from the University of Chicago and has served as a U.S. Public Health Service fellow at Yale University. He is a member of both the Massachusetts and the District of Columbia Bars and Editor-in-Chief of the *Family Law Quarterly*. He is the author of *When Parents Fail: The Law's Response to Family Breakdown* (Beacon Press) and was the editor of *Creativity and Social Work: Selected Writings of Lydia Rapoport* (Temple University Press) and *The Youngest Minority: Lawyers in Defense of Children* (*American Bar Association*).

Eva Manoff Russo, who received her BA from Antioch College, is Research Assistant, Child Welfare League of America, responsible for League-funded surveys involving administrative data. She formerly was Research Assistant, Columbia University School of Social Work.

More CWLA Publications

DATE D

Please remember that this is a library book,
and that it belongs only temporarily to each
person who uses it. Be considerate. Do
not write in this, or any, library book.